Wage and Hour Law

Chester Hanvey

Wage and Hour Law

Guide to Methods and Analysis

 Springer

Chester Hanvey
Berkeley Research Group, LLC
Emeryville, CA, USA

ISBN 978-3-030-09036-4   ISBN 978-3-319-74612-8   (eBook)
https://doi.org/10.1007/978-3-319-74612-8

Printed on acid-free paper

This Springer imprint is published by the registered company Springer International Publishing AG
part of Springer Nature.
The registered company address is: Gewerbestrasse 11, 6330 Cham, Switzerland

Preface

The purpose of this book is to provide a comprehensive reference guide on the methods and analyses to evaluate a variety of specific wage and hour legal issues. Existing academic literature covering these topics is relatively sparse. This book is intended to help fill that void by providing an authoritative resource that will be useful for students, human resources (HR) professionals, external consultants, and experts retained in litigation. Labor and employment attorneys who litigate wage and hour issues may also find the content of this book valuable for developing strategies to evaluate compliance and provide a standard to which work done by experts in litigation can be compared.

I am fortunate to have previously worked with Springer on a related project. In a book I coedited with Kayo Sady, titled *Practitioners Guide to Legal Issues in Organizations* (2015), we included chapters that addressed a variety of specific employment legal issues that are commonly encountered by HR practitioners. Along with Cristina Banks, I co-wrote the chapter called "Wage and Hour Litigation." This book is, in many ways, an extension of that chapter. The space available in this book provided an opportunity to expand on the methodological and analytic approaches we covered previously and provide greater detail on each legal issue.

The range of legal issues that fall under the wage and hour umbrella is quite broad, and many require specialized expertise to properly evaluate compliance. I have invited several colleagues to coauthor chapters, each of whom is an expert in their respective field and was willing to contribute valuable insight. Their contributions added depth and a more robust perspective to the topics addressed in those chapters.

I believe that there is an opportunity for much more academic literature on wage and hour issues. I hope that this book motivates others in the scientific community to study and publish their work on these issues so that our methods can continue to be improved and we can continue to provide valuable contributions to the business and legal communities.

Emeryville, CA, USA   Chester Hanvey

Acknowledgements

I would like to sincerely thank those who contributed to the creation of this book. In particular, I am extremely grateful to chapter coauthors Elizabeth Arnold, Kayo Sady, and Jeremy White for sharing their expertise. In addition, I would like to acknowledge several colleagues who agreed to review portions of this book. Each provided valuable feedback and greatly improved the quality of this book. I would like to express my gratitude to Theodore Alexander, David Dubin, Ari Malka, Alex Milam, Samantha Stelman, and Rob Stewart for their thoughtful contributions. Thank you for contributing your time and expertise. I would also like to thank Springer for giving me the opportunity to write this book. I really appreciate how easy it has been to work with you.

I would also like to acknowledge the contributions of Cristina Banks. Though not directly involved in this book, most of the content is based on approaches she pioneered from the time of wage and hour litigation's infancy. I have learned a great deal from working with her across many years and collaborating with her on previous publications. The guidance and mentorship she has provided, and continues to provide, were instrumental in preparing this book.

I would also like to thank my family and friends for their support during the preparation of this book. I would especially like to thank my beautiful wife, Megan, and always perfectly behaved boys, Charlie (6) and Teddy (3). Time spent working on this book was typically time that I sacrificed with them and I appreciate their willingness to support me. I would also like to acknowledge those friends whose invitations were often a casualty of this book. Thank you for understanding. Then again, perhaps none of these people wanted to spend time with me, in which case I retract their acknowledgement. Of course, I must also acknowledge Vince Young, the greatest of all time.

Disclaimer

The views and opinions expressed in this book are those of the author and do not necessarily reflect the opinions, position, or policy of Berkeley Research Group, LLC or its other employees and affiliates.

Contents

The original version of this book was revised. A correction to this book can be found at
https://doi.org/10.1007/978-3-319-74612-8_10

About the Author

Chester Hanvey, PhD is an Associate Director at Berkeley Research Group (BRG) where he provides consulting services and expert testimony on labor and employment legal issues. Dr. Hanvey has worked with more than 100 organizations across a range of industries including public and private sectors. He specializes in designing and conducting job analyses and conducting statistical analyses to evaluate wage and hour compliance, appropriateness of class certification, allegations of discrimination, and damages. Dr. Hanvey's wage and hour experience includes the evaluation of FLSA exemptions, meal and rest break compliance, employment status, and off-the-clock work. His experience with employment discrimination claims includes the measurement of adverse impact and test validation in the contexts of hiring, promotion, performance evaluation, layoffs, and compensation to evaluate alleged discrimination on the basis of protected class membership and disability. Dr. Hanvey has been retained by plaintiffs and defendants as an expert witness to provide testimony on issues including wage and hour compliance, statistical sampling, statistical analysis, damages calculations, adverse impact, and test validity. He has authored chapters and scholarly articles and regularly presents his work at professional conferences on the topics of wage and hour litigation, class certification, and statistical analyses. Dr. Hanvey received his Ph.D. in industrial/organizational (I/O) psychology with a minor in quantitative methods (statistics) from the University of Houston and a B.A. in psychology with a minor in Spanish from the University of Texas at Austin.

About the Contributors

Elizabeth Arnold, MS is a director in the Labor and Employment Practice at Berkeley Research Group. She has been advising clients on issues related to employment practices and wage and hour compliance for more than 16 years. She provides expert services to clients at leading law firms and companies nationwide on state and federal class action litigation and advisory projects across industries ranging from retail and transportation to food processing and healthcare. Ms. Arnold develops and implements customized research methodologies that address complex legal compliance issues, such as misclassification (i.e., exempt vs. nonexempt employees, independent contractor), donning and doffing, off-the-clock work (compensable time), and missed meal and rest break claims. Ms. Arnold provides expert testimony and has conducted more than 150 job analyses to address employment law compliance issues. Her engagements often include national research projects to determine the tasks and responsibilities of employees. Clients use results from her studies to evaluate internal policies and practices and at multiple stages of active litigation.

Kayo Sady, PhD is an industrial/organizational psychologist and associate principal consultant at DCI Consulting Group, Inc. (DCI) where his practice centers on employee selection matters and compensation equity evaluation. Dr. Sady's primary areas of expertise are job analysis, employee selection practices, validation strategies, compensation practices, and quantitative methods in the equal employment context.Dr. Sady received his M.A. and Ph.D. in industrial/organizational psychology with an emphasis on quantitative methods (statistical analysis) from the University of Houston. Prior to joining DCI, he worked at Valtera Corporation (now Gartner Inc.) as a consultant in the Assessment and Selection Group. At Valtera, Dr. Sady managed validation projects employing criterion-, content-, and construct-validation strategies and advised clients based on complex HR risk management analytics. His work at DCI has expanded to include questions of compensation equity and services related to expert consulting in EEO litigation and OFCCP audits. At DCI, Dr. Sady leads a team of consultants with Ph.D.s in industrial/organizational psychology.Dr. Sady regularly presents on EEO and other personnel selection matters at national conferences such as the annual SIOP and NILG conferences. He is also a coeditor and contributor to a published volume titled *Practitioner's Guide to Legal Issues in Organizations*. This edited book includes guidance on a range of topics including physical abilities testing, job analysis, validation research, cut-score setting, disparity analyses, and other legally sensitive HR issues. In addition to his consulting practice, Dr. Sady serves as an adjunct faculty member at University of Maryland Baltimore County (UMBC) Shady Grove campus, where he teaches graduate courses in both introductory and advanced statistics.

Jeremy White, Esq a partner at McDermott Will & Emery, has over 15 years of experience representing a wide range of clients in complex litigation matters, including in the wage and hour and employment discrimination areas. He counsels employers on a full spectrum of workplace issues, including personnel policies and practices, worker classification, employee separations, performance management, internal complaints and investigations, and arbitration programs. Jeremy was the recipient of the Washington Lawyers' Committee Outstanding Achievement Award in 2007 and 2014 and has been recognized by Chambers USA since 2015. He received his J.D. from Washington University in St. Louis School of Law.

Chapter 1
Wage and Hour Legal Context

Chester Hanvey and Jeremy White

1.1 Introduction

Compliance with wage and hour laws within the USA requires familiarity with many different statutes and regulations. In addition to federal requirements, many states and even some local municipalities have additional wage and hour requirements that also must be followed by companies with employees in those jurisdictions. Government enforcement agencies at the federal and state level also release publications to clarify their positions and interpretations of wage and hour requirements. In addition, numerous court decisions over the years have impacted the way in which these laws and regulations are interpreted in the court system. As a result, understanding an employer's wage and hour obligations requires navigating a complicated and evolving legal landscape. In this chapter, we provide an overview of the legal landscape to help clarify employers' wage and hour obligations.

We also note that the issues which fall within the realm of "wage and hour" are quite broad and include issues such as child labor, minimum wage, and even administrative issues such as recordkeeping requirements. This book is intended for internal and external organizational consultants, experts, and human resources (HR) practitioners, and we therefore focus our attention on issues that are frequently litigated and can be addressed using systematic methods from industrial/organizational (I/O) psychology or related disciplines.

The original version of this chapter was revised. A correction to this chapter can be found at
https://doi.org/10.1007/978-3-319-74612-8_10

© Springer International Publishing AG, part of Springer Nature 2018   1
C. Hanvey, *Wage and Hour Law*, https://doi.org/10.1007/978-3-319-74612-8_1

1.2 Fair Labor Standards Act

Federal wage and hour laws in the USA are based primarily on the Fair Labor Standards Act (FLSA), which can be found in Title 29 of the United States Code.[1] Enacted during the Great Depression in 1938, the FLSA provides workers with certain protections such as minimum wages, overtime pay, and child labor standards.[2] President Franklin D. Roosevelt, who signed the Act into law, stated that "[e]xcept perhaps for the Social Security Act, [the FLSA] is the most far-reaching, far-sighted program for the benefit of workers ever adopted here or in any other country."[3]

In addition to creating a Wage and hour Division (WHD) within the US Department of Labor (DOL) to administer and enforce the FLSA with respect to private employers and certain government agencies,[4] the FLSA granted the DOL authority to promulgate regulations to define certain aspects of the FLSA. Those regulations can be found in Title 29 of the US Code of Federal Regulations.[5] Together with the FLSA, DOL regulations establish employers' legal obligations at the federal level.

While the original version of the FLSA only applied to about one-fifth of the labor force,[6] today the FLSA applies to nearly all US workers. In 2009, the DOL estimated that over 130 million US workers were covered by the FLSA.[7] Coverage under the FLSA is determined by considering whether an employer or employee falls within the broad definitions set forth in the statute.[8] However, as discussed throughout this book, one of the challenges in studying wage and hour compliance is applying existing statutes and regulations—some of which have been around for nearly 80 years—to the modern workforce.

The FLSA and associated DOL regulations include four basic requirements for employers. First, employers are required to pay covered non-exempt employees no less than $7.25 per/h, which is the federal minimum wage effective July 24, 2009.[9] Second, the FLSA requires employers to pay non-exempt employees an overtime rate of at least one and one-half times the regular rate of pay for all hours worked in excess of 40 h per workweek.[10] Third, the FLSA and federal regulations forbid

---

[1] 29 U.S.C. §§ 201–219. The statute can be accessed online at https://www.dol.gov/whd/regs/statutes/FairLaborStandAct.pdf

[2] Grossman (n.d.).

[3] Pederson (2006).

[4] US Department of Labor (2016a).

[5] 29 C.F.R. §§ 500–899. This section of the Code of Federal Regulations can be accessed online at https://www.dol.gov/dol/cfr/Title_29/Chapter_V.htm

[6] See Grossman (n.d.).

[7] US Department of Labor (2009).

[8] US Department of Labor (2009).

[9] 29 U.S.C. § 206; US Department of Labor (n.d.a).

[10] 29 U.S.C. § 207.

"oppressive child labor," restricting children under the age of 18 from being employed in certain "hazardous" jobs, such as coal mining or working with power machines, and limiting the hours children under the age of 16 are allowed to work.[11] Fourth, employers must maintain specific employment records related to wages and hours, such as the employee's name, age and address, hours worked each day and week, regular hourly pay rate, weekly earnings, deductions, and total wages paid each pay period.[12] The DOL regulations also include several sections that provide specific guidance on topics related to these four main requirements, such as who is covered by the FLSA,[13] what should be considered hours worked,[14] how the "regular rate of pay" should be calculated,[15] and what defines a workweek.[16]

1.3   State and Local Wage and Hour Laws

Many states also have their own wage and hour laws, which may be the same as, or more expansive than, the FLSA.[17] When federal and state laws differ, the more restrictive and employee-friendly law controls.[18] Therefore, employers must be familiar and compliant with wage and hour requirements within all states in which they have employees. State laws may set more restrictive thresholds for protections than the FLSA, like higher minimum wages, or may have requirements that are not even covered by the FLSA, such as meal and rest break laws.

In recent years, wage and hour lawsuits have been on the rise. Indeed, in 2016, wage and hour lawsuits surged across the country, which suggests that employers need to be familiar with state wage and hour laws and regulations and kept abreast of new developments in the law. Due to the unique legal landscape in California, wage and hour laws for employees in this state are discussed later in this chapter.

In addition to federal- and state-level requirements, many local municipalities have recently begun adopting their own wage and hour laws for companies operating within their jurisdiction.[19] For example, a growing number of cities and counties have passed minimum wage laws that are higher than the state and federal minimum wage.[20] Several cities, including Chicago, Los Angeles, New York City, Philadelphia, San Diego, San Francisco, and Seattle, also have laws requiring private employers

---

[11] 29 U.S.C. § 212; 29 C.F.R. § 570; US Department of Labor (2013).

[12] 29 U.S.C. § 211; 29 C.F.R. § 516; US Department of Labor (2008a).

[13] 29 C.F.R. § 541.

[14] 29 C.F.R. § 785.

[15] 29 C.F.R. § 778.

[16] 29 C.F.R. § 778.

[17] For links to specific state laws, *see* US Department of Labor (n.d.b) available at https://www.dol.gov/whd/state/state.htm

[18] 29 U.S.C. § 218(a).

[19] *See, e.g.*, Department of Industrial Relations (2016).

[20] *See* UC Berkeley Labor Center (2017).

to provide paid sick leave to their employees.[21] Additionally, while only a handful of states have laws mandating paid family leave (which provides benefits to employees who need to take time off work to care for a seriously ill family member or to bond with their newborn or newly adopted child),[22] cities such as San Francisco are beginning to implement their own local paid family leave laws that go beyond state and federal requirements.[23] The vast number of state and local wage and hour laws creates a significant compliance challenge for employers who operate in different locations throughout the country. As a result, large employers, like national retail chains, must stay up to date with new laws in every city and state in which they operate in order to ensure compliance with this ever-changing legal landscape.

1.4   Exemptions from the FLSA

While nearly all US workers are covered by the FLSA, there are employees who are exempted by the Act. One of the most commonly disputed wage and hour issues in the past few decades has been the proper classification of employees as "exempt" or "non-exempt" from FLSA (or state law) protections. Some employees are exempt from the FLSA's overtime pay provisions, and others are exempt from both the overtime pay and minimum wage provisions. To qualify for an exemption, an employee must meet several specific criteria and have been classified by their employer as "exempt." Employees who are exempt from the FLSA's overtime and minimum wage protections and are paid a fixed salary, regardless of the number of hours they work. These "salaried" employees are thought to make enough money that FLSA protections are unnecessary, whereas non-exempt, hly employees are considered to be more vulnerable to wage and hour abuse by their employers.

"Misclassification" occurs when an employer classifies an employee as exempt even though the employee does not meet all the criteria required to fall within an exemption. When an employee is misclassified in violation of federal or state laws, he or she is denied protections such as overtime pay. Employees who believe they have been misclassified as exempt can notify their employer or initiate litigation in an attempt to recover monetary damages. However, misclassification lawsuits can be expensive for both parties, regardless of the outcome. While a majority of misclassification lawsuits settle prior to a decision on the merits, it is not uncommon for settlements involving large classes of employees to exceed $10 million. Perhaps the most well-known misclassification case that advanced to trial is *Bell v. Farmers Insurance Exchange*, in which a class of plaintiffs were awarded over $90 million in damages when the court determined that insurance claims adjusters were non-exempt administrative employees entitled to overtime pay.

---

[21] National Partnership for Women and Families (2017).

[22] National Conference of State Legislatures (2016).

[23] City and County of San Francisco Office of Labor Standards Enforcement (n.d.).

Table 1.1 Summary of exemption criteria for the "white-collar" exemptions[a]

Exemption (federal regulation)	Criteria (must meet all)
Executive (29 C.F.R. § 541.100)	1. Paid a salary of $455 or more per week 2. Primary duty is management of the enterprise, department, or subdivision 3. Manages at least two or more full-time employees 4. Has the authority to hire or fire others (or whose recommendations are given particular weight)
Administrative (29 C.F.R. § 541.200)	1. Paid a salary of $455 or more per week 2. Primary duty is the performance of office or nonmanual work directly related to the management or general business operations of the employer or the employer's customers 3. Primary duty includes the exercise of discretion and independent judgment with respect to matters of significance

Professional (29 C.F.R. § 541.300)	1. Paid a salary of $455 or more per week
	2. Primary duty meets one of the following criteria:
	   (a) Primary duty is work requiring advanced knowledge (i.e., "learned professional")
	   (b) Primary duty is work requiring invention, imagination, originality, or talent in an artistic or creative field (i.e., "creative professional")

[a]This table is a summary of the criteria specified in the federal regulations. See 29 C.F.R. § 541

The DOL regulations define the criteria that must be met for an employee to be classified as exempt from the FLSA.[24] The three most common exemptions are the executive, administrative, and professional exemptions, which have become known collectively as the "white-collar" or "EAP" exemptions. These exemptions apply to white-collar workers, such as those employees in management or highly skilled positions. Other exemptions outlined in the regulations include computer professionals,[25] outside salespeople,[26] and "highly compensated" employees.[27] While the specific requirements of each exemption differ, all exemptions, under the FLSA and state laws, are based on two broad requirements: (1) the amount and method of compensation the employee receives (known as the "salary test") and (2) the employee's job duties (known as the "duties test"). Table 1.1 summarizes the criteria for the FLSA's so-called white-collar exemptions. Some states have "salary test" and "duties test" requirements that are more stringent than the FLSA.

An evaluation of exempt status requires a detailed understanding of the work that employees perform. This assessment requires precise measurements of the amount of time employees actually spend performing the various types of work described in the exemption criteria. In addition, the level of authority and discretion that employees exercise related to matters of significance is also a relevant factor that can be

[24] 29 C.F.R. § 541; *see also* US Department of Labor (2008b).

[25] 29 C.F.R. § 541.400.

[26] 29 C.F.R. § 541.500.

[27] 29 C.F.R. § 541.601.

studied. These evaluations, which are discussed in Chap. 3, typically involve the use of observational methods, self-report questionnaires, or structured interviewing techniques to collect detailed information regarding factors relevant to one or more of the exemptions.

1.4.1   Proposed Revisions to Exemption Criteria

Although the criteria listed in Table 1.1 are accurate as of the time this chapter was written, the DOL recently undertook an effort to revise regulations that define exemption criteria. This action was initiated by President Obama's 2014 directive to the Secretary of Labor to "modernize and streamline" the white-collar exemption criteria.[28] In response, the DOL released a final rule that would increase the minimum salary threshold for the white-collar exemptions from $455 per week ($23,660 per year) to $913 per week ($47,476 per year) and included an automatic mechanism for increasing the salary threshold every 3 years.[29] The final rule was scheduled to go into effect on December 1, 2016.

However, on September 20, 2016, numerous states jointly filed a lawsuit against the DOL challenging the constitutionality of the new overtime rule.[30] On November 22, 2016, a few weeks after Donald Trump won the presidential election and a few days before the final rule was scheduled to go into effect, a Texas federal judge granted a nationwide preliminary injunction which prevented the DOL from implementing or enforcing the rule.[31] On August 31, 2017, the same judge permanently blocked the rule, reasoning, in part, that the proposed salary level in the final rule was so high that it essentially rendered the duties test irrelevant because nearly all employees who meet the new salary test would also meet the duties test. The diminished role of the duties test was found to be inconsistent with the intent of the FLSA.

The DOL under the Trump Administration issued a request for information (RFI) in July 2017 to assist the department in preparing a new proposal to revise the FLSA regulations.[32] Based on the DOL's announcement of its fall regulatory agenda, there may be a new overtime rule proposed in October 2018. Indications are that the DOL will propose an increase in the salary level but at a level lower than what was previously proposed. It is unknown whether changes to the duties test will also be proposed.

---

[28] Executive Office of the President (2014).

[29] US Department of Labor (2016b).

[30] *Nevada v. US Dep't of Labor*.

[31] *Nevada v. US Dep't of Labor*; *see also* US Department of Labor (2017a).

[32] US Department of Labor (2017b).

1.5 Independent Contractors

In order for FLSA protections to apply to a worker, he or she must be an "employee" of the employer. Under the FLSA, the term "employ" has been defined broadly as "suffer or permit to work," meaning that the employer directs the work or allows the work to take place.[33] In contrast, workers who are classified as "independent contractors" are, by definition, self-employed and therefore *not* employees of the company for whom they perform work. Therefore, these independent contractors are not protected by any of the FLSA provisions, including minimum wage and overtime pay. In addition to the loss of FLSA protections, employees misclassified as independent contractors do not receive employee-type benefits such as family and medical leave and unemployment compensation insurance. Misclassification also results in financial losses to the federal government and state governments in the form of lower tax revenues and less contributions to unemployment insurance and workers' compensation funds.[34]

In recent years, classification of workers as independent contractors has faced increased scrutiny, and legal disputes have arisen as a consequence. The DOL has described the misclassification of employees as independent contractors as "one of the most serious problems facing affected workers, employers and the entire economy."[35] As a result, the WHD has worked with the US Internal Revenue Service (IRS) and 37 states by sharing information and coordinating enforcement to reduce misclassification of employees as independent contractors.[36] In the last few years of the Obama Administration, the DOL was particularly active in this area. For example, in 2015, the DOL issued an Administrative Interpretation that narrowly defined an independent contractor and concluded that "most workers are employees"; however, this guidance was withdrawn by the Trump Administration's DOL on June 7, 2017.[37]

Individual plaintiffs can file lawsuits against employers that they believe misclassified them as independent contractors. Unlike a government enforcement action, these public lawsuits can take an extensive amount of time, require significantly more disclosure of documents and deposition testimony, and can result in unwanted stories in the press. Misclassification lawsuits are often brought against well-known companies as class or collective actions with a large number of plaintiffs. In the end, damages and settlements can be high, especially for start-up companies that are pushing the boundaries of what it means to be an employee in today's virtual world.[38] With the rise of the virtual economy, the proper classification of workers becomes even more challenging.

---

[33] US Department of Labor (2014).

[34] US Department of Labor (n.d.c).

[35] US Department of Labor (n.d.c).

[36] US Department of Labor (n.d.c).

[37] US Department of Labor (2017c); US Department of Labor (2017d).

[38] *See, e.g.*, *O'Connor v. Uber Technologies, Inc. et al.*

While many workers bring lawsuits to gain "employee" status under the FLSA, others seek to maintain their flexibility as independent workers. Many workers welcome being free of the restrictions and rigidity that come with being an employee. As independent contractors, they often operate as their own small business owners, with the freedom to manage their days, goals, and hours as they see fit.

To determine whether a worker is properly classified as an independent contractor, there are various factors that should be considered, and no one factor is dispositive. For example, the DOL previously used a multi-factor "economic realities test" that assesses whether a worker is truly in business for himself or herself or is economically dependent on the employer (i.e., independent contractor vs. employee). Other federal agencies, such as the IRS, along with some state agencies, like the California Employment Development Department, have published separate guidance on how to determine whether a worker is an employee or independent contractor. In addition, each year state and federal courts issue decisions in independent contractor misclassification cases. These decisions shape the way the law is interpreted and applied. The relevant factors from these sources, along with methods for evaluating them, are discussed in more detail in Chap. 4.

Evaluation of most independent contractor criteria requires a detailed understanding of the work performed by the worker and the degree and nature of the interaction between the worker and the company. In many cases this involves collecting data from multiple sources, including company leadership, the workers themselves, and the internal employees who serve as points of contact for the workers.

1.6 Off the Clock Work

The FLSA requires employees to be paid a minimum wage for all hours worked and be paid at the overtime rate (e.g., one and a half times the regular rate of pay) for all hours worked over 40 in a workweek.[39] In some states, including Alaska, California, and Nevada, overtime may have to be paid for hours worked in excess of 8 h during any workday.[40] The terms "hours worked" or "compensable time" are defined by the DOL as the time an employee must be on duty, on the employer's premises, at any other prescribed place of work, or any additional time the employee is allowed (i.e., suffered or permitted) to work.[41]

The number of hours worked by non-exempt employees is typically tracked using a time card system in which employees record the time they began and finished working each shift. Employees are often said to be "on the clock" between the time they clock in for their shift and the time they clock out at the end of their shift,

---

[39] 29 U.S.C. §§ 206–207 (2012).

[40] Alaska Stat. §§ 23.10.050–23.10.150 (2016); Cal. Lab. Code § 510 (2016); Nev. Rev. Stat. § 608.018 (2016).

[41] US Department of Labor (2008c); see also US Department of Labor (2008d).

that is, the time for which they are being paid. The time before or after an employee's shift is referred to as off the clock. When employees are performing compensable work during a time for which they are not being paid, they are said to be performing "off the clock work," which may result in the employee initiating litigation to recover unpaid wages and overtime.

Off the clock work can occur in a variety of ways. Some of the more common allegations include employees starting work before clocking in, clocking out before finishing work, performing work from home but not reporting the time (including phone calls or emails), working through unpaid meal breaks, donning or doffing required uniforms or equipment before or after their shift, time shaving (i.e., paying employees for fewer h than actually worked), or improper time clock "rounding" practices. Employers can be liable for significant damages for not paying all time worked.

Evaluating off the clock claims often involves understanding not only *what* activities performed by employees but also *when* the work is performed. When faced with allegations that an employee worked off the clock, employers must compare the amount of time the employee worked to the amount of time for which the employee was paid. While this comparison is a simple task conceptually, it is often challenging in practice. The primary cause of difficulty is that time worked is rarely recorded separately from paid time. When an employee alleges that the time worked is not equal to the paid time, the challenge is to generate reliable data that shows the actual time worked. Chapter 5 provides discussion of some existing sources of data that may be useful for this purpose, along with some methods for collecting data to estimate the amount of time actually worked.

1.6.1 De Minimis

For both employers and employees, it can be impractical to record off the clock time worked if it is of an insignificant or "de minimis" value. The DOL has acknowledged in regulations that when there are "uncertain and indefinite periods of time involved of only a few seconds or minutes duration, and where the failure to count such time is due to considerations justified by industrial realities," that time can be considered de minimis and does not need to be compensated for by the employer.[42] However, an employer cannot arbitrarily fail to count any portion of an employee's regular working time, even if it only amounts to $1 per week, because in the aggregate this practice could encourage abuse.[43] The DOL further explains that, for purposes of recording or computing time, employers may round to the nearest 5 min, one tenth, or one quarter of an hour, so long as that process does not result in the "failure to compensate the employees properly for all of the time they have actually

---

[42] 29 C.F.R. § 785.47 (2016); *see also Anderson v. Mt. Clemens Pottery Co.*

[43] *Addison v. Huron Stevedoring Corp.*

worked" over a period of time.[44] The Supreme Court of California is currently grappling with how to apply the FLSA's de minimis doctrine to claims for unpaid wages under the California Labor Code.[45]

1.7   Meal and Rest Breaks

Although there are no federal requirements establishing meal and rest breaks, many states provide employees with these added protections. Some states, such as Florida and Texas, do not mandate that employers provide minimum meal or rest breaks to employees who work shifts of a certain length, but others require that employers provide up to an hour of break time to employees who work an 8-h shift. For example, employees in states such as California, Colorado, Massachusetts, Nebraska, Nevada, Tennessee, and Washington are entitled to a 30-min unpaid meal break when they work a shift ranging between 5 and 8 h, depending on the state.[46] In addition, employees in states such as California, Colorado, Kentucky, Nevada, Oregon, and Washington are entitled to two paid 10-min rest breaks in an 8-h shift.[47] In other states, employees are entitled to meal and rest breaks of different lengths (e.g., West Virginia, Illinois) or the break requirements depend on the particular circumstances (e.g., Kentucky, Maine) or industry (e.g., New York, Massachusetts).

Litigation arises when employees allege that they did not receive the meal and/or rest breaks to which they were legally entitled, or the break they received was shorter than the minimum break required. Another potential for non-compliance is when employees are interrupted to perform work tasks during their breaks or have certain activities restricted during their break, making them not relieved of all duties, as required by many states. Evaluating these issues can be done in a variety of ways, including analysis of existing time clock data or other sources of electronic data, designing and administering self-report surveys to collect information from employees about meal and rest break compliance, or conducting observational studies to determine the length of breaks actually taken and whether compensable work was performed during breaks. The strategies for evaluating meal and rest break compliance are discussed in Chap. 6.

---

[44] US Department of Labor (2008e).

[45] Green (2016); *Troester v. Starbucks Corp.*

[46] US Department of Labor (2017e); HR360 (2017).

[47] US Department of Labor (2017f).

1.8 Special Wage and Hour Issues in California

Due to the highly restrictive nature and unique requirements of California's wage and hour laws, many resources on wage and hour laws discuss California's laws separately from other states. Historically, more wage and hour lawsuits have been filed in California than any other state, and the range of protections for California employees is far broader than other states. Two of the most impactful differences in California are the "job duties" test for exempt employees and the California Fair Pay Act (which went into effect on January 1, 2016),[48] both of which are significantly more restrictive than their federal equivalents. The job duties test is discussed in more detail in Chap. 3, and issues of pay equity legislation are covered in Chap. 9.

California's wage and hour laws are contained in two sets of regulations: the California Labor Code[49] and the Industrial Welfare Commission (IWC) Wage Orders.[50] The Department of Labor Standards Enforcement (DLSE) is the enforcement agency for California's wage and hour laws. The DLSE interprets laws and creates guidelines for companies to ensure compliance with the law. As part of its responsibilities, the DLSE publishes and regularly revises the Enforcement Policies and Interpretations Manual,[51] which summarizes the agency's policies and interpretations of wage and hour laws and regulations. It also regularly publishes opinion letters to clarify the agency's perspective on various issues.[52]

Minor compliance or technical errors, like a missed meal break or omitted information on a pay stub, can result in significant financial consequences for employers. Passed in 2004, the Private Attorneys General Act (PAGA) provides employees the power to sue their employers on behalf of themselves, other employees, and the State of California for violations of the California Labor Code. PAGA lawsuits increased by more than 400% from 2005 to 2013, and an excess of 6,000 PAGA notices are received by the State of California each year.[53] Because PAGA permits plaintiffs to recover legal costs and attorneys' fees if they prevail, plaintiffs' attorneys have been able to use it as a vehicle to file a wave of wage and hour lawsuits against California employers. For example, obscure labor laws, like the requirement

---

[48] The California Fair Pay Act prohibits California employers from paying their employees less than employees of the opposite sex for "substantially similar" work unless the employer can show that the pay gap is justified by a factor other than sex, such as seniority, merit, a system that measures production, or differences in education, training, or experience (Department of Industrial Relations, 2017). Effective January 1, 2017, the Act was expanded to cover unequal pay as to race and ethnicity. *See* Wage Equality Act of 2016.

[49] *See* Cal. Lab. Code, available at http://leginfo.legislature.ca.gov/faces/codesTOCSelected.xhtml ?tocCode=LAB&tocTitle=+Labor+Code+-+LAB

[50] *See* Cal. Code Regs., available at https://www.dir.ca.gov/IWC/WageOrderIndustries.htm

[51] Division of Labor Standards Enforcement (2017).

[52] The opinion letters are available online at https://www.dir.ca.gov/dlse/OpinionLetters-bySubject.htm

[53] Saltsman (2017).

for employers to provide "suitable seats" to employees when "the nature of the work reasonably permits,"[54] have recently brought multimillion dollar lawsuits against large employers in California.[55] Chapter 7 provides the latest legal updates on suitable seating requirements in California along with some methods that can be used to evaluate relevant criteria.

1.9   Class Certification

The vast majority of high-profile wage and hour lawsuits are brought as class or collective actions. In these cases, the named plaintiffs seek to represent a group of other current or former employees who they allege have common claims or are similarly situated. Before a case can proceed as a class or collective action, it must be "certified," that is, the court must decide whether the claims of all class members are similar enough that they can be resolved on a class-wide basis. Plaintiffs argue in favor of class certification, while employers generally want to defeat the creation of a class of plaintiffs. A certified class creates much greater financial exposure for the employer and typically settles before trial because employers are motivated to resolve the case to avoid the risk of large monetary awards if unsuccessful. While cases that are not certified can proceed as individual plaintiff cases, many plaintiffs choose not to pursue them further because of the high cost of litigation, uncertain outcome, and relatively small financial awards, even if they prevail in the end. As a result, many cases are won or lost at the class certification stage and before the issue of liability is litigated. Wage and hour classes can be certified under two legal processes: Section 216(b) of the FLSA[56] and Rule 23 of the Federal Rules of Civil Procedure ("Rule 23").[57] The certification standards under these two processes differ, and therefore each one will be discussed separately.

Multi-plaintiff FLSA cases are certified under Section 216(b) of the FLSA. If certified, the case is called a collective action. Current and former employees must actively opt in to the collective action to join the lawsuit. The certification standard for FLSA classes is whether the putative collective action members are "similarly situated."[58] While the FLSA does not define "similarly situated" nor does it establish a process for certifying a collective action, courts generally apply a two-stage process in certifying a collective action under Section 216(b). The first stage is the "notice stage" where the case is first "conditionally certified" based on a lenient standard for the purpose of sending notice of the action to potential opt-in

---

[54] I.W.C. Wage Order 7-2001 § 14.

[55] *See, e.g.*, Lee (2017).

[56] 29 U.S.C. § 216(b).

[57] Fed. R. Civ. P. 23, available at https://www.federalrulesofcivilprocedure.org/frcp/title-iv-parties/rule-23-class-actions/

[58] 29 U.S.C. § 216(b).

plaintiffs.[59] In the second stage, after all evidence has been presented, the court determines whether the case should proceed to trial as a collective action. A more stringent standard is applied at the second stage and is where evidence from experts is considered.

While FLSA collective actions must proceed in federal court, class actions under state wage and hour laws may be filed in either federal or state court. Although states have their own criteria for certifying class actions,[60] many states, including California,[61] look to Rule 23 of the Federal Rules of Civil Procedure for guidance in the certification process. The most significant difference between class actions brought under Rule 23 and collective actions brought under Section 216(b) is that, in a class action, class members are generally bound by the judgment or settlement unless they choose to "opt out," whereas in a collective action, individuals who want to be part of the class must "opt in" to participate and be bound by the judgment. Given that inactivity does not preclude an individual from being a part of the Rule 23 class, the size and value of class actions tend to be much higher than collective actions.

In contrast to the FLSA's "similarly situated" requirement, Rule 23 sets forth four basic prerequisites for a class action: (1) numerosity, (2) typicality, (3) commonality, and (4) adequacy of representation.[62] In addition to these four requirements, a class action must satisfy one of the three requirements of Rule 23(b), which for class claims seeking damages (such as unpaid overtime), the analysis involves whether common questions predominate and a class action is superior to individual actions.[63] In a well-known decision that impacts wage and hour class actions, *Wal-Mart Stores, Inc. v. Dukes*, the US Supreme Court made it clear that plaintiffs must not merely plead the existence of the Rule 23 requirements but rather must prove them, thereby requiring courts to perform a "rigorous" analysis to determine whether the Rule 23(a) prerequisites are satisfied. In the *Wal-Mart* case which involved allegations of systemic gender discrimination, the Supreme Court articulated that commonality in a Rule 23 class action "requires the plaintiff to demonstrate that the class members 'have suffered the same injury.'"[64] Simply put, it is not whether a well-crafted class action complaint includes allegations that raise *common questions* but whether a class-wide proceeding will generate *common answers*.[65] The plaintiffs in *Wal-Mart* could not point to any specific employment policy or practice of class-wide application (such as an inherently biased testing procedure) that directly affected women across different stores. Therefore, the Supreme Court held that commonality was lacking because plaintiffs could not demonstrate that they had all suffered the same injury and not merely a violation of their rights under

[59] *See, e.g., Hoffman-La Roche, Inc. v. Sperling* (vesting district courts with the authority and discretion "to implement 29 U.S.C. § 216(b) . . . by facilitating notice to potential plaintiffs").

[60] *See, e.g.,* Cal. Code of Civ. Pro. § 382.

[61] *Vasquez v. Superior Court.*

[62] Fed. R. Civ. P. 23(a).

[63] Fed. R. Civ. P. 23(b)(3).

[64] *Wal-Mart Stores, Inc. v. Dukes* (quoting *Gen. Tel. Co. of Sw. v. Falcon*).

[65] *Wal-Mart Stores, Inc. v. Dukes.*

the same law. As a result, the *Wal-Mart* decision set a higher bar for plaintiffs to certify a class in employment and wage and hour cases.

The "similarly situated" criterion under Section 216(b) and "commonality" criterion under Rule 23 are generally where methods from I/O psychology (or other related disciplines) are most directly applicable. Both criteria require plaintiffs to show similarity in the claims for putative collective action or class action members. For example, this similarity may be shown when a uniformly implemented company policy resulted in employees working off the clock or all employees within a job title performing the same duties in the same way and spending the majority of their work time performing non-exempt work. Thus, I/O methods are useful to evaluate certification under both processes because the underlying issue is the degree of variability between putative class members on factors such as the tasks employees actually perform and the time spent on those tasks. The goal of the evaluation is to determine whether the members of the putative class do in fact vary from person to person with respect to the issues in the case to the extent that class certification is inappropriate because their claims cannot be resolved on a class-wide basis.

1.10 Trends in Wage and Hour Litigation

From 2000 to 2015, the number of wage and hour lawsuits filed in federal court increased by approximately 358%.[66] During this time period, there have also been high volumes of wage and hour cases in state courts. While federal filings decreased for the first time in 2016, it was still the second-highest number of wage and hour cases ever filed.[67] Additionally, wage and hour settlement values increased significantly in 2016, up to $695.5 million from $463.6 million in 2015 for the top ten largest settlements.[68]

At least one commentator attributed the surge in wage and hour litigation to the decline of union-related litigation.[69] Another possible factor is that, under the Obama Administration, the DOL and Equal Employment Opportunity Commission (EEOC) were widely considered to be pro-employee and they placed a greater focus on wage and hour issues, which contributed to increased filings.[70] While wage and hour enforcement is expected to be less aggressive under the Trump Administration, a more employer-friendly DOL may result in "litigation gaps" that are filled in by private lawsuits or increased enforcement at the state level. Because these wage and hour litigation trends are likely to continue, it is essential for employees to know their rights and for employers to understand the myriad of current laws and regulations that impact their businesses.

---

[66] DePillis (2015).

[67] Teachout (2017).

[68] Ramirez (2017).

[69] *See* DePillis (2015).

[70] *See* Ramirez (2017).

1.11   Conclusion

This chapter provided the legal background for each of the issues discussed in this book. Each topic covers an area of wage and hour compliance that is frequently litigated and also addressed using methods from I/O psychology such as job analysis. Chapter 2 provides the foundation for the methods that are regularly used to address these issues. The remaining chapters each address a specific wage and hour issue, which includes a description of the issue and methods for evaluating compliance.

Acknowledgment We would like to thank Theodore E. Alexander, a student at the George Washington University Law School, for his contributions.

References

City and County of San Francisco Office of Labor Standards Enforcement. (n.d.). *San Francisco labor laws: Citywide*. Retrieved from http://sfgov.org/olse/san-francisco-labor-laws-citywide

Department of Industrial Relations. (2016). *Minimum wage*. Retrieved from http://www.dir.ca.gov/dlse/FAQ_MinimumWage.htm

Department of Industrial Relations. (2017). *California Equal Pay Act: Frequently asked questions*. Retrieved from https://www.dir.ca.gov/dlse/California_Equal_Pay_Act.htm

DePillis, L. (2015, November 25). Why wage and hour litigation is skyrocketing. *The Washington Post*. Retrieved from https://www.washingtonpost.com/news/wonk/wp/2015/11/25/people-are-suing-more-than-ever-over-wages-and-hours/?utm_term=.14e3293ce750

Division of Labor Standards Enforcement. (2017). *The 2002 update of the DLSE enforcement policies and interpretation manual (Revised)*. Retrieved from http://www.dir.ca.gov/dlse/DLSEManual/dlse_enfcmanual.pdf

Executive Office of the President. (2014). *Updating and modernizing overtime regulations: Memorandum for the Secretary of Labor (79 FR 15209)*. Retrieved from https://federalregister.gov/a/2014-06138

Green, K. (2016, August 18). California justices take on time issue in Starbucks wage suit. *Law360*. Retrieved from https://www.law360.com/articles/830228/calif-justices-take-on-time-issue-in-starbucks-wage-suit

Grossman, J. (n.d.). *Fair Labor Standards Act of 1938: Maximum struggle for minimum wage*. Retrieved from https://www.dol.gov/oasam/programs/history/flsa1938.htm

HR360. (2017). *Meal and rest breaks in all 50 states*. Retrieved from https://www.hr360.com/statelaws/Connecticut/Meal-and-Rest-Breaks-In-All-50-States.aspx

Lee, S. (2017, November 7). Bank of America to pay $15M to end tellers' seating suit. *Law360*. Retrieved from https://www.law360.com/articles/860087/bank-of-america-to-pay-15m-to-end-tellers-seating-suit

National Conference of State Legislatures. (2016). *State family and medical leave laws*. Retrieved from http://www.ncsl.org/research/labor-and-employment/state-family-and-medical-leave-laws.aspx

National Partnership for Women and Families. (2017). *Interactive map: Paid sick days campaigns, statistics and stories [Web log post]*. Retrieved from http://www.paidsickdays.org

Pederson, W. D. (2006). *Presidential profiles: The FDR years*. Retrieved from https://www.e-reading.club/bookreader.php/142104/Pederson_-_Presidential_Profiles__The_FDR_Years.pdf

Ramirez, J. C. (2017). *Surveying the class action landscape*. Retrieved from http://www.hreonline.com/HRE/print.jhtml?id=534361759

Saltsman, M. (2017, June 4). Private Attorneys General Act is another burden to California small businesses. *The Orange County Register.* Retrieved from http://www.ocregister.com/2017/06/04/private-attorneys-general-act-is-another-burden-to-california-small-businesses/

Teachout, R. (2017). *Fewer wage and hour class actions filed, but value of settlements spikes.* Retrieved from https://www.shrm.org/resourcesandtools/legal-and-compliance/employment-law/pages/class-action-wage-and-hour-2016.aspx

U.S. Department of Labor. (2008a). *Fact sheet #21: Recordkeeping requirements under the Fair Labor Standards Act (FLSA).* Retrieved from https://www.dol.gov/whd/regs/compliance/whdfs21.pdf

U.S. Department of Labor. (2008b). *Fact sheet #17A: exemption for executive, administrative, professional, computer & outside sales employees under the Fair Labor Standards Act (FLSA).* Retrieved from https://www.dol.gov/whd/overtime/fs17a_overview.pdf

U.S. Department of Labor. (2008c). *Off-the-clock references.* Retrieved from https://www.dol.gov/whd/offtheclock/

U.S. Department of Labor. (2008d). *Fact sheet #22: Hours worked under the Fair Labor Standards Act (FLSA).* Retrieved from https://www.dol.gov/whd/regs/compliance/whdfs22.pdf

U.S. Department of Labor. (2008e). *Opinion letters - Fair Labor Standards Act, FLSA2008-7NA.* Retrieved from https://www.dol.gov/whd/opinion/FLSANA/2008/2008_05_15_07NA_FLSA.htm

U.S. Department of Labor. (2009). *Fact sheet #14: Coverage under the Fair Labor Standards Act (FLSA).* Retrieved from https://www.dol.gov/whd/regs/compliance/whdfs14.pdf

U.S. Department of Labor. (2013). *Child labor provisions for nonagricultural occupations under the Fair Labor Standards Act.* Retrieved from https://www.dol.gov/whd/regs/compliance/childlabor101_text.htm

U.S. Department of Labor. (2014). *Fact sheet #13: Am i an employee? Employment relationship under the Fair Labor Standards Act (FLSA).* Retrieved from https://www.dol.gov/whd/regs/compliance/whdfs13.pdf

U.S. Department of Labor. (2016a). *Handy reference guide to the Fair Labor Standards Act.* Retrieved from https://www.dol.gov/whd/regs/compliance/wh1282.pdf

U.S. Department of Labor. (2016b). *Defining and delimiting the exemptions for executive, administrative, professional, outside sales and computer employees (81 FR 32391). [Final Rule].* Retrieved from https://federalregister.gov/a/2014-06138

U.S. Department of Labor. (2017a). *Important information regarding recent overtime litigation in the U.S. District Court of the Eastern District of Texas.* Retrieved from https://www.dol.gov/whd/overtime/final2016/litigation.htm

U.S. Department of Labor. (2017b). *Defining and delimiting the exemptions for executive, administrative, professional, outside sales and computer employees (82 FR 34616). [Request for Information].* Retrieved from https://www.federalregister.gov/documents/2017/07/26/2017-15666/request-for-information-defining-and-delimiting-the-exemptions-for-executive-administrative

U.S. Department of Labor. (2017c). *Administrator interpretation letter – Fair Labor Standards Act.* Retrieved from https://www.dol.gov/WHD/opinion/adminIntrprtnFLSA.htm#foot

U.S. Department of Labor. (2017d). *News release.* Retrieved from https://www.dol.gov/newsroom/releases/opa/opa20170607

U.S. Department of Labor. (2017e). *Minimum length of meal period required under state law for adult employees in private sector.* Retrieved from https://www.dol.gov/whd/state/meal.htm

U.S. Department of Labor. (2017f). *Minimum paid rest period requirements under state law for adult employees in private sector.* Retrieved from https://www.dol.gov/whd/state/rest.htm.

U.S. Department of Labor. (n.d.-a). *Minimum wage.* Retrieved from https://www.dol.gov/whd/minimumwage.htm.

U.S. Department of Labor. (n.d.-b). *State labor laws.* Retrieved from https://www.dol.gov/whd/state/state.htm.

U.S. Department of Labor. (n.d.-c). *Misclassification of employees as independent contractors.* Retrieved from https://www.dol.gov/whd/workers/misclassification/

UC Berkeley Labor Center. (2017) *Inventory of U.S. City and County minimum wage ordinances.* Retrieved from http://laborcenter.berkeley.edu/minimum-wage-living-wage-resources/inventory-of-us-city-and-county-minimum-wage-ordinances/

Statutes and Regulations

29 C.F.R. § 541 (2016).
29 C.F.R. § 541.400 (2016).
29 C.F.R. § 541.500 (2016).
29 C.F.R. § 541.601 (2016).
29 C.F.R. § 570 (2016).
29 C.F.R. § 778 (2016).
29 C.F.R. § 785 (2016).
29 C.F.R. § 785.47 (2016).
29 C.F.R. §§ 500–899 (2016).
29 U.S.C. § 206 (2012).
29 U.S.C. § 207 (2012).
29 U.S.C. § 216(b) (2016).
29 U.S.C. § 218(a) (2012).
29 U.S.C. §§ 201–219 (2012).
29 U.S.C. §§ 206–207 (2012).
Alaska Stat. §§ 23.10.050–23.10.150 (2016).
Cal. Code of Civ. Pro. § 382.
Cal. Lab. Code § 510 (2016).
Fed. R. Civ. P. 23.
Fed. R. Civ. P. 23(a).
Fed. R. Civ. P. 23(b)(3).
I.W.C. Wage Order 7-2001, § 14 (2005).
Nev. Rev. Stat. § 608.018 (2016).
Wage Equality Act of 2016, S.B. 1063 (Cal. 2016).

Court Cases

Addison v. *Huron Stevedoring Corp.*, 204 F. 2d 88, 95 (2d Cir. 1953).
Anderson v. Mt. Clemens Pottery Co., 328 U.S. 680 (1946).
Gen. Tel. Co. of Sw. v. Falcon, 457 U.S. 147, 157 (1982).
Hoffman-La Roche, Inc. v. Sperling, 493 U.S. 165, 169 (1989).
Nevada v. U.S. Dep't of Labor, 227 F. Supp. 3d 696 (E.D. Tex. 2017).
O'Connor v. Uber Technologies, Inc. et al., C13-3826 EMC (N.D. Cal.).
Troester v. Starbucks Corp., No. S234969 (Cal.).
Vasquez v. Superior Court, 4 Cal. 3d 800, 821 (1971).
Wal-Mart Stores, Inc. v. Dukes, 564 U.S. 338 (2011).

Chapter 2
Data Collection Methods

Chester Hanvey

This chapter describes the underlying foundation for several data collection methods that are commonly used to evaluate wage and hour compliance. The resolution of nearly all wage and hour disputes covered in this book requires detailed measurement of the work employees perform, the amount of time spent on that work, and the context in which work is performed. In the past 15 years, consultants and experts have been successfully applying job analysis techniques to collect data to address these issues.[1] The core methodologies are applicable to multiple wage and hour disputes. However, the general approaches described in this chapter are often customized to address the unique legal questions associated with each wage and hour issue. In later chapters, methodological considerations specific to a particular wage and hour issue are addressed.

As Guion and Highhouse (2006) put it, "fundamentally, all job analysis consists of observing what can be seen and asking questions about what cannot."[2] Consistent with that framework, the data collection methodologies discussed in this chapter fall into two general categories: observational methodologies and self-report methodologies. Both approaches are grounded in well-established job analysis techniques.

2.1 Measurement

The concept of measurement plays a significant role in the context of wage and hour litigation. Within the sciences, researchers generally strive to maximize the precision of measurement, as more precise measurements are more useful for making

---

The original version of this chapter was revised. A correction to this chapter can be found at https://doi.org/10.1007/978-3-319-74612-8_10

[1] See Banks and Cohen (2005).

[2] Guion and Highhouse (2006) (p. 25).

© Springer International Publishing AG, part of Springer Nature 2018

C. Hanvey, *Wage and Hour Law*, https://doi.org/10.1007/978-3-319-74612-8_2

accurate inferences.[3] Historically, measurement has served one of two purposes: assign numeric quantities to objects and define whether an object falls within a certain category or group.[4] Both are applicable within the realm of wage and hour compliance. It is generally accepted that measurement accuracy can have consequences for the quality of decision-making in various areas of Human Resources (HR).[5] What is unique about the wage and hour context is that even small measurement errors can have major consequences in litigation; that is, small measurement errors can make the difference in the outcome of a lawsuit and potentially millions of dollars in financial liability. Without precise and accurate measurement of relevant factors, the data collected may be unable to answer key questions or, worse, lead to erroneous conclusions.

It is important to draw a distinction between the quality of the data used in a statistical analysis and the quality of the statistical analysis itself. The meaningfulness of results from a statistical analysis is dependent on the quality of the underlying data. Many wage and hour cases, for example, involve extrapolating statistics from a small sample of employees to a large population of employees. Thus, small measurement errors are magnified when they are extrapolated to the population. Issues related to sampling, statistical analysis, and extrapolation are covered in Chap. 8. The focus of this chapter is to provide strategies for gathering valid and reliable data that address key legal questions. The methods described in this chapter were chosen because they tend to produce the most precise measurement of concepts directly related to the legal questions in wage and hour disputes.

2.2   Job Analysis

Knowledge of the work employees perform, time spent performing work, and the context in which it's performed are critical components in the resolution of most wage and hour disputes. For more than a century, various job analysis techniques have been developed to gather this information in a systematic manner. There are many excellent texts that provide extensive detail on various job analysis techniques.[6] I do not intend to provide a complete summary of all job analysis techniques. Rather, the discussion below is focused on job analysis methods that are applicable in the wage and hour context.

The term job analysis refers to "a wide variety of systematic procedures for examining, documenting, and drawing inferences about work activities, worker attributes, and work context."[7] Job analysis is one of the most commonly used orga-

---

[3] Guion and Highhouse (2006); Babbie (1990).

[4] Nunnally and Bernstein (1994).

[5] See Gatewood, Feild & Barrick (2007).

[6] See, e.g., Sackett, Walmsley, and Laczo (2013); Wilson, Bennett, Gibson, and Alliger (2012); Morgeson and Dierdorff (2011); Brannick, Levine, and Morgeson (2007); Sanchez and Levine (2001); Harvey (1991); Gael (1988).

[7] Sackett et al. (2013), p. 61.

nizational data collection techniques[8] and can provide a basis for variety of HR applications (e.g., selection, training, performance appraisal) and non-HR applications (e.g., ergonomics, human factors).[9] In recent decades, job analysis techniques have become commonplace when evaluating many different wage and hour disputes.[10]

2.2.1 Toward an FLSA-Relevant Job Analysis

Conducting a job analysis requires many methodological choices throughout the process. There are many different uses for job analysis data, and the purpose of the study drives these methodological decisions. Sackett et al. (2013) highlighted many of these choices including two that are especially relevant in the wage and hour context.

The first is whether the focus of the job analysis is the work performed ("work-oriented" approach) or the attributes required to perform that work ("worker-oriented" approach). Addressing wage and hour disputes typically requires the researcher to take a work-oriented approach such as a task inventory.[11] Information about worker attributes, such as knowledge, skills, and abilities (KSAs) required to successfully perform the job, are relevant in many applications (e.g., employment selection) but are typically not applicable to resolve wage and hour disputes.[12]

The second choice is the degree of specificity or generality at which data will be collected. Many job analyses methods are not designed to collect data at a sufficient level of detail to determine compliance with wage and hour laws. An analysis of exemptions from the Fair Labor Standards Act (FLSA), for example, may require a calculation of the percent of time that an individual employee spends performing exempt tasks. A job analysis questionnaire which shows that employees in general perform many exempt tasks "frequently" does not allow this required calculation. In addition, class certification decisions are usually based on the degree of similarity between employees on factors such as the job duties they perform and time spent in performing them. Overly generalized descriptions of work can make dissimilar employees appear similar, while overly specific descriptions of work can make similar employees appear different.[13]

An additional methodological issue when conducting a job analysis for wage and hour purposes is the unit of measurement. Most job analyses have the goal of

---

[8] Morgeson and Campion (1997).

[9] Sanchez and Levine (2001).

[10] Banks and Aubry (2005); Banks and Cohen (2005); Ko and Kleiner (2005); Honorée, Wyld, and Juban (2005).

[11] See Gatewood et al. (2007); Gael (1988).

[12] One exception is the applicability of the professional exemption, which is impacted by the educational background required to perform the job. This issue is discussed in Chap. 3.

[13] Sackett (1991) provides actual examples of this issue.

describing the work performed by a "typical" employee, not an individual employee. This is preferred in many situations, such as when decisions are made based on job title (e.g., selection criteria, performance criteria). Wage and hour cases, on the other hand, typically require decisions to be made at the *individual* level,[14] creating the need for an individual differences approach to job analysis. It does not matter if employees in the job *generally* perform exempt tasks, for example; it matters if *each* employee performs exempt tasks.

Along similar lines, it is important to consider how differences between employees should be treated. There has been debate in the literature regarding whether variability in job analysis ratings represent inaccuracy or meaningful differences.[15] When job analysis data are used in the context of a class certification decision, a critical question is whether meaningful differences exist between employees. Methods that describe a typical employee or treat within-title variability as measurement error do not provide information valuable to this inquiry. The method used must at least acknowledge *the possibility* that meaningful differences exist between employees and be able to describe the degree to which employees differ. This approach is consistent with recent literature that suggests actual differences in work can be the sources of differences between employees, rather than measurement error.[16]

In the following section, I describe many considerations that frequently influence methodological choices when designing and executing a job analysis to study wage and hour issues.

2.3   Choosing an Appropriate Method

One of the most important decisions to make when studying a wage and hour issue is determining the appropriate method for collecting data. The decision will have significant impact on the execution of the study and may impact the legal defensibility of the study results. The methodology should be driven by the goal of collecting valid and reliable data that can address relevant legal questions. Often, more than one method can achieve this goal, and practical or logistical factors such as cost, time, or client preferences are considered. Below, I list several factors that often impact the choice of method:

- *The specific violation at issue.* Some methods are better suited to capture relevant data for a specific violation than others. In the next few chapters, these potential violations will be described along with the methods that are used to address them.
- *Stage in litigation.* As described in Chap. 1, class action lawsuits typically go through three phases: class certification, merits/liability, and damages. The legal

---

[14] 29 C.F.R. §541.2.

[15] See Harvey and Wilson (2000); Morgeson and Campion (2000); Sanchez and Levine (2000).

[16] Lievens, Sanchez, Bartram, and Brown (2010); Dierdorff and Morgeson (2007).

questions at each stage of litigation differ, and it's important to design a study that will address relevant questions. Studies that are conducted prior to class certification are typically conducted with the goal of determining the degree of similarity or variability between putative class members. A study conducted after the class has been certified typically has the goal of determining whether violations occurred. These two goals are related but require a slightly different focus that may impact the methodology. In addition, direct contact with incumbents may be prohibited post-certification which can limit some methodological options.

- *Type of job.* Jobs that involve high complexity or primarily consist of mental tasks are not as well suited for an observational approach.[17] An employee who works on a computer for a large portion of their day, for example, is challenging to observe because it may be difficult to reliably determine what task they are performing at any given time.

- *Size of the putative class.* The size of the class may impact the amount of data desired. Generally, more data can be collected using self-report methodologies such as questionnaires. When a class consists of a relatively small number of people, an observational approach can gather data from a significant portion of the class members. When the class includes thousands of employees, it can be extremely costly to gather observational data from a large proportion of the class. If this is desirable (in some cases, the portion of class members sampled is not important), self-reported questionnaires are often the preferred option.

- *Geographic disparity of class members.* Some methods require job analysts to be physically present at the workplace to collect data (e.g., observational approaches), while others do not (e.g., questionnaires, structured interviews). The geographic disparity can have implications for travel time, travel expenses, and the speed with which data can be collected. All of these factors may play a role in the choice of method.

- *Degree to which the job has changed over time.* Another consideration is the degree to which the job being studied has changed within the relevant time period (e.g., different processes, different staffing models, reallocation of responsibilities). Observational methods are capable of describing how work is performed currently. For jobs that have not changed significantly, these data are informative about how the job used to be performed. However, for jobs that have undergone significant changes, information about how the job is performed now will be less informative as to how the job was performed before the changes. Self-report approaches are often designed to collect retrospective data and therefore may be able to provide reliable information about how a job was performed in the past.

- *Existing company policies and practices.* Some companies regularly conduct job analyses observations or administer internal questionnaires and surveys. Employees may have developed a comfort with these approaches, and systems are already in place to communicate about the study and execute the data collection. It may make sense in these situations to use a method familiar to employees to minimize operational disruption.

---

[17] Guion and Highhouse (2006).

- *Language fluency of incumbents*. In some companies, the language ability of the employees from whom data will be collected plays a role in the methodology. Questionnaires require a minimum level of reading ability, and structured interviews require a minimum level of verbal ability. When employees are not fluent in English, these methods are more challenging.[18] Questionnaires can be translated into other languages, but this can introduce new challenges. Professional translations might be problematic in some companies because employees tend to use informal terminology to refer to various work processes. This is often the case in the restaurant industry, for example. In some companies, employees have low levels of language ability, regardless of their native language, which requires self-report instruments to be designed with low complexity.

The appropriate method is often based on these and many other factors unique to the company. In the following sections, I describe the methods that are typically used to collect data relevant to wage and hour compliance.

2.4   Observational Approaches

One of the most commonly used methods to collect data to evaluate wage and hour compliance is through direct observation. This method is a systematic process in which a job analyst directly observes incumbents performing their work and documents detailed information about that work such as the tasks performed and the duration of tasks. Direct observation is a well-accepted technique to learn about the work employees perform, especially for jobs that involve physical or otherwise observable work.[19]

There are different types of observation methodologies that are applicable to wage and hour cases. Broadly, these can be categorized as either "live" observations or video observations. Live observations require a job analyst to be physically present to observe and record tasks performed and time spent on tasks. Video observations involve analyzing video recordings of employees performing work. There are advantages associated with each type of observation. The choice of observational approach is typically driven by the specific wage and hour issue and therefore the relevant legal questions. For example, live observations are well suited for situations that require detailed information about what an employee does on the job including the sequence of tasks, the content of conversations, and the work context. Alternatively, video observations are well suited for situations that require precise timing of employee movements within the same physical location. Each is described in more detail in later sections.

---

[18] The real issue is when the language spoken by the researcher is different from the language spoken by employees. The primary language spoken by researchers may differ by country.

[19] Pande and Basak (2015); Guion and Highhouse (2006).

2.4.1 Sampling Considerations

Observations of all varieties are time-intensive and costly, thus making sampling necessary. In addition to the factors that are used to determine *who* should be observed,[20] observation studies may also require attention to *when* they should be observed, such as day of the week and shift time. As an example, consider an observation study of managers at a chain of restaurants. At most restaurants, weekends tend to have more customers (i.e., more tasks related to customer service), and mid-week days tend to have fewer customers (i.e., more administrative tasks). In addition, morning shifts tend to involve different tasks (e.g., setting up tills, receiving deliveries, preparing the bank deposit, checking food temperatures) than a mid or closing shift (e.g., cashing out servers, inspecting side work, and completing accounting reports). Because restaurants typically differ in customer flow across days of the week and times of the day, and therefore require employees to perform different tasks across days of the week, all of these factors should be reflected in the sample of restaurants observed. In general, objective differences in the sample observed (e.g., shifts, days of the week) should mirror the range of differences found in the population. Disproportionality in observed days or shifts may result in a biased view of how the job is performed.

2.4.2 Live Observations

Live observations capture a detailed description of a "day in the life" of incumbents by adapting time and motion methods that have been used since the 1890s.[21] Time and motion methods were initially developed to determine the time required to perform a repetitive task such as assembling a part. However, time and motion methods adapted for wage and hour compliance have some key differences. Although both involve an observer tracking the duration of tasks, the goal of a wage and hour observation study is to describe what work an employee performs across an entire day or workweek, as opposed to describing how much time it takes for a group of employees to perform a single task or set of tasks. This technique may also be called the continuous clock, continuous workday, or continuous observation[22] method. Full-day observations almost always result in the description of unique tasks and time transitioning from one task to the next (e.g., walking to the office to get a report), information that would not be included in a traditional time and motion study. The adapted time and motion method is now regularly used to capture all the tasks performed by a single employee and the duration of each task across a fixed period of time.

---

[20] Issues related to sampling are covered in Chap. 8.

[21] Pigage and Tucker (1954).

[22] *See, e.g.*, Kahn and Perkoff (1977).

Usually this technique involves one observer being assigned to "shadow" a single employee and track the tasks they perform either for an entire workday or some portion of a workday. However, there may be some circumstances where multiple observers are used simultaneously or one observer can observe multiple employees simultaneously. For example, in a large facility, multiple observers can be used to avoid observers following employees throughout the facility. In other circumstances, a single observer may be able to reliably observe multiple employees such as when only a small number of tasks are being tracked which always occur in the same location (e.g., clocking in/out, donning, and doffing).

Through observation, observers are able to capture highly detailed descriptions of the work incumbents perform and the amount of time spent performing categories of tasks (e.g., exempt vs. non-exempt tasks). Observers follow the employee wherever they go during the shift. Observers are also close enough to the employee to capture detail regarding the tasks performed such as the reports being reviewed or what is being said to other employees. Without that level of detail, coding a task into legally relevant categories (e.g., exempt or non-exempt) is challenging. Observers also capture important contextual information because they can see and hear what is going on around them which may be important for properly interpreting the task performed and, thus, the proper coding of that task. Observers also ask clarifying and probing questions when it is necessary for understanding what the incumbent is doing. However, interaction with the incumbent is minimized to avoid influence the observer may have on the work the incumbent performs. Therefore, observers interact with the incumbent only when it is crucial for properly understanding the work an incumbent is performing. The key steps of a live observation study are listed in Table 2.1, and some are described in more detail in the next section:

Communication Process In most observation studies, particularly when the observer is in close proximity to the employee for an extended period of time (such as when conducting a full-shift observation), it is advisable to inform the employees selected for observation about the study in advance using a structured communication plan. A structured communication plan is helpful for notifying key employees about the study and for ensuring standardization of information received by those being observed. Formally scripted communication can help to avoid incumbents speculating about the reasons for, or implications of, the study due to the absence of complete information about the study. The value of the data is dependent on the job analyst's ability to observe the incumbent's behavior on the job as it is normally performed; a properly scripted communication plan helps ensure that this occurs. In particular, it should be clearly communicated to those being observed that their performance is not being evaluated and that they should perform their job normally during the observation. This helps to minimize the likelihood that incumbents will purposely distort their behavior during the observation to project a favorable image. This message is most impactful when it is repeated multiple times by several company representatives and especially by their direct supervisor and the job analyst.

Table 2.1 Steps in a typical observation study

Number	Step	Description
1	Conduct background research	Review existing company materials and conduct site visits and interviews with subject matter experts (SMEs) to become familiar with the organization and job
2	Prepare task list	Develop a comprehensive list of tasks employees may perform to guide coding of observed tasks
3	Develop an observation protocol	Create written observation protocol to standardize data collection
4	Select observation sample	Select a representative sample that will allow inferences to be made to the population or reach conclusions about the degree of variability between employees
5	Develop a communication plan	Develop and implement a communication plan to standardize the information that observation participants receive
6	Schedule observations	Schedule observations such that each workday/shift is appropriately represented
7	Conduct observation	Conduct observation to collect detailed information about the work performed such as task description and duration
8	Code tasks	Assign tasks to appropriate categories to facilitate statistical analysis and review coding for consistency
9	Analyze data	Perform statistical analysis on data collected

Though generally recommended, there could be situations in which prior communication with study participants may not be necessary or appropriate. In a study where job analysts observe employees from a distance and do not interact with them, the absence of formal notification might not impact the ability to collect reliable data. In other situations, employees could be aware of the active litigation and may have a desire to purposely changing their behavior to manipulate the data and influence the outcome of a lawsuit (which could have a direct benefit to them financially). The decision not to formally notify employees about the study in advance may be advisable in some circumstances to maximize the reliability of the data.

Conducting an Observation The observation requires a trained job analyst to observe an employee for a pre-determined period of time, often an entire workday which can last 8 or more hours. The observer records every task the employee performs along with the start and stop time of each task. Despite technological advancements such as software that allows data to be recorded electronically using a mobile device or tablet, there are distinct advantages to recording data using an old-fashioned pen and paper. Most important is the ability to record detailed task statements that describe exactly what the job analyst observes—information that cannot be pre-programmed into electronic devices. Recording data using smartphones or tablets may enable greater precision in the time stamping of tasks, but the use of these technologies generally requires observers to report what tasks are performed by selecting from a pre-defined list, thus not allowing the observer to report precisely what was observed. The trade-offs are an important consideration when

Table 2.2 Example observation record

Task start	Task end	Duration	Task
14:43:40	14:44:00	0:00:20	Wipe off condiments counter
14:44:00	14:44:30	0:00:30	Wipe off computer station
14:44:30	14:45:30	0:01:00	Unlock supply door for employee
14:45:30	14:46:00	0:00:30	Inspect cleanliness of bar
14:46:00	14:49:20	0:03:20	Answer phone and help customer with directions to restaurant
14:49:20	14:51:20	0:02:00	Talk with guests about whether they were satisfied with their meal
14:51:20	14:52:30	0:01:10	Monitor dining room
14:52:30	14:52:50	0:00:20	Answer employee question about where to seat large party
14:52:50	14:53:50	0:01:00	Answer phone and answer questions about restaurant hours
14:53:50	14:54:40	0:00:50	Tell hostess to inform Manager when large party arrives
14:54:40	14:55:20	0:00:40	Sign certificate for guest to have free appetizer
14:55:20	14:57:30	0:02:10	Talk to other manager about sales for the night
14:57:30	14:58:40	0:01:10	Make correction to guest's bill in POS system
14:58:40	15:00:10	0:01:30	Put voided check in office
15:00:10	15:01:30	0:01:20	Monitor dining room
15:01:30	15:02:30	0:01:00	Check on hostess to see if she needs any assistance
15:02:30	15:03:00	0:00:30	Direct server to replace lunch menus with dinner menus
15:03:00	15:03:20	0:00:20	Talk to employee about restaurant dress code
15:03:20	15:04:40	0:01:20	Greet guests at host station

deciding which method will generate the most useful data. Table 2.2 contains portion of an example observation record for a restaurant manager.

The level of desired precision in the timing of tasks in an observation study must also be determined. This largely depends on the issue being studied. When studying FLSA exemptions (such as the example in Table 2.2), observations typically last 8 or more hours. For this issue, recording data in 10-s increments is common and usually provides a sufficient level of detail to answer relevant legal questions. Recording data in 10-s increments (e.g., as opposed to 1-s increments) enables the observer to capture a greater level of detail in the tasks performed, which is often important for purposes of classifying tasks. In other circumstances, such as a study of off the clock work, greater precision in timing may be preferred over more detailed task statements. In some off the clock cases, the amount of time in dispute may only be a min or less, and it may be desirable to record activities to the nearest second. Greater precision in measurement is usually at the expense of detail about the tasks performed, so it's important to consider these options when determining how to collect data that will answer relevant legal questions.

Coding and Analyzing Observation Data For most wage and hour issues, the observed data is coded to generate meaningful statistical results. For an exemption analysis, observed tasks are coded into exempt or non-exempt groups, yielding a total time spent for exempt and non-exempt work. To determine how much time is spent performing work off the clock, tasks observed before clock-in or after clock-out are coded as compensable or non-compensable.

Coding observation data should follow a clear and systematic approach to maximize reliability. A written protocol to guide data coding is useful in many studies to standardize the process. This often includes guidelines that clarify potential ambiguities. Coding is typically completed by multiple independent coders to minimize coding errors, increase standardization, and evaluate the reliability of the coding. Once the observation coding is finalized, an observation record is generated for each incumbent, and this record contains all tasks performed, the duration of each task, and the coding of all tasks. Coded data can be analyzed to generate numeric estimates that address relevant criteria.

Controlling for the Hawthorne Effect A potential concern when conducting an observational study is the well-known psychological phenomenon called the Hawthorne effect[23] or, alternatively, the Heisenberg effect.[24] That is, without proper controls, the observation itself may influence the employee to alter his or her behavior. It is advisable to implement controls to minimize if not entirely eliminate these potential effects. First, as noted, it is helpful to communicate to employees that their performance is not being evaluated, and they are expected to perform their job as they normally would. It may also be useful to ask incumbents at the end of the observation whether they would have done anything different if they hadn't been observed. In my experience, very few incumbents are able to identify anything they would have done differently. Second, observers should minimize interactions with the incumbent and to stay out of the incumbent's line of sight as much as possible. By implementing these controls, incumbents generally habituate to the observation and go about their typical job duties.

Advantages and Limitations One of the primary advantages of an observation study is that it results in a record of work performed that is extremely rich in detail. Some attorneys and judges find data collected using this method particularly persuasive because it paints a very clear picture of what employees actually do. The method also does not rely on the memory or language ability of incumbents to gather reliable and valid data. Moreover, it is difficult for a motivated employee to purposefully distort the data resulting from an observation study. This is because it would require the employee to make significant changes to their behavior while working with other employees and being expected to accomplish work tasks. Also, this method of data collection does not take employees away from their jobs, a feature that is very important to operations managers from a cost perspective.

There are a few limitations associated with observations. Observations provide a "snapshot" of the work an incumbent performs at one point in time. To the extent that the job an incumbent performs changes significantly over time, the observation

---

[23] *See* Roethlisberger and Dickson (1939).

[24] Heisenberg (1927).

record may not be generalizable to all other periods of time. Another limitation is that an observer can only record tasks that can be observed and cannot record most mental tasks. Observation studies in the context of exemptions tend to underestimate the amount of exempt time as a result of this limitation, as most mental tasks are considered exempt. Still another limitation is that this method is focused on tasks performed on the job and does not indicate directly the role of the incumbent in hiring, firing, or exercising discretion on the job—other criteria that would be important to know in evaluating exemption status. Observational data alone are unlikely to be sufficient to establish whether employees do have this authority.

2.4.3   Video Observation

Observational data can also be collected using video technology. This method involves capturing video of employees performing work, coding the activites performed, and analyzing the data. Video observations have several advantages. Video observations can be used to capture data regarding employee tasks and activities over a designated period of time. Two contexts where this method is particularly useful are determining meal and rest break compliance and occurrence of off the clock work.

Video data also can be collected to precisely measure the duration of certain activities. This information is especially useful when determining the amount of time that employees spent donning or doffing uniforms and personal protective equipment (PPE). This is important when time data are required to resolve whether the amount of paid compensated time allocated by the company is sufficient to cover the actual time it takes to don and doff uniforms and PPE. Data can be collected from many employees simultaneously to capture the range of time it takes to don and doff, giving the court the information it needs to make a decision about the occurrence and duration of off the clock work and whether the amount of uncompensated time is de minimis.

Depending on the physical layout of the work location, a small number of cameras could capture the movements of many or all employees. After the data are captured, it must be reviewed, coded, and then analyzed. The coding process is made easier by coders' ability to review the video as many times as needed for coding accuracy. Multiple coders can also code the same video to verify the reliability of data coding.

There are practical advantages to video observations. Unlike live observation, the costs associated with collecting additional data are minimal. Once the video cameras are purchased and installed, no other significant costs will be incurred by letting the cameras run over time. This is an advantage when a large amount of data is desired. The marginal costs associated with additional coding time are minimal as coders can be deployed relatively inexpensively.

There are also limitations to video observations that should be considered. Most importantly, data can be collected only when employees are in the cameras' view; when employees move outside of the cameras' view, data are lost. Even when employees are within view of the camera, it may be difficult to record much detail about what work they are performing. For example, it is difficult to tell what information an employee is reading (e.g., sales report or personal email) or the content of their conversations (e.g., taking a customer's order or evaluating customer service)—both of which may be important pieces of information, depending on the issue being studied. In addition, privacy laws in some states may restrict the use of video and audio recording in the workplace by placing restrictions which prevent the placement of cameras in specific locations (e.g., changing rooms) or require the posting of a notification that the area is under video surveillance. All of these limitations should be considered when applying this method as it may compromise one's ability to collect crucial data.

2.5 Self-Report Approaches

Asking employees or other knowledgeable persons to self-report their work experiences can be an effective way to collect reliable data relevant to wage and hour disputes. There are two broad methodological approaches described in this section: (1) job analysis questionnaires and (2) structured interviews. Both of these approaches involve employees self-reporting their work experiences but in a different format. Questionnaires allow employees to report their experiences nonverbally (hardcopy or online), whereas structured interviews allow employees to report their experiences verbally. Each approach is described in more detail in later sections.

A particularly useful reference to consult when collecting self-report data in the context of litigation is the *Reference Manual on Scientific Evidence* (2011), currently on its third edition.[25] The chapter titled "Reference Guide on Survey Research" offers detailed guidance for conducting a study through self-report in a legal setting.[26] The chapter covers several broad topics including the purpose and design of the study, population definition and sampling, questions and structure, use of interviewers, data entry, and reporting. The chapter combines perspectives from social sciences and law to provide specific guidance on the design of a self-report instrument that is legally defensible. Many of these recommendations are incorporated throughout this section.

2.5.1 Biases and Limitations in Retrospective Reports

An underlying assumption of all self-report methods is that participants will accurately recall and report past events. However, research has shown that in certain situations, one's ability to accurately report retrospective information is limited.[27] In

---

[25] The book was created to help fulfill the mission of the Federal Judicial Center to "develop and conduct educational programs for judicial branch employees."

[26] Diamond (2011).

[27] *See, e.g.*, Belli (1998).

order to collect meaningful data, these limitations should be addressed to maximize data quality. In many cases, issues related to memory can be minimized through the design of the study. There is a vast body of research literature on the topic of human memory as it relates to one's ability to accurately self-report information.[28] I do not intend to cover that body of research here. However, one of the most useful practical implications from that literature to enhance accurate recall comes from research on the event history calendar.[29] The event history calendar taps into the hierarchical nature of human memory by tying less memorable events to more memorable events that occurred around the same time. For example, an event history calendar exercise can be inserted at the beginning of a questionnaire to improve memory for the relevant time period. The calendar can include well-known events that occurred during specific years, and participants can be asked to recall memorable events in their personal lives during the relevant time frame. Many studies have demonstrated that exercises like that can increases the accuracy of self-report data.[30] In addition, strategies such as reducing the referenced time frame and breaking questions down to their constituent parts, called "decomposition,"[31] have also been proposed as strategies for overcoming memory limitations and increasing accuracy.[32]

In addition, several studies suggest that survey participants tend to overestimate the amount of time they spent performing work tasks. For example, researchers have compared the number of hours employees reported working per workweek to employer reports[33], time records[34], and time diaries[35]. Each study found that employees tend to overestimate the number of hours worked per week. The magnitude of the error was larger for professional and managerial employees and for employees who reported working more total hours. These findings are significant in the wage and hour context because, often, the amount of time spent performing certain tasks is a critical issue in the dispute. One way to avoid this error is to ask participants to report relative time spent performing tasks, rather than absolute time. That is, in an exemption study, participants can report the percent of time they spent performing groups of tasks, rather than the actual number of hours. Percentage estimates are unlikely to suffer from the same bias because percentages cannot be consistently overestimated and still sum to 100%. In other circumstances, estimates of absolute time are necessary. When possible, verifying self-reports of absolute time with external data will strengthen the amount of confidence in the accuracy of the data.

---

[28] *See, e.g.,* Schwarz (2007) for a summary.

[29] Belli (1998).

[30] Belli, Smith, Andreski, and Agrawal (2007); Freedman, Thornton, Camburn, Alwin, and Young-DeMarco (1988); Schwarz (2007); VanDerVaart and Glasner (2007).

[31] *See* Cannell, Oksenberg, Kalton, Bischoping, and Fowler (1989).

[32] Krosnick and Presser (2010).

[33] Mellow and Sider (1983).

[34] Duncan and Hill (1985).

[35] Robinson and Bostrom (1994).

2.5.2 Confidentiality and Anonymity

Study designs may differ based on whether data will be collected confidentially or anonymously. Many survey participants do not recognize a difference between these two terms, so it may be useful to clearly describe how their identities will be protected. Anonymity means that the identity of the participant is not known to the person collecting data. Even if the researcher wanted, they would not be able to determine who provided the response. In contrast, confidentiality means that the identity of each participant is known to the researcher, but they do not disclose that information. Confidentiality is often protected by taking precautions such as reporting results in aggregate, not sharing individual responses with the employee's supervisor, securely storing data, and using numeric codes rather than participant names to conceal identities. In either case, the researcher is responsible for protecting the identities of participants, especially when revealing their identity would harm them in some way.[36]

The choice between the two forms of participant protection can have important consequences when study results are involved in litigation and should be discussed with clients to make an informed decision. Although anonymous surveys may increase honesty and response rates, confidentiality is typically preferred in the wage and hour context when possible. One reason is that circumstances in the litigation may change, creating an unanticipated need to identify certain individuals in the sample. As an example, suppose that data are collected anonymously from a group of employees in response to a nationwide lawsuit. After data are collected, the class definition is revised to only include employees in Texas. Data collected from employees in all other states are no longer relevant to the case and should be excluded. However, the results cannot be updated to reflect the response of Texas employees only because the data were collected anonymously. A potential solution in this example would have been asking employees to report the state in which they work as part of the study. However, it is not always possible to anticipate which factors will become relevant to the litigation prior to the study. Similarly, any factors used in sample selection would need to be included in an anonymous survey. Without this information, it is not possible to know whether the sample is representative when the response rate is less than 100%. This may add length and time to the survey.

In some circumstances, self-report data are required to determine the amount of economic damages owed to individuals. In this situation, class members' self-reports (e.g., hours worked per week) can result in personally receiving large sums of money. Anonymity may exacerbate this bias because participants are not accountable for their responses[37].

Another factor to consider is whether an anonymous survey is acceptable to the court. Researchers are generally expected to produce all questionnaires so that the

---

[36] Babbie (1990).

[37] Petersen, Allman and Lee (2015).

opposing party has an opportunity to evaluate the raw data. Conflicts often arise when one party also requests the names of those who provided data in the study, a request that researchers often resist.[38] This presents a difficult dilemma for the researcher to which there is not really a satisfactory solution. Though promising confidentiality to participants is common, those promises cannot prevent a lawful inquiry.[39] It is possible that a judge could require the names to be provided or rule the entire study inadmissible. At the same time, the use of the study in litigation does not relieve the researcher of their responsibility to participants.[40] As a practical matter, the names of participants are often provided to both parties in the lawsuit, but not made publicly available. However, instances in which disclosing participant identities raises legitimate concerns about harm to the participants may justify a decision not to disclose names.[41]

2.5.3   Threats to Data Quality

The quality of the data and the accuracy of inferences made from the data are dependent on individuals' ability and willingness to provide accurate information. There are several ways in which data quality can be compromised and precautions should be taken to eliminate or minimize these issues. In this section, I discuss some of the most common threats to data quality in collecting self-report data in the wage and hour context along with potential strategies to address them.

The first threat is purposeful distorting of data by participants. Employees may be motivated to provide false job analysis data for many reasons, but in the context of litigation, one concern is that participants have a desire to influence the outcome of the lawsuit. Participants directly involved in the litigation might have financial incentive to provide data that favors plaintiffs. Employees with strong loyalty to the company may be motivated to provide data that favors defendants. Purposeful distortion is only possible when (a) participants are aware of litigation, (b) participants are willing to provide false data, and (c) participants know enough about the legal issues in the case to be able to distort data in one direction. It is useful to investigate whether there is a general awareness about the litigation among employees early in the project. In larger companies, it is rare that a typical employee is aware of the litigation, making this issue moot. In addition, the typical employee may not know the legal issues at a level of detail that would enable them to distort data, even if they were motivated to do so. Nonetheless, it is wise to implement controls into the study design to detect and eliminate this issue. One strategy is to embed "lie items"

---

[38] Diamond (2011).

[39] Diamond (2011).

[40] Diamond (2011).

[41] For example, the court in *Walter v Western Hockey League, et al.* (2016) found that participants had a legitimate fear of reprisal if their identities were known and allowed self-report data to be collected anonymously and used as evidence.

(sometimes called "distractor items" or "validity checks") into the questionnaire. These are items, typically multiple choice, in which the correct answer is known to the researcher in advance. An example may be, "How frequently do you review and analyze the Red Report?" In this example, the Red Report does not exist in this company, so participants who report performing this task frequently may be providing false data. It is advisable to include multiple lie items throughout the questionnaire, around 4–6 depending on the length of the questionnaire. Of course, it's critical to ensure the answers are known in advance and will not be misinterpreted by participants. Using the previous example, store managers whose weekly performance scorecard appears in red text if they are not meeting their targets may think the "Red Report" is another term for the scorecard and truthfully report that they perform that task.

Participants may also provide false information, not because they are motivated to distort the results, but because they are *not* motivated to devote sufficient attention to the questionnaire, called "satisficing."[42] This may occur to varying degrees, based on the effort required by the participant, the participant's ability, and their motivation.[43] These participants may respond carelessly or randomly to complete the task as quickly as possible. Lie items are also an effective way to identify these individuals. In addition, some participants simply select the same rating for all questions to complete the questionnaire as quickly as possible. Reponses can also be analyzed to determine the frequency with which the same rating was selected. If 250 tasks are all rated on a 7-point Likert scale and an employee selects a rating of 5 on more than 95% of the tasks, that suggests the employee may not be responding in a careful manner which could justify removing their responses from the dataset.

Another threat to data quality is the language ability, specifically reading comprehension, of the participants. This is more likely to be an issue when studying an issue that impacts non-exempt employees such as off the clock work or meal and rest break compliance because reading comprehension is often required to be an effective management employee. For example, plaintiffs in a lawsuit against a fast food chain in California alleged that non-exempt employees (e.g., cooks, cashiers) were not provided meal and rest breaks. The majority of this population had limited reading comprehension, especially in English. To preserve data quality, the questionnaire was translated to Spanish, and the wording of both version was simplified to maximize comprehension. Prior to administration, feedback from employees confirmed the revised questions were clear and understandable. In the end, a questionnaire was administered that was clear to participants and still able to directly address the legal issues.

There are a variety of sources available that offer guidance on survey design.[44] This literature covers far more topics than can be included here. Most important is that questions are clear, unbiased, and not leading[45] and properly address a relevant

---

[42] Krosnick and Presser (2010).

[43] Krosnick (1991).

[44] *See, e.g.*, Marsden and Wright (2010); Babbie (1990).

[45] *See* Krosnick and Presser (2010) for more details about question wording.

legal question. For example, consider a survey intended to assess meal break compliance in California. The survey includes the following question: "Do you take a meal break on every shift that you work." An affirmative response seems to indicate compliance, while a negative response seems to indicate non-compliance. However, the question wording does not properly address the legal questions for at least two reasons. First, employees may only be only eligible for a meal break if they work five or more hours. An employee who works less than 5 h would respond negatively even though no violations have occurred. Second, compliant meal breaks often must be at least 30 consecutive min. An employee who routinely takes breaks less than 30 min or is interrupted during their breaks would respond affirmatively to the question, even though their meal breaks on non-compliant. This example demonstrates how the questions themselves can compromise the ability to make accurate inferences about relevant legal questions.

2.6 Job Analysis Questionnaires

Job analysis questionnaires are used to collect systematic self-report data about tasks and activities performed, individual attributes required to perform those tasks, working environment, and other characteristics about the job or the workers performing the job.[46] This method offers several advantages. First, a large amount of data can be collected more quickly when compared to other methods like observations. Also, information can be collected retrospectively. That is, employees can report their work experiences currently but also can provide valuable information about prior work experiences. This is an important feature when the study results may be used in litigation because the relevant time period typically goes back several years. Another advantage is that information can be collected about non-observable features of a job such as role in decision-making processes, reasons for performing certain work, or company policies and procedures.

2.6.1 Administration Method

Job analysis in this context is usually administered using hardcopy questionnaires or online. Surveys in other contexts may also administered by phone.[47] However, for most wage and hour issues, the type of detailed information being elicited in the questionnaires requires the employee to view the instructions and the questions and refer to definitions and examples as needed. An interview that requires assistance from visual materials is not feasible by phone.[48]

---

[46] Gatewood et al. (2007).

[47] Diamond (2011).

[48] Diamond (2011).

Hardcopy surveys are printed and participants complete them by hand (also called "paper and pencil"). Questionnaires can either be mailed or hand-delivered to individual employees, or employees can meet at a centralized meeting location to complete the questionnaire. The latter offers some important advantages when the study results may be used in litigation. An in-person administration can be closely controlled by a proctor. Proctors receive training along with a written protocol and scripts to standardize their behavior during administration. Part of the process can include reading all instructions aloud to participants and demonstrating how to complete each section. Proctors are also able to answer questions that participants have about the questionnaire. This process is time-consuming but ensures that all participants in all locations have received the proper instructions and understand how to complete the questionnaire.

Alternatively, administering surveys online has become increasingly common. There are various online survey vendors that have made the task of programing an online survey relatively simple. Even surveys that require branching and logic to determine which questions are asked can be implemented fairly easily. There are several advantages to administering the questionnaire online. First, it is much easier to collect data from a large number of employees using this method. The survey URL can be emailed to employees in any location with internet access. Another advantage is that all data are electronic and no data entry is required. This is not only faster and less expensive but also eliminates the possibility that data entry errors introduce unreliability into the dataset. In addition, questions or response options can be randomized to avoid potential order effects.[49] However, participants for an online administration are perhaps less likely to read all instructions and less likely to put forth the effort to contact the researcher if they have a question. A person completing an online questionnaire may also be more likely to multitask rather than devoting their full attention to the questionnaire. Online questionnaires are only an option when employees have access to computers with internet access and a minimum level of comfort using computers.

When implementing an online questionnaire for current employees, it is advisable to work with the internal IT department to ensure that employees will have access to the survey from their work computers. Many companies, especially larger companies, have network security protections that may prevent employees from accessing an online survey. It's recommended to address these issues early in the process as they may take time to resolve.

Questionnaires relevant to most wage and hour issues tend to be very detailed and may require a significant time commitment to complete them. It is not uncommon for questions to take 1–2 h for employees to complete them. Typically the questionnaire includes multiple sections, each designed to address different components of the legal issue. For example, a questionnaire designed to study an FLSA exemption will usually include a section measuring relative time spent on individual tasks, a section measuring percent of time spent on groups of exempt or non-exempt

---

[49] Diamond (2011); Krosnick and Presser (2010).

Table 2.3 Steps in a typical questionnaire study

Number	Step	Description
1	Conduct background research	Review existing company materials and conduct site visits and interviews with subject matter experts (SMEs) to become familiar with organization and job
2	Develop questions	Develop questions that address the key aspects of the legal issue
3	Design questionnaire layout	This may be done online or hardcopy.This also includes the written instructions throughout the questionnaire
4	Conduct pilot test	Administer the questionnaire to a small group of "pilot" participants and collect their feedback
5	Finalize the questionnaire	Incorporate feedback and prepare final version of the questionnaire
6	Select sample	Select a sample of employees to complete the questionnaire that will allow desired inferences to be made based on results
7	Invite employees to participate	Prepare a communication plan to invite selected employees to complete the questionnaire
8	Administer questionnaire	Administer questionnaire online or in person and address questions from participants
9	Analyze data	Perform statistical analysis on data collected

tasks, and a section measuring decision-making authority. Other sections may also be included, such as demographics to the extent they are relevant.

2.6.2   Job Analysis Questionnaire Development

The process to design and execute a job analysis questionnaire contains several broad steps, and some modifications to the process could be necessary depending on the specifics of the company or the issue being studied. Table 2.3 provides an outline of typical steps.

A preliminary step in most job analyses is a review of existing company materials. In some companies, it is also helpful to talk to SMEs and physically see the workplace and observe work being performed. This background research is helpful for designing a questionnaire that asks appropriate questions and uses appropriate terminology that employees will clearly understand and will interpret consistently. For example, some restaurants refer to their customers as "guests" and employees as "team members." Using these terms in the questionnaire will help ensure that participants are able to understand the questions.

The next step is to prepare the questions. The content of the questions will vary greatly not only based on the legal issue being studied but also on the company. When studying whether employees are exempt from the FLSA (see Chap. 3), the "questions" often include a task list with an instruction for the participant to indicate the amount of time spent on each task. When studying independent contractor classification (see Chap. 4), questions would likely ask about the forms of control exerted by the company over different aspects of the work. Depending on the industry and the company, the way in which control is exerted varies, and questions should be crafted to be most relevant to the participant.

Because of the detailed nature of these questionnaires, it is important that instructions are sufficient for employees to clearly understand what they are being asked and how they are supposed to respond. It is often helpful to also provide definitions of key terms when there is potential that they could be misinterpreted.

An important step in a high-quality survey is pre-testing or "pilot" testing.[50] This step helps identify any issues that exist prior to the full administration, such as questions that are confusing, instructions that are not clear, or response options that are inadequate. For online surveys, the pilot test may also uncover technical issues that prevent employees from the completing the survey. Usually, a small sample of employees are selected to participate in the pilot. My experience has been that a sample of 6–10 employees who are diverse with respect to key factors such as geography, location type, sales volume, etc. is sufficient to gather quality pilot data.[51] The pilot participants are told they are participating in the pilot program and will be asked for their feedback after they complete the questionnaire. For an in-person questionnaire, a pilot administration is completed, and participants can provide feedback in a group discussion. For an online questionnaire, a job analyst contacts each participant, often by phone, to collect their feedback on many different aspects of the questionnaire. It is useful to prepare a list of questions in advance to guide these feedback discussions and ensure all aspects are covered. To maximize the utility of the pilot, the pilot version of the questionnaire should be as close as possible to the actual administration.

Based on feedback from pilot participants (or others who have reviewed the questionnaires), it is common that some changes are necessary, which often include rewording questions and adding or clarifying instructions. Not every suggestion received from the pilot should be accepted. Participants generally do not have expertise in the legal issues being investigated or survey design. Additionally, one participant's feedback may conflict with others. Incorporating feedback requires professional judgment to balance competing needs and ensure the final survey is able to accomplish its intended goal.

Details regarding the sample selection process are discussed Chap. 8. Please refer to that chapter for a discussion of this process. Once the sample is selected, the selected group must be notified about the study. Similar to the process used in an observation study, a prescripted communication plan is helpful for this process. This ensures that the correct people are notified about the study and that each party receives complete, accurate, and standardized information prior to participation.

---

[50] Diamond (2011); Krosnick and Prosser (2010); Presser et al. (2004); Krosnick (1999).

[51] Some have recommended using larger pilot samples. For example, Diamond (2011) recommends a pilot sample of 25–75. The size of the pilot sample depends on the type of study being conducted. Smaller samples, provided they are diverse, are generally considered sufficient in this context.

Once participants are notified, the administration can begin. When using an online platform, administration effort is minimal as it consists primarily of providing the URL to participants. The trade-off is the loss in control over the administration such as whether participants are reading the instructions or multitasking while completing the questionnaire. Most of the effort in administration of an online questionnaire are addressing participant's questions or technical issues. In addition, the administration often occurs over a period of time which may require regularly tracking participation rates and following up with those who have not completed a questionnaire. Participation rates tend to spike when the administration begins and right before the deadline. Participation can often be increased by setting an artificial deadline (e.g., 2 weeks) and then extending it a week at a time until participation rates are acceptable.[52]

The final step in the process is to analyze and summarize data. The analysis of questionnaire data mostly involves descriptive statistics and frequency counts. In addition, measures of reliability and validity are important to demonstrate the quality of the data. This may involve calculating statistics such as Cronbach's alpha to test the internal consistency of responses,[53] calculating similarity in responses to similar items or groups of items, or comparing responses to external data (e.g., comparing self-reported start time to timeclock data).

2.7 Structured Interviews

The second self-report approach that can applied in wage and hour cases is structured interviews. Interviews are a frequently used job analysis method[54] and have recently begun to be applied to address wage and hour issues. A structured interview allows a researcher to systematically collect employees' verbal reports of their work at a high level of detail. This is useful when studying jobs that are highly technical (e.g., silicon chip development, financial analysis) or involve tasks that are complex and vary widely person to person. Structured interview methods involve asking the same set of questions in a specific order to a group of participants. Typical self-report questionnaires preload questions about the work performed; a structured interview may better reflect the potentially large range of tasks involved and skill sets required to perform such complex work.

The same foundations of job analysis practice are used to form the basis of the structured interview. However, unlike questionnaire which typically contains mostly closed-ended (i.e., fixed-scale) questions, the structured interview contains mostly open-ended questions. Open-ended questions have several notable advantages[55]

---

[52] Some issues related to response rates, and specifically non-response bias, are discussed in Chap. 8.

[53] See Cortina (1993) for a discussion on appropriate application of this statistic.

[54] Gatewood et al. (2007).

[55] Diamond (2011); Krosnick and Prosser (2010).

such as giving the employee an opportunity to provide unlimited detail about their work to provide rich, in-depth information about tasks performed that otherwise would not be captured by standardized, fixed-format methods, thus enabling the job analyst to capture each employee's job uniquely and precisely. These types of interviews can result in interesting and illustrative examples of different scenarios and circumstances. In addition, follow-up questions can be built into the tool to capture the drivers that lead to different employee behaviors. Some interviews may incorporate both open- and closed-ended questions which can expedite the interview and provide numeric data to analyze.

It may be easier to collect data that directly addresses certain legal questions using this method. Evaluation of the administrative and professional exemptions or employment status, for example, often requires contextual information about the work performed, such as the purpose that tasks are performed, the impact of the work on the company's business operations, and the specific KSAOs required to perform the job effectively. This information is often easier to communicate in an interview because of the open-ended format and the ability to ask probing questions to clarify responses.

Given the large number and detailed nature of questions, structured interviews can take a significant amount of time to execute. Depending on the environment, this time requirement can limit the number of employees who can be interviewed.

2.7.1 Elements of Structure

Interviewing is a commonly used technique is various areas of HR management. Perhaps the most widely studied application of interviewing is for the purpose of employment selection.[56] The literature on employment selection interviewing places a strong emphasis on the degree to which the interview is "structured." Interview structure can be loosely defined by the degree to which the process is standardized. For example, Campion, Palmer, and Campion (1997) list a variety of factors that increase structure in an employment selection interview. Many of these features apply in this context as well, such as asking the same questions, limiting prompting, and controlling ancillary information.

Generally, structured interviews are preferred to unstructured interviews[57] as they are consistently shown to increase the quality of the data and inferences that can be made from the data.[58] Many different aspects of the interview process can be standardized including the questions asked, the visual materials shown, and the method used. In addition, written guidelines and interviewer training can increase standardization of interviewer behavior during the interview.[59] Written scripts

---

[56] Posthuma, Morgeson, and Campion (2002); Eder and Harris (1999).

[57] Gatewood et al. (2007).

[58] *See, e.g.*, Schmidt and Hunter (1998); Huffcutt and Arthur (1994).

[59] Diamond (2011).

including responses to frequently asked questions can be used to ensure all interviewers provide the same information to participants. Guidelines for the interviewers' appearance (when in person), attitude, and demeanor can also be standardized to the extent possible as these factors may also impact responses.[60] Interviewer guidelines for asking follow-up or "probing" questions during the interview may also be important.[61] Participants may provide responses to open-ended questions that are unclear, are incomplete, or do not actually answer the question. In these cases, it is appropriate for the interviewer to follow up to get additional information. Providing written guidelines improves structure by ensuring that interviewers are asking follow-up questions at the appropriate time and asking appropriate questions.

Standardizing the process serves two primary purposes. First, it allows meaningful comparisons to be made across employees. This is often necessary when conducting a study before a class is certified.[62] At this stage in litigation, the primary legal question is related to the degree of similarity or variability between putative class members. Standardizing the interview process helps rule out the possibility that the interview itself resulted in different responses, as opposed to actual difference between employees. Second, standardizing interviewer behaviors minimizes the possibility of biasing the results by "leading" participants to a particular response. This is a common critique from attorneys when the study is used in litigation and documenting the process is one way to demonstrate the validity of the data.

2.7.2   Documenting Interview Responses

The manner in which interview responses are documented can play an important role in the legal defensibility of a study. In particular, the degree to which interview responses are summarized should be carefully considered. Responses that are overly summarized are more vulnerable to critiques that study results are biased by the interviewer's interpretation of the actual responses. To avoid this concern, two features can be included in the interview design. First, responses should be recorded as close to verbatim as possible. Second, interviews can be designed to allow the participant to review and edit all answers recorded by the job analyst. This allows the researcher to verify that answers are recorded accurately and in the interviewee's own words. This can be accomplished by conducting the interview in person or using online meeting software that allows the interviewee to view and comment on the job analyst's recorded answers in real time. Computerized data collection during survey interviews has become a common practice[63] and falls within the definition of what has been labeled as a computer-assisted interview (CAI) or computer-assisted

---

[60] Babbie (1990).

[61] Diamond (2011).

[62] See Chap. 1 for more detail about this process.

[63] Wright and Marsden (2010).

telephone interview (CATI).[64] Using this platform avoids problems with opposing parties' objections to the data, alleging that answers were not recorded accurately. The questions can be presented, and the data can be recorded using a variety of applications, including customized software, online survey tools, or even widely used applications such as Microsoft Excel or Word. Generally, using an application that produces a database with all interview responses is preferred because data in this form can be filtered, categorized, and analyzed much more quickly and efficiently. These applications sometimes require a time investment on the front end, but this is usually outweighed by the time savings on the back end.

2.7.3   Analyzing Interview Data

Responses to open-ended questions can be detailed and lengthy. Depending on the number of interviews conducted, the amount of interview data can be substantial. Whereas the amount of detail is one of the primary advantages of this method, the data typically need to be summarized in order to be communicated to a client or the court. This can be accomplished using a content analysis approach, a technique for extracting quantitative data from qualitative data.[65]

Generally, a content analysis involves identifying relevant information within the detailed responses and assigning numeric codes. The coding process should be executed in a way that produces high reliability, typically measured by interrater agreement. Training raters is one way to increase rating reliability by ensuring that each rater has a consistent understanding of the responses they are coding, the coding scheme and rules, and how to assign and record their codes. Training usually includes a calibration exercise to ensure that raters are applying consistent codes. All raters review and code the same responses which are then compared and discussed. This process can be repeated until all raters are assigning consistent codes.

To code the interview responses, multiple raters are typically assigned to independently code each response. After both coders have completed their coding, the codes can be compared and interrater reliability can be calculated. There is no widespread agreement on the minimum level of acceptable agreement. For coding schemes that are less complex, greater than 90% agreement is usually a reasonable expectation. For more complex coding schemes, agreement of 70% or higher may be acceptable. When there is a coding discrepancy between the two raters, a structured process can be used to resolve them. There are several strategies for resolving coding discrepancies. The two raters can have a discussion to reach a consensus code, or a third rater could be used to resolve the discrepancy. In reality, the method of resolving discrepancies usually has a minimal impact on the study

---

[64] *See* Diamond (2011); Babbie (1990).

[65] *See* Krippendorff (2013) for a more complete coverage of the content analysis methodology.

results, especially when interrater agreement is high. This is consistent with research on similar rating schemes.[66] Of course, the actual responses are preserved and will not be impacted by the coding.

2.8   Conclusion

This chapter provides the foundations for several data collection methods that are commonly used to evaluate wage and hour disputes. The basic methods are typically customized to address specific legal issues, and discussions about what modifications are necessary are described in later chapters. In addition to the type of issue being studied, methods are typically customized to best fit a particular industry, company, and job included in the study.

References

Babbie, E. R. (1990). *Survey research methods* (2nd ed.). Belmont, CA: Wadsworth.

Banks, C. G., & Aubry, L. W. (2005). How to conduct a wage and hour audit for exemptions to overtime laws. *Bender's Labor & Employment Bulletin*, 292–302.

Banks, C. G., & Cohen, L. (2005). Wage and hour litigation: I-O psychology's new frontier. In F. J. Landy (Ed.), *Employment discrimination litigation*. San Francisco: Jossey-Bass/Pfeiffer.

Belli, R. F. (1998). The structure of autobiographical memory and the event history calendar: Potential improvements in the quality of retrospective reports in surveys. *Memory, 6*, 383–406.

Belli, R. F., Smith, L. M., Andreski, P. M., & Agrawal, S. (2007). Methodological comparisons between CATI event history calendar and standardized conventional questionnaire instruments. *Public Opinion Quarterly, 71*, 603–622.

Brannick, M. T., Levine, E. L., & Morgeson, F. P. (2007). *Job Analysis: Methods, research, and applications for human resource management* (2nd ed.). Thousand Oaks, CA: Sage.

Campion, M. A., Palmer, D. K., & Campion, J. E. (1997). A review of structure in the selection interview. *Personnel Psychology, 50*, 655–702.

Cannell, C. F., Oksenberg, L., Kalton, G., Bischoping, K., & Fowler, F. J. (1989). *New techniques for pretesting survey questions* (Research Rep.). Ann Arbor, MI: Survey Research Center, University of Michigan.

Cortina, J. M. (1993). What Is coefficient alpha: An examination of theory and applications? *Journal of Applied Psychology, 78*, 98–104.

Diamond, S. S. (2011). Reference guide on survey research. In*Reference manual of scientific evidence* (3rd ed.). Washington, DC: National Academies Press.

Dierdorff, E. C., & Morgeson, F. P. (2007). Consensus in work role requirements: The influence of discrete occupational context on role expectations. *Journal of Applied Psychology, 92*, 1228–1124.

Duncan, G., & Hill, D. (1985). An investigation of the extent and consequences of measurement error in labor-economic survey data. *Journal of Labor Economics, 3*, 508–532.

Eder, R. W., & Harris, M. M. (1999). *The employment interview handbook*. Thousand Oaks, CA: Sage.

---

[66] Pynes and Bernardin (1992).

Freedman, D., Thornton, A., Camburn, D., Alwin, D., & Young-DeMarco, L. (1988). The life history calendar: A technique for collecting retrospective data. *Sociological Methodology, 18,* 37–68.

Gael, S. (1988). *The job analysis handbook for business, industry, and government.* New York: Willey.

Gatewood, R. D., Feild, F. S., & Barrick, M. (2007). *Human resource selection* (7th ed.). Mason, OH: South-Western.

Guion, R. M., & Highhouse, S. (2006). *Essentials of personnel assessment and selection.* New York: Lawrence Erlbaum Associates.

Harvey, R. J. (1991). Job analysis. In M. D. Dunnette & L. M. Hough (Eds.), *Handbook of industrial and organizational psychology* (Vol. 2, pp. 71–63). Palo Alto, CA: Consulting Psychologists Press.

Harvey, R. J., & Wilson, M. A. (2000). Yes, Virginia, there is an objective reality in job analysis. *Journal of Organizational Behavior, 21,* 829–854.

Heisenberg, W. (1927). Uber den anschaulichen Inhalt der quantentheoretischen Kinematik und Mechanik. *Zeitschrift für Physik, 43,* 172–198. English translation in (Wheeler and Zurek, 1983), pp. 62–84.

Honorée, A. L., Wyld, D. C., & Juban, R. L. (2005). A step-by-step model for employers to comply with the fairpay overtime initiative under the Fair Labor Standards Act (FLSA). *Equal Opportunities International, 24*(2), 54–66.

Huffcutt, A. I., & Arthur, W. (1994). Hunter and Hunter (1984) revisited: Interview validity for entry-level jobs. *Journal of Applied Psychology, 79,* 184–190.

Kahn, W. P., & Perkoff, G. T. (1977). Comparability of two methods of time and motion study used in a clinical setting: Work sampling and continuous observation. *Med Care, 15*(11), 953–960.

Ko, H. Y., & Kleiner, B. H. (2005). Analysing jobs to determine exempt or non-exempt status. *Equal Opportunities International, 24*(5/6), 93–100.

Krippendorff, K. (2013). *Content analysis: An introduction to its methodology* (3rd ed.). Thousand Oaks, CA: Sage.

Krosnick, J. A. (1991). Response strategies for coping with the cognitive demands of attitude measures in surveys. *Applied Cognitive Psychology, 5,* 213–236.

Krosnick, J. A. (1999). Survey research. *Annual Review of Psychology, 50,* 537–567.

Krosnick, J. A., & Presser, S. (2010). Questions and questionnaire design. In P. V. Marsden & J. D. Wright (Eds.), *Handbook of survey research* (2nd ed.). Bingley, UK: Emerald.

Lievens, F., Sanchez, J. I., Bartram, D., & Brown, A. (2010). Lack of consensus among competency ratings of the same occupation: Noise or substance? *Journal of Applied Psychology, 95,* 562–571.

Marsden, P. V., & Wright, J. D. (2010). *Handbook of survey research* (2nd ed.). Bingley, UK: Emerald.

Mellow, W., & Sider, H. (1983). Accuracy of response in labor market surveys: Evidence and implications. *Journal of Labor Economics, 1*(4), 331–344.

Morgeson, F. P., & Campion, M. A. (1997). Social and cognitive sources of potential inaccuracy in job anlysis. *Journal of Applied Psychology, 82*(5), 627–655.

Morgeson, F. P., & Campion, M. A. (2000). Accuracy in job analysis: Toward an inference-based model. *Journal of Organizational Behavior, 21,* 819–827.

Morgeson, F. P., & Dierdorff, E. C. (2011). Work analysis: From technique to theory. In S. Zedeck (Ed.), *APA handbook of industrial and organizational psychology* (Vol. II, pp. 3–43). Washington, DC: American Psychological Association.

Nunnally, J. C., & Bernstein, I. H. (1994). *Psychometric theory* (3rd ed.). New York: McGraw-Hill.

Pande, S., & Basak, S. (2015). *Human resource management: Text and cases* (2nd ed.). New Delhi, India: Vikas Publishing.

Petersen, J. S., Allman, P. H., & Lee, W. C. (2015). Surveys in class action wage and hour cases and the use of anonymous respondents. *Journal of Legal Economics, 22*(1), 25–38.

Pigage, L. C., & Tucker, J. L. (1954). Motion and time study. *Institute of Labor and Industrial Relations Bulletin, 24*, 9–48.

Posthuma, R. A., Morgeson, F. P., & Campion, M. A. (2002). Beyond employment interview validity: A comprehensive narrative review of recent research and trends over time. *Personnel Psychology, 55*, 1–81.

Presser, S., Rothgeb, J. M., Couper, M. P., Lessler, J. T., Martin, E., Martin, J., & Singer, E. (Eds.). (2004). *Methods for testing and evaluating survey questionnaires.* New York: Wiley.

Pynes, J. E., & Bernardin, H. J. (1992). Mechanical vs consensus-derived assessment center ratings: A comparison of job performance validities. *Public Personnel Management, 21*(1), 17–28.

Robinson, J., & Bostrom, A. (1994). The overestimated workweek? What time diary measures suggest. *Monthly Labor Review, 117*(1), 11–23.

Roethlisberger, F. J., & Dickson, W. J. (1939). *Management and the worker: An account of a research program conducted by the Western Electric Company, Hawthorne Works, Chicago.* Cambridge, MA: Harvard University Press.

Sackett, P. R. (1991). Exploring strategies for clustering military occupations. In A. K. Wigdor & B. F. Green (Eds.), *Performance assessment for the workplace* (pp. 305–330). Washington, DC: National Academy Press.

Sackett, P. R., Walmsley, P. T., & Laczo, R. M. (2013). Job and work analysis. In N. Schmitt & S. Highhouse (Eds.), *Comprehensive handbook of psychology, volume 12: Industrial and organizational psychology.* New York: Wiley.

Sanchez, J. I., & Levine, E. L. (2000). Accuracy or consequential validity: Which is the better standard for job analysis data? *Journal of Organizational Behavior, 21*, 809–818.

Sanchez, J. I., & Levine, E. L. (2001). The analysis of work in the 20th and 21st centuries. In N. Anderson, D. S. Ones, H. K. Sinangil, & C. Viswesvaran (Eds.), *Handbook of industrial, work & organizational psychology* (pp. 71–89). London: SAGE.

Schmidt, F., & Hunter, J. (1998). The validity and utility of selection methods in personnel psychology: Practical and theoretical implications of 85 years of research findings. *Psychological Bulletin, 124*(2), 262–274.

Schwarz, N. (2007). Cognitive aspects of survey methodology. *Applied Cognitive Psychology, 21*(2), 277–287.

VanDerVaart, W., & Glasner, T. (2007). Applying a timeline as a recall aid in a telephone survey: A record check study. *Applied Cognitive Psychology, 21*, 227–238.

Walter v. Western Hockey League, et al. (2016). *Court file no. 1401-11912, Court of Queen's Bench of Alberta (Canada).*

Wilson, M. A., Bennett, W., Gibson, S. G., & Alliger, G. M. (Eds.). (2012). *The handbook of work analysis in organizations: The methods, systems, applications, and science of work measurement in organizations.* New York: Routledge.

Wright, J. D., & Marsden, P. V. (2010). Survey research and social science: History, current practice, and future prospects. In P. V. Marsden & J. D. Wright (Eds.), *Handbook of survey research* (2nd ed.). Bingley, UK: Emerald.

Statutes and Regulations

29 C.F.R. §541.2.

Chapter 3
FLSA Exemptions

Chester Hanvey

3.1 Introduction

In the past few decades, one of the most common and costly wage and hour legal disputes has been the classification of employees as "exempt" or "non-exempt" from Fair Labor Standards Act (FLSA) coverage. Unless exempt, all US employees are covered by the FLSA and thus entitled to certain protections, such as minimum wage and overtime pay. In many states, non-exempt workers are entitled to additional protections, such as meal and rest breaks. The FLSA permits employers to classify employees as exempt from the FLSA, provided several specific criteria are met. Typically, exempt employees are paid a fixed salary regardless of the number of hours they work and do not receive overtime.

Litigation arises when one or more employees dispute their exempt classification, claiming the exemption criteria are not met. Litigation involving the classification of employees as exempt is typically brought as a class action, in which one or more plaintiffs seek to represent a class of employees who they believe have similar claims. The "class" is frequently defined as all current or former employees with a certain job title or job titles during a specific time period. For example, an exempt store manager at a national retail chain may file litigation against his or her employer on behalf of all store managers in the company. If the lawsuit is to proceed as a class, it must first be "certified" by the court. Certification decisions are often based on the degree of variability between putative class members with respect to the claims in the litigation. The more variability between putative class members (e.g., time spent performing exempt work), the more challenging it will be for the court to

---

The original version of this chapter was revised. A correction to this chapter can be found at
https://doi.org/10.1007/978-3-319-74612-8_10

© Springer International Publishing AG, part of Springer Nature 2018   47
C. Hanvey, *Wage and Hour Law*, https://doi.org/10.1007/978-3-319-74612-8_3

resolve the claims of all class members and the less likely the litigation will be certified as a class action.[1]

Evaluating exemption status requires detailed knowledge about an employee's job duties. FLSA regulations and case law provide clear guidance that exemption status must be determined based on actual job duties, not job title. An evaluation of proper classification includes data that demonstrates work characteristics such as the work employees perform, the context in which work is performed, the nature of the work, and the time spent on that work. Job analysis methods are commonly used to gather these data in a systematic manner.[2]

A component of the law that has important consequences for measurement of job duties is that classification decisions must be made on an individual basis, as opposed to a group basis, such as job title. This means that exemption status is determined employee by employee based on the work each employee performs on the job. Exemption status is not based on the job description or what employees in the job generally or typically do. This is a critical component of the law and one that those who conduct job analyses should find particularly meaningful. For many applications, a job analysis results in a generalized description of the work employees typically perform. However, a job analysis that is conducted to evaluate exemption status is focused on a single individual and therefore requires an individual-level job analysis.

In this chapter, I'll first clarify terminology used in this context. I'll then provide a discussion of some broad issues applicable to all exemptions before providing more detail about individual exemptions. In addition to the factors discussed in Chap. 2, the design of the data collection method to evaluate exemption status largely depends on which exemption is being challenged, and I'll also provide commonly used practices for evaluating each exemption.

3.2   Terminology

A challenge sometimes encountered when discussing FLSA exemption is the use of overlapping or inconsistent terminology. Exempt employees are often called "salaried" employees within the workplace because they are typically paid on a fixed salary basis. Conversely, non-exempt employees are often called "hourly" employees in the workplace because they are paid based on the number of hours they work. Exempt employees may also be called "overtime ineligible" or "managerial" while non-exempt employees be called "overtime eligible"[3] or

---

[1] See Chap. 1 for further discussion about the class certification process.

[2] Banks and Aubry (2005); Banks and Cohen (2005); Honorée et al. (2005); Ko and Kleiner (2005). Chapter 2 provides an overview of applicable job analysis methods. In later sections, aspects of those methods that are related to FLSA exemption classification are highlighted.

[3] The Department of Labor suggested the use of "overtime eligible/overtime protected" and "overtime ineligible/not overtime protected" in response to frustration expressed by stakeholders over the nonintuitive nature of "non-exempt" and "exempt" terminology (U.S. Department of Labor, 2015).

Table 3.1 Terminology used for exempt and non-exempt employees

Exempt	Non-exempt
Salaried	Hourly
Overtime ineligible	Overtime eligible
Not overtime protected	Overtime protected
Managerial	Nonmanagerial

"nonmanagerial." In most cases, all of these terms (listed in Table 3.1) refer to the same thing: whether the employee is exempt from the FLSA or non-exempt from (i.e., covered by) the FLSA.

Another potential source of confusion stems from the term "misclassification." Employees who do not meet the criteria for an exemption but are nonetheless considered exempt by their employer are said to be misclassified. However, workers can also be misclassified with respect to other legal classifications. For example, employees may be misclassified as independent contractors, an issue discussed in more detail in Chap. 4. Therefore, it may be necessary to specify the type of misclassification when discussing these issues.

Finally, different terminology is sometimes used to refer to exemptions from the FLSA. Although there are multiple exemptions for which an employee can qualify, the three most common are the executive, administrative, and professional exemptions. These three exemptions are collectively referenced as the "white-collar" exemptions or alternatively the "EAP" exemptions. Some may also use the term "541 exemptions" to refer to all exemptions which are defined in Section 541 of the federal regulations (i.e., 29 C.F.R. §541).

3.3 Duties Test and Salary Test

The criteria for the three white-collar exemptions are summarized in Table 3.2. Although the specific criteria differ by exemption, all exemptions are based on two broad factors: the manner and amount of pay the employee receives ("salary test")[4] and the employee's job duties ("duties test"). An employee must surpass the minimum thresholds for both tests to be exempt from the FLSA. To satisfy the salary test, an employee must be paid a minimum salary of $455 or more per week ($23,660 per year). To satisfy the duties test, the employee's "primary duty" must meet certain characteristics which is where job analysis methods are applicable. The focus of this chapter is to provide methodological approaches to evaluate the duties test. An evaluation of "primary duties" requires an understanding of what work employees perform, the context in which it's performed, the nature of the work, and the time spent on that work.

---

[4] The salary test is sometimes further broken up into two components: the "salary basis test" and the "salary level test" (*see, e.g.*, Miller (2016)).

Table 3.2 Summary of exemption criteria for the "white-collar" exemptions[a]

Exemption (federal regulation)	Criteria (must meet all)
Executive (29 C.F.R. §541.100)	1. Paid a salary of $455 or more per week 2. Primary duty is management of the enterprise, department, or subdivision 3. Manages at least two or more full-time employees 4. Has the authority to hire or fire others (or whose recommendations are given particular weight)
Administrative (29 C.F.R. §541.200)	1. Paid a salary of $455 or more per week 2. Primary duty is the performance of office or nonmanual work directly related to the management or general business operations of the employer or the employer's customers 3. Primary duty includes the exercise of discretion and independent judgment with respect to matters of significance
Professional (29 C.F.R. §541.300)	1. Paid a salary of $455 or more per week 2. Primary duty meets one of the following criteria: (a) Primary duty is work requiring advanced knowledge (i.e., "learned professional") (b) Primary duty is work requiring invention, imagination, originality, or talent in an artistic or creative field (i.e., "creative professional")

[a]This table is a summary of the criteria specified in the federal regulations. Readers should refer to the actual regulations (29 C.F.R. §541 et seq.) for additional explanation and guidance

3.4 Defining "Primary Duty"

A critical term used in all three white-collar exemptions is "primary duty." In federal courts, primary duty has been interpreted qualitatively. This means that there is no accepted numeric threshold for the percent of time that an employee needs to spend performing exempt duties to qualify as a primary duty. Other factors, such as importance of the work performed, may be considered in addition to the percent of time spent when determining an employee's primary duty. Because of this qualitative focus, employees may be considered exempt under the FLSA even if they spend less than half of their time performing exempt work.

This is one area where the FLSA can differ from state law in a critical way. In California, for instance, employees must be "primarily engaged" in exempt work to qualify for an exemption, a requirement that goes beyond the FLSA's "primary duty" requirement. "Primarily engaged" is consistently interpreted quantitatively, meaning that an employee must spend more than 50% of his or her time on exempt tasks each workweek to be considered exempt under California state law. In other words, an employee who spends 40% of his or her time on exempt duties may be considered exempt under the FLSA but not under California law. Therefore, it is more difficult to meet the exemption criteria in California than it is to meet the

FLSA exemption criteria. When state and federal requirements differ, the more restrictive standard applies.[5] Therefore, employers operating in California must comply with the higher state standard.

3.5   Executive Exemption

To qualify for the executive exemption, an employee must be "employed in a bona fide executive capacity."[6] The specific criteria for the executive exemption are summarized in Table 3.2. Of the exemption criteria, job analysis methods are most commonly applied to evaluate whether an employee's "primary duty" is the "management of the enterprise." This evaluation requires at least two broad steps. The first is determining which tasks qualify for "management of the enterprise" (i.e., exempt tasks), and the second is determining degree to which these tasks represent the employee's "primary duty."

Federal regulations provide guidance on which tasks are exempt by specifying examples of activities and jobs that are generally considered exempt.[7] These include typical management functions such as hiring, scheduling, planning, or reviewing performance. The list of activities found within the regulations is provided in Table 3.3. Although these examples provide a useful starting point, most jobs involve many activities that are not included in the regulations, which can create uncertainty about whether those additional activities are considered "management."

If exemption status is litigated, the court has the authority to decide which job duties are exempt. However, as a practical matter, tasks must be classified as part of the job analysis order to calculate the percent of time employees spend performing exempt work or when an evaluation is conducted proactively (i.e., no active litigation). When exemption status is challenged, the classification of tasks is likely to be scrutinized. Due to the nuances involved in classifying tasks as exempt or non-exempt and the importance of the classification, an employer may benefit from an independent review of the classification of tasks early in the evaluation process. Some employers obtain input from a third-party legal expert in wage and hour classification (often an attorney) to assist with the classification of tasks. Once tasks are classified as exempt or non-exempt, job analysis data can be collected to evaluate whether the employee's "primary duty" is exempt work, a determination usually based on time spent performing exempt work and the importance of that work for successful job performance.

The executive exemption is intended to apply to management employees with substantial management responsibilities. First-line supervisor positions with "management-like" job titles (e.g., assistant manager, department manager, shift supervisor) sometimes cannot meet the executive exemption criteria and have been

---

[5] 29 U.S.C. §218(a).
[6] 29 C.F.R. §541.100.
[7] See 29 C.F.R. §541.102.

Table 3.3 Examples of job duties and job titles referenced by federal regulations[a]

Exemption	Generally exempt job duties	Job titles
Executive	• Interviewing, selecting, and training of employees • Setting and adjusting their rates of pay and hours of work • Directing the work of employees • Maintaining production or sales records for use in supervision or control • Appraising employees' productivity and efficiency for the purpose of recommending promotions or other changes in status • Handling employee complaints and grievances • Disciplining employees • Planning the work • Determining the techniques to be used • Apportioning the work among the employees • Determining the type of materials, supplies, machinery, equipment, or tools to be used or merchandise to be bought, stocked, and sold • Controlling the flow and distribution of materials or merchandise and supplies • Providing for the safety and security of the employees or the property • Planning and controlling the budget • Monitoring or implementing legal compliance measures	None specified
Administrative	Work in functional areas such as: • Tax • Finance • Accounting • Budgeting • Auditing • Insurance • Quality control • Purchasing • Procurement • Advertising • Marketing • Research • Safety and health • Personnel management • Human resources • Employee benefits • Labor relations • Public relations • Government relations • Computer network, internet, and database administration • Legal and regulatory compliance	*Examples that generally meet the exemption:* • Insurance claims adjusters • Employees in the financial services industry • Employees who lead a team assigned to complete major projects • Executive assistant to a business owner or senior executive • Human resources managers • Purchasing agents *Examples that generally do not meet the exemption:* • Ordinary inspection work • Examiners or graders • Comparison shoppers • Public sector inspectors or investigators

(continued)

Table 3.3 (continued)

Exemption	Generally exempt job duties	Job titles
Professional (learned)	• None specified	*Examples that generally meet the exemption:* • Registered or certified medical technologists • Nurses • Dental hygienists • Physician assistants • Accountants • Executive chefs and sous chefs • Athletic trainers • Funeral directors or embalmers • Teachers • Physicians *Examples that generally do not meet the exemption:* • Practical nurses and other similar health-care employees • Accounting clerks and bookkeepers • Cooks • Paralegals and legal assistants

[a]Note that these are examples from the regulations that *generally* qualify as exempt. There are many circumstances that could impact these general classifications

the frequent subject of misclassification lawsuits under this exemption. Employees in these positions often perform some managerial duties, but they may also perform some of the same nonmanagerial duties as the non-exempt employees they manage.[8] In later sections, I describe methods that are typically used to evaluate the executive exemption.

3.5.1 Employer's Realistic Expectation

There are times when employees perform their job in a manner that is inconsistent with their employer's expectations. As an example, an exempt manager may choose not to perform any of their managerial duties and instead focus on non-exempt duties that are typically performed by non-exempt employees. This would probably make that employee a poor performer, but does it also make the company legally

---

[8] *See* Banks (2004).

liable for misclassifying that employee? In evaluating exemption status, courts have considered whether the employee's practice diverges from the employer's realistic expectations[9] and whether there was any expression of employer displeasure over an employee's performance. In other words, employees should not be able to "underperform" their way out of an exemption.

This issue may arise when allegations of misclassification involve a single plaintiff as opposed to a class action. This typically occurs when the court does not certify a class action but an individual plaintiff chooses to pursue their claims anyway. In this situation, collecting data on the work performed by other employees may not be able to precisely describe how the plaintiff performed his or her job. Instead, data collected from other employees can be useful for assessing whether the company's expectation for employees in the plaintiff's position to perform the job in an exempt manner is realistic. Data showing that the majority of employees in the plaintiff's position spent most of their time performing exempt work provides evidence that the expectation to perform the job in this manner is realistic.

3.5.2 Methods to Evaluate the Executive Exemption

There are a few reasons why an assessment of exemption status is conducted: to determine the appropriate classification for employees, to audit existing classifications, and to provide evidence in litigation. The methods used to gather relevant data are generally the same for all purposes. However, the data collection method is likely to encounter substantial scrutiny when conducted for purposes of litigation. In addition, the outcomes associated with the evaluation in litigation are considerably higher stakes than a similar study conducted in a non-litigation environment.

There are three primary methods to study the executive exemption: observational studies, self-report questionnaires, and structured interviews. The foundations for each of these methods are discussed in Chap. 2. Please refer to that chapter for more detail about these methods. In this section, I will expand on the information presented previously by addressing some considerations specific to evaluating the executive exemption.

Observation Observational studies have become one of the most commonly used approaches in the past few decades to determine whether employees meet the criteria for the executive exemption. An observational approach is typically used to study jobs that consist primarily of tasks that are either physical or otherwise observable. Observations are often used in industries such as retail, food service, and grocery where job analysts can clearly understand and describe the tasks employees perform. Observations are either conducted by a live observer or by analyzing prerecorded video footage. Live observations are typically more effective

---

[9] See Ramirez v. Yosemite Water Co.

than video observations in this context because live job analysts are able to capture subtle aspects of the work environment that impact the classification of tasks as exempt or non-exempt. Details such as the content of conversations or phone calls, printed or electronic information the employee is reviewing, or the reasons the employee is performing a task can provide critical information and can be obtained more easily by a live observer. In addition, live observers can easily move with the employees when they move within the premises and especially when they leave the premises (e.g., attend an off-site meeting).

An observation study usually begins with the creation of a detailed task list that includes all tasks the employee may perform.[10] The task list is compiled based on various sources including existing documents (e.g., job descriptions, operation manuals, performance criteria), preliminary observations or "site visits," interviews with subject matter experts (SMEs), or external resources such as O*NET.[11] A typical task list consists of 200–300 discrete tasks although the number of tasks can vary by job. Each task begins with a verb in the present tense and describes an observable[12] unit of work (e.g., "process customer transaction at register"). Tasks are then grouped into homogenous groups or "task areas" (e.g., serving customers"). Grouping tasks that serve a similar function is a common practice in job analysis, but the groupings serve an additional function in the evaluation of exemption status. Each task area consists of tasks that are also homogeneous with respect to exempt status, so that group-level data can be used to calculate the percent of time spent performing exempt work. That is, each task area is comprised entirely of exempt tasks or entirely of non-exempt tasks. This often requires some functions to be split into two separate task areas, one non-exempt and one exempt. For instance, a restaurant manager's responsibility for "customer service" usually consists of some exempt and some non-exempt tasks. The non-exempt portion ("serving customers") includes tasks that servers or hosts typically perform, such as showing customer to their table, taking food and drink orders, and delivering food to the customer. The exempt portion ("overseeing customer service") consists of managerial duties that servers or hosts do not typically perform, such as approving discounts or special pricing, evaluating customer's satisfaction with their service ("table touching"), or resolving customer complaints. Table 3.4 contains an example of the task list structure for managerial jobs in the retail and food service industries.

Often, the breadth of a managers' responsibility within their establishment results in a task list with more exempt task areas than non-exempt task areas. However, the number of exempt task areas does *not* bias the study results to overestimate the amount of non-exempt time. The task list reflects the comprehensive

---

[10] This approach is similar to what has previously been described as a job task analysis (JTA). *See* Gael (1988) for additional detail on this approach.

[11] O*NET is publically available at https://www.onetonline.org/

[12] Tasks beginning with verbs such as "verify" or "ensure" do not describe observable behavior and can be problematic if used in an observational study.

Table 3.4 Examples of task list structure

Retail store manager	Restaurant manager
Task area (exempt/non-exempt)	**Task area (exempt/non-exempt)**
• *Example tasks*	• *Example tasks*
Directing customer service (exempt) • Assist cashier with questions • Review customer service survey results	Overseeing and directing guest service (exempt) • Direct server to run food to customer • Resolve guest complaints
Serving customers (non-exempt) • Greet customers in the store • Process customer transactions at register	Serving guests (non-exempt) • Seat customer at the table • Take customer's food order
Overseeing inventory (exempt) • Direct associates to restock merchandise on sales floor • Review displays in the store compared to plan	Monitoring food preparation (exempt) • Evaluate appearance of food • Check temperature of food
Stocking products (non-exempt) • "Front and face" products on shelves • Restock merchandise on sales floor	Preparing food (non-exempt) • Add garnish to plated food • Pull product from freezer to thaw
Supervising merchandise delivery process (exempt) • Review and sign delivery invoice • Inspect quality of delivered merchandise	Training and developing staff (exempt) • Provide training to new employees • Conduct coaching session with employees
Receiving and processing deliveries (non-exempt) • Unload merchandise from delivery truck • Scan delivered merchandise using handheld	Managing HR and personnel (exempt) • Update employee personnel file • Advertise open positions
Training and coaching staff (exempt) • Review employee completion of online training modules • Provide performance feedback to employees	Controlling inventory (exempt) • Place food and supply order • Verify and sign for accuracy of deliveries
Managing hiring (exempt) • Review job applications • Conduct job interviews	Analyzing labor hours (exempt) • Prepare labor hours forecast • Evaluate labor hour usage report
Analyzing store performance (exempt) • Review store performance metrics • Analyze sales trends	Analyzing store sales (exempt) • Analyze store sales reports • Complete profit and loss (P&L) report
Scheduling and planning work (exempt) • Prepare employee's work schedules • Assign daily tasks to employees	Overseeing handling cash (exempt) • Count and reconcile cash in safe • Pull change from safe for servers or bartenders
Overseeing cash handing and loss prevention (exempt) • Take cash deposit to the bank • Investigate cash discrepancies	Monitoring customer and employee's safety (exempt) • Conduct safety inspection • Prepare accident report

(continued)

Table 3.4 (continued)

Retail store manager	Restaurant manager
Task area (exempt/non-exempt)	**Task area (exempt/non-exempt)**
• *Example tasks*	• *Example tasks*
Handling cash (non-exempt) • Verify cash in register at start of shift • Request change for register	Overseeing facility maintenance and repair (exempt) • Inspect cleanliness of kitchen equipment • Contact IT department to report issues with POS system
Monitoring safety (exempt) • Conduct safety meetings • Perform store safety inspection	Cleaning and sanitizing facility (non-exempt) • Wipe down tables • Clean exterior windows
Overseeing store cleaning and maintenance (exempt) • Call vendor to request repairs to equipment • Direct employee to sweep the floor	
Cleaning and maintaining store (non-exempt) • Sweep the floor • Take garbage to dumpster	

range of tasks employees *could* perform. The study results reflect the tasks employees *actually* perform and how much time they spend on those tasks. If an employee spends the majority of his or her time performing non-exempt tasks, the study results will reflect that, regardless of how many exempt tasks and non-exempt tasks are on the task list.

After the task list is created, the observation sample is selected and notified about the study, and observations are conducted as described in Chap. 2. Once the data are collected, each task is coded into one of the task areas. Based on the duration of each observed task, the amount of time spent performing work in each task area can be calculated. Because each task area is either entirely exempt or entirely non-exempt, the exempt task areas are summed to determine the total percent of time spent performing exempt work.

Questionnaire Job analysis questionnaires can be designed to measure many of the critical components of the executive exemption, including the percent of time an employee spends performing exempt tasks and the importance of that work. Although the percent of time spent on exempt work is a critical component of the exemption, estimating this value may be a difficult task for some employees as it requires them to recall all the work they perform, categorize that work as either exempt or non-exempt, and estimate the percent of time they spend performing the tasks within each group. To minimize the cognitive demand and maximize the accuracy of self-reports, the questionnaire can separate this process into a few distinct steps.

The first step asks employees to estimate time spent on individual tasks (task ratings). A key component of the questionnaire is a task list, which closely resembles what was described for an observational study in the previous section. The individual

Table 3.5 Example rating scale for task ratings

Use the scale below to indicate *how much time* you have spent in an *average week* performing each task *compared to all other tasks*. When selecting your rating, consider all the tasks you have performed in your job—Not just the ones in the task area.
1. Have not performed this task
2. Very small amount of time
3. Small amount of time
4. About the same amount of time as other tasks
5. Large amount of time
6. Very large amount of time

tasks, grouped by task area, are included in the questionnaire, and employees are asked to report the relative amount of time they personally spend performing each task compared to all other tasks.[13] A useful rating scale for this purpose is provided in Table 3.5.

The primary purpose for collecting task ratings is to remind the employee of all the tasks they may perform in their job and thus reduce the cognitive burden associated with unaided recall of all tasks performed. Like an observation study, task areas consist entirely of tasks that are exempt or entirely of tasks that are non-exempt which also removes the cognitive burden associated with properly distinguishing between exempt and non-exempt tasks. As discussed in an earlier section, the classification of tasks as exempt or non-exempt can be nuanced and sometimes requires a legal expert. Allowing the typical employees to make their own classifications may result in unreliable data. Pre-classifying task as exempt or non-exempt greatly enhances the reliability of the data.

After providing task ratings, the next step is for employees to report the percent of time they personally spend performing different aspects of their job. Because it's not feasible for employees to report the percent of time spent on each individual task, employees can report the percent of time they spend performing tasks in each task area. When there are many task areas, this can be done in two steps. First, employees report the amount of time they spend performing work in larger groups or work categories that include several related task areas. See Table 3.6 for an example of the work category and task area structure for a retail store manager. Once the employees have allocated their time among the larger work categories, they can then allocate their time among the smaller task areas within that work category. The groupings of tasks in the previous step (task ratings) help define the work that is included in each task area for the employee. When possible, employees should be able to see all the tasks within each task area to refresh their memory if needed. See Table 3.7 for an example.

To calculate the percent of total work time spent on each task area, the percent of time spent on the work category is combined with the percent of time spent on each

---

[13] Harvey (1991) questions the usefulness of this type of scale because it doesn't allow for comparisons across jobs. However, cross-job comparisons are rarely of interest in this context.

Table 3.6 Example of work category and task area structure

Work category	Task area
Customer service	Directing customer service (exempt)
	Serving customers (non-exempt)
Inventory	Overseeing inventory (exempt)
	Stocking products (non-exempt)
	Supervising merchandise delivery process (exempt)
	Receiving and processing deliveries (non-exempt)
Human resources	Managing hiring (exempt)
	Analyzing store performance (exempt)
	Scheduling and planning work (exempt)
Cash management	Overseeing cash handing and loss prevention (exempt)
	Handling cash (non-exempt)
Facility and equipment	Monitoring safety (exempt)
	Overseeing store cleaning and maintenance (exempt)
	Cleaning and maintaining store (non-exempt)

Table 3.7 Example of question to report percent of time spent in task areas

Work category	Task area	Percent of time working in task area
Inventory	Overseeing inventory (pp. 7–9)	%
	Stocking products (pp. 10–12)	%
	Supervising merchandise delivery process (pp. 13–14)	%
	Receiving and processing deliveries (pp. 15–17)	%
	Total of inventory =	100%

Instructions: Estimate the percent of time *from 0 to 100%* that you have spent in each *task area within each work category* over the last 12 months as an account manager

The percentages for task areas within each work category *must total 100%*. If you need to refresh your memory, review the tasks included in each task area (page numbers are included for your reference)

task area within that work category. For example, if an employee reports spending 50% of his or her time on the "inventory" work category and 20% of that time on the "overseeing inventory" task area, the total percent of time spent on the "overseeing inventory" task area is 10% ($0.50 \times 0.20 = 0.10$ or 10%). An advantage to this approach is that participants do not need to be aware of the classification of task areas as exempt or non-exempt. Participants' lack of awareness of this distinction is not only acceptable but often desirable, as it prevents employees from purposely distorting results.[14] Total time spent on exempt and non-exempt tasks is then calculated by summing the percent of time spent on task areas that were predetermined to be comprised entirely of exempt tasks.

---

[14] See Chap. 2 for additional discussion on purposeful distortion.

Structured Interviews Structured interviews to evaluate the executive exemption usually follow the same structure as the questionnaire. The primary difference is that structured interviews are administered verbally. A structured interview typically includes open-ended questions, and interviewers have an opportunity to ask probing questions to clarify responses or extract more detail. For some jobs that are highly complex or specialized, it is not feasible to generate a comprehensive task list that can be loaded into a survey or questionnaire. The structured interview allows the employees to provide customized descriptions of their job.

The structured interview follows the same logic as the questionnaire. Rather than providing a task rating section with pre-generated tasks, employees can describe the work they perform within each category in their own words. Example tasks and task area definitions are helpful for ensuring that employees are grouping the work they perform appropriately. Employees may also add additional components of work (e.g., new task areas) that were not previously included.

Employees can also provide numeric estimates for the percent of time they spend performing work in each of the task areas. The interviews are administered according to the procedures described in Chap. 2. Once data are collected, numeric data are analyzed in the same manner as questionnaire data to determine the percent of time spent on each task area and the total percent of time spent on exempt work. Non-numeric data is reviewed and in some cases analyzed using a content analysis strategy to summarize the information, identify response trends, or identify illustrative examples.

3.6   Administrative Exemption

To qualify for the administrative exemption, an employee must be "employed in a bona fide administrative capacity."[15] The specific criteria to qualify for the administration exemption are summarized in Table 3.2. Of the exemption criteria, two are commonly evaluated using job analysis methods: (1) the employee's primary duty is "the performance of office or nonmanual work directly related to the management or general business operations of the employer or the employer's customers," and (2) the employee's primary duty "includes the exercise of discretion and independent judgment with respect to matters of significance." These factors require detailed information about how the employee's work supports management or contributes to the company's general business operations and the frequency and level of authority exercised by the employee. Job analysis methods are applicable for evaluating both of these factors.

According to federal regulations, administratively exempt work is defined as "assisting with the running or servicing of the business,"[16] which means the

---

[15] 29 C.F.R. §541.200.
[16] See 29 C.F.R. §541.201 (a).

employee's function is to support the fundamentals of the business such as finance, human resources (HR), and administration. Administratively exempt work is distinguished from production work (e.g., manufacturing, production line work) or sales work (e.g., retail or customer service work). Federal regulations also provide several examples of job duties that are generally considered administratively exempt including work in functional areas such as accounting, marketing, and human resources.[17] The full list is provided in Table 3.3.

One of the challenges associated with evaluating jobs under the administrative exemption is the importance placed on the nature of the work. Not only is the actual work that employees perform important, but the purpose of that work may impact whether the job is administratively exempt. What an employee does physically may not project the precise meaning of that work without an in-depth understanding of the context of the work. For instance, it may not be obvious that an employee who designs a new computer chip is doing something more than programming. Instead, the employee may be creating something new that enables the company to be more competitive in the marketplace by introducing a new feature. In essence, the employee is enabling the company in a material way to advance its business operations—an aspect of administratively exempt work.

To facilitate understanding of this exemption, the regulations offer examples of jobs that generally meet and do not meet the duties requirements for the administrative exemption, which are also listed in Table 3.3. Examples include employees in the financial services industry, executive assistants, and purchasing agents. However, recall that job duties, not job title, determine whether an employee is exempt. There have been multiple, high-profile lawsuits challenging the exemption status of insurance claims adjusters, a job title listed in the regulation as one that generally meets the requirements for the administrative exemption.[18] The outcomes of these cases have been inconsistent, with some courts finding these employees to be exempt[19] and others finding them to be non-exempt.[20] These outcomes illustrate the need to fully understand what work employees actually perform and the nature of that work.

3.6.1   Administrative/Production Dichotomy

Similar to other exemptions, California's version of the administrative exemption is more restrictive, requiring, among other things, that employees are "primarily engaged" in duties which meet the definition of administratively exempt. In the past, the administrative exemption was evaluated in California courts by assessing the

---

[17] See 29 C.F.R. §541.201 (b).

[18] 29 C.F.R. §541.203 (a).

[19] *See, e.g.,* Hodge v. Aon Ins. Services; Harris v. Superior Court.

[20] Bell v. Farmers Insurance Exchange.

percent of time that employee spent time performing either "administrative" work or "production" work, an analysis called the "administrative/production dichotomy."[21] More recently, California courts have not used a strict application of this analysis, a trend that was highlighted by a 2011 California Supreme Court decision in *Harris v. Superior Court,* which rejected the appellate court's use of the administrative/production dichotomy. In doing so, the Supreme Court stressed the importance of other factors, such as the amount of discretion and independent judgment exercised by employees. However, a more recent decision by the ninth Circuit departed from the California Supreme Court and applied a form of the administrative/production dichotomy in evaluating whether mortgage underwriters met the administrative exemption under the FLSA.[22] This decision creates a potential conflict in the appropriate analysis for employers within California which may ultimately be resolved by the US Supreme Court.[23]

3.6.2 Methods to Evaluate the Administrative Exemption

Multiple methods may be appropriate for evaluating the administrative exemption. In some circumstances, observations provide the most useful data. The focus of observation for the administrative exemption is typically to determine the time employees spend performing work that either supports the general business operations or involves discretion and independent judgment. For instance, job analysts may ask employees during observations to describe their decision-making process (e.g., alternatives considered, reason for decisions), which may provide insight into the employee's authority to make decisions.

Though observation may be applicable in some situations, self-report approaches are more frequently used to evaluate the administrative exemption. One reason is that an employee's level of authority to make decisions and the potential consequences of those decisions are difficult to observe directly, as decisions may occur infrequently and are primarily mental tasks (i.e., not observable). Self-report approaches, on the other hand, can be designed to characterize these aspects of an employee's work. In particular, structured interviews are well suited to address the administrative exemption because the open-ended nature enables employees to provide highly detailed information about the work they perform, how that contributes to business operations, and their role in decision-making. Because the work that may be considered administratively exempt is likely to differ by industry, company, or job, the general approach described here can be customized to capture all relevant aspects of an employee's work.

---

[21] *Bell v. Farmers Insurance Exchange.*

[22] *McKeen-Chaplin v. Provident Savings Bank, FSB.*

[23] Petersen, Giovannone, and Finkel (2017).

Structured Interview Consistent with other job analysis methods, a useful stating point is background research about the position and organization, which usually includes activities such as site visits, SME focus groups, and a review of internal documents. The nature of the work performed and the business' operations and structure are especially important when studying the administrative exemption. Understanding how an employee's work contributes to the organization's operations, for example, is a key area of interest at this phase and differs across organizations. Effort invested in the early stages of the project to understand the organization broadly will be beneficial for developing of interview questions that properly tap into administratively exempt aspects of a job.

Interview questions can also be developed to measure the degree to which the employee performs work that involves discretion and independent judgment. Discretion and independent judgment are typically operationalized as the type of decisions in which the employee is involved, his or her role in decision-making (e.g., final decisions or giving recommendations), the importance of the decisions, and the frequency of the decisions. All employees make numerous decisions throughout the day ranging in importance from what to have for lunch to whether to acquire another company. The application of the administrative exemption is based on an employee's decision-making authority related to "matters of significance." Whether an employee plays a significant role in trivial decisions is unlikely to be relevant to exemption status.

It is important to recognize that employees' role in decision-making can be more nuanced than a dichotomous classification of whether or not they make final decisions. This is illustrated by examining typical employee responses to questions about whether they have the authority to terminate an employee (a factor cited in the regulations). Nearly all managers in companies with a sophisticated HR department report that they do not have final authority to terminate employees. A closer examination shows that most managers are required to contact the human resources department, which reviews the termination and ensures proper procedures are followed to protect the company legally (e.g., proper documentation, justified rationale). In most cases, the termination will be approved as long as the proper procedures were followed. Regulations consider an employee to have exercised discretion and independent judgment, even if their decisions or recommendations are reviewed at a higher level.[24] It is therefore necessary to capture this level of detail to accurately evaluate the exemption. An example of a response scale to accomplish this goal is provided in Table 3.8.

---

[24] 29 C.F.R. §541.202 (c).

Table 3.8 Scale to assess role in decision-making

Please use the following scale to indicate your *role* in making each decision:
1. I have made final decisions
2. I have made recommendations that were regularly followed
3. I have made recommendations that were occasionally followed
4. I have no involvement in this decision

3.7 Professional Exemption

There are two versions of the professional exemption for which an employee can qualify: "learned professional" and "creative professional."[25] The criteria to meet each are summarized in Table 3.2 and described below. Evaluating the learned professional exemption is where job analysis methods most useful and therefore the focus of this section. To qualify for the learned professional exemption, an employee's primary duty must be work "requiring knowledge of an advanced type in a field of science or learning customarily acquired by a prolonged course of specialized intellectual instruction."[26] This factor includes three components, all of which much be present.[27] First, the employee's primary duty requires advanced knowledge. This means that work is primarily intellectual in nature and involves consistent exercise of discretion and judgment. Second, the advanced knowledge must be in a "field of science or learning." These include law, medicine, accounting, and engineering,[28] because they have a recognized professional status as opposed to mechanical arts or skilled trades. Third, the advanced knowledge must be "customarily acquired by a prolonged course of specialized intellectual instruction." In other words, the knowledge must be academic in nature, as opposed to knowledge acquired through experience (e.g., on the job training). Jobs such as nurses, teachers, and physicians are listed in federal regulations as examples of job titles that are generally considered exempt under the professional exemption.[29] The full list of job tiles cited in the regulations is provided in Table 3.3.

A potential dispute is whether an advanced degree is *required* to perform a job or simply *preferred*. Even when all current employees in the job have an advanced degree, questions may still remain as to whether the degree is required or whether someone without the degree would capable of performing the job effectively. Several companies in the high-tech industry have faced litigation related to classification of employees under the professional exemption. The details of the work performed by technical employees are not widely understood, creating a lack of clarity as to whether these employees meet the professional exemption criteria.

---

[25] 29 C.F.R. §541.300.

[26] 29 C.F.R. §541.301.

[27] See 29 C.F.R. §541.301.

[28] See 29 C.F.R. §541.301(c).

[29] 29 C.F.R. §541.301 (e).

Employees in this field may have bachelor's or master's degrees in fields such as electrical engineering or computer science, but it sometimes isn't obvious whether these degrees are necessary to perform the work. In such cases, it is crucial to understand the technical details of the work being performed, how the work is performed, why it is performed, and how the work is connected to in the business before one can determine what knowledge is required to perform that work and where that knowledge is customarily acquired. Even after that determination, it is not clear what level of education meets the exemption criterion. Therefore, it is up to the court to determine what "advanced knowledge" means in each case, based on a detailed description of the work and the knowledge required to perform that work. Job analysis data can contribute significantly to the court's ability to make an accurate determination.

3.7.1 Methods to Evaluate the Learned Professional Exemption

Evaluation of the learned professional exemption involves an understanding of the knowledge, skills, abilities, and other characteristics (KSAOs) required to perform the job successfully and how those KSAOs are typically acquired (e.g., prolonged study of an advanced nature or on the job training). Personnel selection professionals regularly address these same issues when designing systems to hire new employees. Selection systems often include the identification of "minimum qualifications" for job applicants to be considered for a position. The use of minimum qualifications, such as educational degree, as an initial screening tool is a common practice in both public and private sectors.[30] In the context of personnel selection, job analysis data is typically used as evidence to support job-relatedness and validity of the minimum qualifications and enhance the legal defensibility of the selection system. Similar to an evaluation of the learned professional exemption, the goal is to determine whether a specific educational degree is required to perform the work and, if it is, provide reliable data to support that conclusion.

Several authors have proposed customized job analysis methods specifically for the purpose of demonstrating the validity of using minimum qualifications as a screening tool when selecting new employees.[31] These methods have proven useful for determining whether an educational degree, or other experience requirements, is related to the content of a job and have withstood legal scrutiny in multiple instances. Although these approaches have previously been applied for purposes of selection, they provide a useful framework for evaluating the applicability of the professional exemption. The following approach is based on recommendations provided by Buster et al. (2005) but adapted to address issues specific to the professional exemption.

---

[30] Buster, Roth, and Bobko (2005).

[31] *See, e.g.*, Wooten and Prien (2007); Buster et al. (2005); Prien and Hughes (2004); Levine, Maye, Ulm, and Gordon (1997).

An evaluation starts with a job analysis that identifies the tasks and KSAOs that are critical to the job, focusing on those that are required immediately upon entry into the job, as opposed to those that can be learned on the job. Based on these tasks and KSAOs, an initial list of potential educational requirements is developed with input from SMEs. The SMEs independently rate the degree to which specific educational requirements are required to perform the job while considering alternatives such as varying levels of education, professional certifications, or job experience. The educational requirements are then linked to individual tasks and KSAOs identified in the job analysis to document the relationship between the educational degree and the job requirements and to evaluate the proportion of the content domain that is related to the educational degree.

Despite the clear applicability of this approach to address legal questions related to the learned professional exemption, it is yet to be tested in this context. For any method used in litigation, reliance on well-established job analysis techniques and prior acceptance in the court system strengthens the ability to withstand legal scrutiny.

3.8 Other Exemptions

In addition to the "white-collar" exemptions, the federal regulations identify a group of occupations that are also considered exempt. These occupations include teachers, outside salespersons, computer professionals (e.g., programmers, software engineers), public safety employees (police officers), and fire protection employees.[32] Although these jobs are specifically designated as exempt in the federal regulations, the exemption status of employees who hold these job titles has been disputed based on questions regarding employees' actual job duties. As an example, an employee could hold the title of "outside sales" but not actually perform the duties of outside salespersons where the work meets the exemption criteria.[33]

There have been a few notable cases challenging the outside salesperson exemption for pharmaceutical sales representatives, individuals who visit physicians' offices, educate them on the drugs they represent, provide drug samples to the physicians to use with their patients, and encourage physicians to prescribe these drugs for their patients. A key issue in such cases is whether the act of meeting with physicians and gaining nonbinding commitments to use the representatives' drugs constitutes "sales." A representative's performance is judged by how many prescriptions of the representative's drugs the physician writes and how many prescriptions are filled by a local pharmacy. No sales are directly made by the representative, but rather the actual sale occurs sometime later, following the representative's visit to the physician. Legally, are these activities sales activities? The US Supreme Court ruled in 2012 that this activity did constitute sales and

---

[32] 29 C.F.R. §541.3.
[33] See 29 C.F.R. §541.500.

therefore pharmaceutical sales employees are properly classified as exempt.[34] These exemptions again highlight the need for in-depth and thorough understanding of the work performed by employees.

3.9   The Future of FLSA Exemptions

Starting in March 2014, the US Department of Labor (DOL) engaged in an effort, at the direction of President Obama, to "modernize and streamline" the regulations that define the white-collar exemptions.[35] After a lengthy rulemaking process, the Department of Labor released a final rule in May 2016 which was scheduled to take effect on December 1, 2016.[36] The primary change in the final rule was a substantial increase in the minimum salary for exempt employees: from $455 per week ($23,660 per year) to $913 per week ($47,476 per year). The new minimum was set at the Fortieth percentile of earnings of full-time salaried workers in the lowest-wage census region. Therefore, all exempt employees who previously qualified under one of the white-collar exemptions and earned less than $47k per year would no longer meet the salary test and will become non-exempt. Notably, no changes to the duties test were included in the final rule, despite being discussed by the DOL as a possibility and receiving considerable attention.

However, a group of 21 states filed litigation over the legality of the final rule, and days before the new rule was to take effect, a federal judge placed a temporary injunction on the final rule, preventing it from taking effect.[37] Eventually, in August 2017, the judge permanently blocked the rule, in part because the new salary was so high that it essentially rendered the duties test irrelevant (nearly all employees who meet the new salary would also meet the duties test) which is inconsistent with the intent of the FLSA.[38] The ruling emphasized the importance of evaluating employee job duties in determining which employees are exempt.

Although the proposed rule change did not take effect, indications at the time of this writing are that the DOL intends to pursue alternative revisions. The DOL issued a Request for Information (RFI) in July 2017 to assist the department in preparing a new proposal to revise FLSA regulations. The labor secretary has stated that he believes the previous salary was too high,[39] but the department has appealed one part of the ruling that blocked the previous final rule to confirm the agency's authority to set a salary threshold, something that was called into question by the ruling.[40] Therefore, it is expected that the DOL will propose an increase in the salary level but

---

[34] *Christopher v. SmithKline Beecham Corp.*

[35] Executive Office of the President (2014).

[36] US Department of Labor (2016).

[37] *State of Nevada* et al. *v. U.S. Department of Labor* et al. (2016).

[38] *State of Nevada* et al. *v. U.S. Department of Labor* et al. (2017).

[39] Campbell (2017a).

[40] Campbell (2017b).

at a level lower than what was previously proposed. It is unknown whether changes to the duties test will also be proposed. Based on the DOL's announcement of its fall regulatory agenda, there may be a new overtime rule proposed in October 2018.

3.10 Conclusion

This chapter was intended to provide readers an overview of exemptions from FLSA coverage for which employees can qualify along with the specific criteria associated with each exemption. The three most common exemptions (executive, administrative, and professional) were discussed in detail, and I discussed methodological options to evaluate each exemption. Evaluation of exempt status requires detailed job analysis data that addresses the key legal issues involved, and this chapter can serve as a useful reference for those conducting such an evaluation.

References

Banks, C. G. (2004). Keeping exempt jobs exempt. *HR Advisor: Legal and Practical Guidance*, 21–27.

Banks, C. G., & Aubry, L. W. (2005). How to conduct a wage and hour audit for exemptions to overtime Laws. *Bender's Labor & Employment Bulletin*, 292–302.

Banks, C. G., & Cohen, L. (2005). Wage and hour litigation: I-O psychology's new frontier. In F. J. Landy (Ed.), *Employment discrimination litigation*. San Francisco: Jossey-Bass/Pfeiffer.

Buster, M. A., Roth, P. L., & Bobko, P. (2005). A process for content validation of education and experience=based minimum qualifications: An approach resulting in federal court approval. *Personnel Psychology, 58*, 771–799.

Campbell, B. (2017a, November 15). House committee presses Acosta on OT, fiduciary rules. *Law360*. Retrieved from https://www.law360.com/articles/985740/house-committee-presses-acosta-on-ot-fiduciary-rules

Campbell, B. (2017b, October 30). DOL to appeal invalidation of white collar overtime rule. *Law360*. Retrieved from https://www.law360.com/articles/979597/dol-to-appeal-invalidation-of-white-collar-overtime-rule

Executive Office of the President. (2014). *Updating and modernizing overtime regulations: Memorandum for the secretary of labor (79 FR 15209)*. Retrieved from https://federalregister.gov/a/2014-06138

Gael, S. (1988). *The job analysis handbook for business, industry, and government*. New York: Willey.

Harvey, R. J. (1991). Job analysis. In M. D. Dunnette & L. M. Hough (Eds.), *Handbook of industrial and organizational psychology* (Vol. 2). Palo Alto, CA: Consulting Psychologists Press.

Honorée, A. L., Wyld, D. C., & Juban, R. L. (2005). A step-by-step model for employers to comply with the fairpay overtime initiative under the Fair Labor Standards Act (FLSA). *Equal Opportunities International, 24*(2), 54–66.

Ko, H. Y., & Kleiner, B. H. (2005). Analysing jobs to determine exempt or non-exempt status. *Equal Opportunities International, 24*(5/6), 93–100.

Levine, E. L., Maye, D. M., Ulm, R. A., & Gordon, T. R. (1997). A methodology for developing and validating minimum qualifications (MQs). *Personnel Psychology, 50*, 1009–1023.

Miller, S. (2016, November 1). *It takes two: Exempt employees must meet both salary and duties tests*. Retrieved from https://www.shrm.org/resourcesandtools/hr-topics/compensation/pages/overtime-salary-duties-tests.aspx

Petersen, K., Giovannone, J., & Finkel, N. (2017). *It's a strange new world in California for the administrative exemption.* Wage & hour litigation blog [web log post]. Seyfarth Shaw LLP. Retrieved from https://www.wagehourlitigation.com/misclassification/strange-new-world-for-administrative-exemption/

Prien, E. P., & Hughes, G. L. (2004). A content-oriented approach to setting minimum qualifications. *Public Personnel Management, 33*(1), 89–98.

U.S. Department of Labor. (2015). *Defining and delimiting the exemptions for the executive, administrative, professional, outside sales and computer employees [notice of proposed rulemaking].* Retrieved from https://www.gpo.gov/fdsys/pkg/FR-2015-07-06/pdf/2015-15464.pdf#page=2

U.S. Department of Labor. (2016). *Defining and delimiting the exemptions for executive, administrative, professional, outside sales and computer employees (81 FR 32391). [final rule].* Retrieved from https://www.federalregister.gov/documents/2016/05/23/2016-11754/defining-and-delimiting-the-exemptions-for-executive-administrative-professional-outside-sales-and

Wooten, W., & Prien, E. P. (2007). Synthesizing minimum qualifications using an occupational area job analysis questionnaire. *Public Personnel Management, 36*(3), 307–314.

Statutes and Regulations

29 C.F.R. §541 et seq.
29 C.F.R. §541.100.
29 C.F.R. §541.102.
29 C.F.R. §541.2.
29 C.F.R. §541.200.
29 C.F.R. §541.201 (a).
29 C.F.R. §541.201 (b).
29 C.F.R. §541.202 (c).
29 C.F.R. §541.203.
29 C.F.R. §541.203 (a).
29 C.F.R. §541.3.
29 C.F.R. §541.300.
29 C.F.R. §541.301.
29 C.F.R. §541.301(c).
29 C.F.R. §541.301 (e).
29 C.F.R. §541.302.
29 C.F.R. §541.500.
29 U.S.C. §218(a).

Court Cases

Bell v. Farmers Insurance Exchange, 87 Cal. App. 4th 805 (2001).
Christopher v. SmithKline Beecham Corp., 567 U. S. ___ (2012).
Harris v. Superior Court (Liberty Mutual Insurance), 2011 WL 6823963 (Cal.), ___P.3d.
Hodge v. Aon Ins. Services, 192 Cal. App. 4th 1361 (Cal. App. 2d Dist. 2011).
McKeen-Chaplin v. Provident Savings Bank, FSB, No. 12-CV03035 (E.D. Cal.).
Ramirez v. Yosemite Water Company, Inc., 20 Cal. 4th 785 (1999).
State of Nevada et al. v. U.S. Department of Labor et al., No. 4:16-cv-00731, (E.D. Tex. 2016).
State of Nevada et al. v. U.S. Department of Labor et al., No. 4:16-cv-00731, (E.D. Tex. 2017).

Chapter 4
Employment Status

Elizabeth Arnold and Chester Hanvey

4.1 Employment Status

Relationships between "employees" and "employers" have grown increasingly complex in the modern workplace. Due to the numerous variants in relationships between the individuals that perform a service and the organization for whom the service is provided, determining who meets the legal standard of an "employee" has become more and more challenging for companies, enforcement agencies, and the courts.

The meaning of the term "employment" has evolved significantly since the Fair Labor Standards Act (FLSA) originally defined it in 1938. In the current workforce, many workers perform services for multiple companies concurrently. This new workforce of "temporary" workers has been described using many different labels, including "freelancers," "temps," "permatemps," "on-call" workers, "contingent" workers, "on-demand" workers, workers in the "gig economy," and workers in the "shared economy," among others. This workforce is large and growing. A 2015 Government Accountability Office (GAO) study estimated that 7.9% of the employed labor force in 2010 was classified as "contingent workers" and that, depending on how "contingent" worker is defined, the actual percentage could be as small as 5% or as large as 33%.[1] The same report also states that if the definition of contingent workers is expanded to include all individuals who are employed in various types of alternative work arrangements (including independent contractors, self-employed workers, and part-time workers), the percentage of the current workforce made up of contingent workers increases to over 40%. Another study suggested that the entire net employment growth in the US economy from 2005 to 2015 has occurred in alternative work arrangements.[2] More recently, a 2016 McKinsey

---

The original version of this chapter was revised. A correction to this chapter can be found at https://doi.org/10.1007/978-3-319-74612-8_10

[1] US Government Accountability Office (2015).

[2] Katz and Krueger (2016).

© Springer International Publishing AG, part of Springer Nature 2018
C. Hanvey, *Wage and Hour Law*, https://doi.org/10.1007/978-3-319-74612-8_4

study showed that 20–30% of the working-age population in the United States and Europe engage in independent work.[3] Other sources indicate that independent contractors alone are expected to represent 40% of the workforce by 2020[4].

The new workforce has created unexpected challenges to well-established assumptions, standards, and laws. According to the former Secretary of Labor Thomas Perez, the "largest question" for the Department of Labor (DOL) under the Trump administration will be how to "ensur[e] a level of workforce protections for participants in the on-demand economy."[5] In his Memorandum to the American People in January 2017, Perez called on the government to enact employment legislation to prepare for the "future of work," stating that, "work arrangements have been undergoing a profound change for decades… in ways that threaten the basic social contract for American workers."[6]

Historically, the majority of the attention on this issue has been devoted to whether workers are employees or independent contractors. One challenge when evaluating the proper status of on-demand workers is determining whether they are in fact "independent contractors." The issue of classification, and claims of misclassification, has spread to almost every industry and sector of the modern workforce, from high tech to entertainment industry performers to workers in the new "gig" economy.

However, in recent years, several other types of nontraditional employment relationships have faced legal scrutiny. These include "joint employment" in which an employee of one company (e.g., subcontractor) is said to be jointly employed by a separate company (e.g., parent company), thus making both companies liable for any wage and hour violations of the subcontractor. Other forms of nonemployment relationships that have been challenged recently include college and minor league athletes, interns, and trainees. In this chapter we provide a background on each of these employment relationships, the legal criteria for classification, and methods for evaluating factors relevant to classification.

4.2   Independent Contractors

The classification of workers as independent contractors has been an area of growing concern for employers and workers in recent years. The DOL has described the misclassification of employees as independent contractors as "one of the most serious problems facing affected workers, employers and the entire economy."[7] While it is difficult to determine exactly how many misclassified workers exist across the country, some studies have found surprisingly high rates. For example, a study of misclassification relating to unemployment compensation commissioned by the

---

[3] Manyika et al. (2016).

[4] "Twenty Trends" (2010).

[5] Lolito and Schuman (2017).

[6] Perez (2017).

[7] US Department of Labor (n.d.a).

DOL in 2000 found that nearly 30% of audited firms in California and 42% of audited firms in Connecticut were found to have employees misclassified as independent contractors.[8] Given how quickly the workplace has changed since that study was published, it is possible that the current rates of misclassification are even higher. More recently, a 2015 study found that between 10 and 20% of employers misclassify at least one worker.[9] There are currently efforts underway by the Bureau of Labor Statistics to collect updated figures on these measures.[10]

In an effort to reduce misclassification of employees as independent contractors, in 2011 the DOL's Wage and Hour Division began to work with the US Internal Revenue Service (IRS)[11] and 37 states[12] by sharing information and coordinating enforcement. Some of these agreements may also include the cooperation of the Employee Benefits Security Administration, Occupational Safety and Health Administration, Office of Federal Contract Compliance Programs, and the Office of the Solicitor.[13] The DOL was also actively working to reduce the numbers of misclassified employees during the last few years of the Obama administration.[14]

In addition to government enforcement action, private plaintiffs can file lawsuits against employers that they believe have misclassified them as independent contractors. These cases are often brought against well-known companies as class or collective actions with a large number of plaintiffs and can result in large damages or settlements.

Some state workforce and tax agencies have also been increasing their regulatory and enforcement efforts in recent years. Multiple states and cities have passed laws recently that have made it more difficult to classify a worker as an independent contractor and have increased the penalties for violations, including New York, Massachusetts, and Illinois.[15] More specifically, New York passed the "Freelance Isn't Free Act (FIFA)" in November 2016. Under this act, independent contractors need to have written contracts with specific terms, and independent contractors can be awarded double damages for companies not paying on time.[16] Some states have coordinated their enforcement effort among various state agencies. In 2015 at least 21 states had created task forces designed to combat independent contractor misclassification.[17]

---

[8] Dickinson et al. (2016).

[9] Carre (2015).

[10] In his Cabinet Exit Memo on January 5, 2017, former Labor Secretary Perez stated that "the Bureau of Labor Statistics will conduct a survey on contingent and alternative employment for the first time since 2005 to help us understand how many of America's workers are participating in 'gig work'—that is, nontraditional work arrangements" (Perez, 2017).

[11] US Department of Labor (2011).

[12] US Department of Labor (n.d.a).

[13] US Department of Labor (n.d.a).

[14] US Department of Labor (2016a).

[15] Bartlett and Young (2016).

[16] Fox (2017).

[17] Reibstein (2015); National Employment Law Project (2017).

4.2.1 Implications of Independent Contractor Classification

The classification of a worker as an employee has significant implications for the company, the worker, and the economy. Among these implications is the applicability of wage and hour employee protections granted by FLSA. This is because the FLSA only applies to workers who are classified as "employees."[18] Independent contractors are, by definition, self-employed and therefore not protected by any of the FLSA provisions, including minimum wage and overtime pay. In addition, they do not receive employee benefits such as medical leave or unemployment compensation insurance. Misclassification also results in financial losses to the federal government and state governments in the form of lower tax revenues and fewer contributions to unemployment insurance and workers' compensation funds.[19]

Avoiding the costs associated with these taxes as well as employee benefits can be a significant economic advantage to companies who classify their workers as independent contractors rather than employees. Indeed, according to David Weil, former administrator of the DOL's Wage and Hour Division, "when misclassification is adopted as a business strategy by some companies, it quickly undermines other, more responsible employers who face costs disadvantages arising from compliance with labor standards and responsibilities."[20]

Employers may also see cost savings from the additional flexibility in compensation practices for independent contractors. For example, some independent contractors are paid on a "piece-rate" basis, meaning that time spent on work tasks that do not result in "production" is not paid. A delivery driver, for example, might be paid for each delivery but may not be paid for time spent on nondelivery work, such as loading the vehicle or waiting in traffic between deliveries. In contrast, a driver who holds the same position but is classified as an employee must be paid at least minimum wage for all time worked, even if they are also compensated on a piece-rate basis.[21] The cost savings for a company using an independent contractor compensation model can be significant.

Working with independent contractors also affords companies increased staffing flexibility. When there are changes to the demand for a company's services, increasing or decreasing the number of independent contractors to perform the work is significantly easier than it would be with employees. Hiring employees can involve an investment in recruiting, applicant assessment, and training, whereas an independent contractor typically can be brought on board and deployed rapidly with a smaller investment in preparatory activities. Further, bringing independent contractors in to perform work can be limited to only when they are actually needed. This flexibility allows companies to respond quickly to changes in the market, minimizing the amount they must pay to workers when they are idle.

---

[18] US Department of Labor (2016b).

[19] US Department of Labor (n.d.a).

[20] Weil (2017).

[21] US Department of Labor (n.d.a).

Employers generally do not reimburse expenses for independent contractors' equipment and tools. The lack of equipment and expense costs could be beneficial to a small company, for example, that lacks the financial resources to purchase equipment necessary for work to be performed. Avoiding these costs can result in financial savings for the employer. Many companies take advantage of this approach according to a 2016 Time Magazine survey of 800 employers which found that more than 80% of companies that use independent contractors reported doing so because they can quickly adjust the size of their workforce, save money on benefits, and tailor the worker to a specific task.[22]

Because of the economic incentives for companies who use contractors, some believe that companies will continue to increase their reliance on independent contractors, despite the risks associated with litigation.[23] Indeed, some studies show that the size of the independent contractor workforce in the USA has increased nearly 25% between 1995 and 2005 and is continuing to grow. [24] Some studies show that many employers plan on using even more contractors in the future.[25] In contrast, other research suggests that while the proportion of independent contractors in California may be growing in some occupations, it is actually declining for others.[26]

While there are clear advantages for companies who work with contractors rather than hiring employees, there are also trade-offs. Most notable are the limits on the amount of control employers can exert over workers. For example, companies are legally prohibited from directly controlling certain aspects of the work that independent contractors perform. In addition, companies are prohibited from providing independent contractors with certain forms of training. These limitations may negatively impact the reliability, consistency, and quality of the services these workers provide, which can be detrimental to the success of some businesses. At MyClean (cleaning service based in New York City), for example, the company attempted to use only contractors to perform its services but quickly discovered that it got better customer ratings if it used permanent staff, according to a 2015 article in *The Economist*.[27]

In addition, there is an increasing legal risk of classifying workers as independent contractors as a result of increased government scrutiny of these relationships and enhanced awareness among independent contractors of their rights. The costs associated with litigation in this area can be substantial.

Though some contractors pursue litigation to become classified as employees, other contractors prefer the independence associated with working as an independent contractor. Contractors operate as their own independent small business owners, with the freedom to set their own schedule, and control their own work. (i.e., determine how best to execute a task, receive little supervision or direction). This

---

[22] Steinmetz (2016).

[23] Dishman (2017).

[24] Hathaway and Muro (2016); US Government Accountability Office (2016).

[25] Steinmetz (2016).

[26] Habans (2016).

[27] "The 'On-Demand Economy'" (2015).

degree of flexibility is highly desirable to some workers, and, to many, it outweighs the potential advantages of being classified as an employee. One study reported that the majority of independent workers in the USA and Europe chose to be contractors and are highly satisfied with their working status.[28] However, the same report states that about 30% of the independent contractors who participated in the study in the USA and Europe would prefer traditional employment if they could secure these full-time, single-employer jobs.[29]

Indeed, many of the factors that typically result in worker retention and satisfaction, such as co-worker relationships, job security, engagement with the organization, and promotion opportunities, are typically not available in gig economy jobs. This may be partially to blame for the high turnover found among on-demand workers. Studies show that more than half of workers for companies which rely on online platforms, such as Uber, leave these jobs within 12 months.[30]

While some workers choose to become independent contractors, others may not have a choice. Depending on the industry and the specific situation, some contractors may not be in a position to question how they are classified when starting a new job. Therefore, not all contractors are in the on-demand economy by choice. Regardless of whether the worker has a preference to be an independent contractor, the company for which they provide services determines how to classify its workers, and those classifications must meet certain legal standards. The following section provides background on the legal standards that dictate when a worker can legally be classified as an independent contractor.

4.2.2 Defining an Independent Contractor

To determine whether a worker may be legally classified as an independent contractor, various factors should be considered, and no one factor is dispositive. One challenging aspect of this issue is that the relevant factors to evaluate who is an independent contractor differ across government agencies, courts, and individual cases. For example, the DOL, Internal Revenue Service (IRS), Equal Opportunity Commission (EEOC), National Labor Relations Board (NLRB), and California's Department of Labor Standards Enforcement (DLSE) have each provided their own interpretations of relevant factors. [31] Some of the similarities and differences are illustrated in the Table 4.1 below. In addition, each year, state and federal agencies and courts issue decisions in independent contractor misclassification cases which influence how these factors are evaluated.

A review of Table 4.1 shows that some factors are considered by all of the agencies listed (e.g., integral to the operations of the business, control of how the work

---

[28] Manyika et al. (2016).

[29] Manyika et al. (2016).

[30] Farrell and Greig (2016).

[31] The DLSE is the California state version of the DOL.

Table 4.1 Comparison of key factors considered in an independent contractor assessment[a]

Factor	DOL (FLSA)	IRS	EEOC	NLRB	DLSE
Does the company provide benefits?	N/A	Yes	Yes	Yes	N/A
Is payment from the company variable and calculated based on job(s)/quantity of work completed?	No	Yes	Yes	Yes	Yes
Does the company control the manner/how the work is performed?	Yes	Yes	Yes	Yes	Yes
Does the company control the sequence of work performed?	N/A	Yes	N/A	Yes	N/A
Does the company control the work schedule?	No	Yes	N/A	Yes	N/A
Is the relationship with the company permanent?	Yes	Yes	Yes	Yes	Yes
Is the worker economically dependent on the company?	Yes	N/A	N/A	N/A	N/A
Is the worker engaged in a distinct occupation or business?	Yes	N/A	Yes	Yes	Yes
Can the worker hire employees?	Yes	Yes	Yes	N/A	Yes
Is the work integral to the operations of the company business?	Yes	Yes	Yes	Yes	Yes
Is the work performed on the company premises?	No	Yes	Yes	Yes	Yes
Does the worker have the opportunity for profit and loss?	Yes	Yes	N/A	Yes	Yes
Does the worker have the ability to work for more than one customer?	Yes	Yes	Yes	Yes	N/A
Does the worker need special skills to perform the work?	Yes	N/A	Yes	Yes	Yes
Does the company supply the tools and equipment needed to perform the work?	Yes	Yes	Yes	Yes	Yes
Does the company provide training?	N/A	Yes	N/A	Yes	N/A
Do the parties believe they are creating an employer-employee relationship?	No	Yes	Yes	Yes	Yes

[a]The information presented in this table is based on an analysis of the language provided by each agency. However, due to the inconsistency in terminology and phrasing used by each agency, some of the categorization shown may be subject to alternative interpretation.

Note. "Yes" indicates that the factor is considered relevant; "N/A" indicates that the factor is not specified as a relevant factor; "No" indicates that the factor is specifically listed as not determinative.

is performed), while others are only considered by half of the agencies (e.g., controls scheduling). This table is a selective illustration of how some relevant factors compare across some agencies and is not intended to be a comprehensive.

Under the FLSA, the term "employ" has been defined broadly as "suffer or permit to work," meaning that the employer directs the work or allows the work to take place. This is a broad definition indicating that most workers should be classified as employees, not independent contractors. At the federal level, the DOL has relied on a multifactor "economic realities test" that assesses whether a worker is truly in business for himself or herself or is economically dependent on the employer (i.e., independent contractor vs. employee). The DOL has identified a number of factors that are generally considered by most courts when evaluating independent contractor status: [32]

1. The extent to which the work performed is an integral part of the employer's business.
2. Whether the worker exercises managerial skills (i.e., hiring workers or investing in equipment) and, if so, whether those skills affect the worker's opportunity for profit and loss.
3. The relative investments in facilities and equipment by the worker and the employer, such that they appear to be sharing the risk of loss.
4. The worker's skill and initiative such that he or she exercises independent business judgment.
5. The permanency of the worker's relationship with the employer.
6. The nature and degree of control by the employer (including who sets pay amount, work hours, how work is performed, and whether the worker generally works free from control).[33]

While federal agencies (such as the DOL) don't make the law, their opinions and rulings are significant because they are responsible for enforcing the regulations. The DOL is the federal agency tasked with enforcing labor laws throughout the country. It also provides guidance and opinions regarding how those laws should be interpreted and how these interpretations should be prioritized in terms of enforcement. The DOL has a significant impact on employee classification regulations and issues "Administrative Interpretation" (AI) and opinion letters periodically to provide clarity on specific topics. These letters are frequently referenced by courts and agencies. However, AIs can be, and have been, removed at the discretion of the current Labor Secretary.[34]

California is often considered the "bellwether" of employment law activity and trends. Due to the large number of start-ups, as well as California's "employee friendly" legal environment, it is not surprising that California companies have seen significant activity in independent contractor (and gig economy in particular) misclassification cases. To define what constitutes an independent contractor, California courts and agencies, such as the DLSE, have relied upon a "multifactor" test based on a seminal ruling from 1989 in *S. G. Borello & Sons, Inc. v Dept. of Industrial Relations*, which focused on the employer's "right to control" the contractor's work. Specifically, the ruling stated that, "[t]he principal test of an employment relationship is whether the person to whom service is rendered has the right to control the manner and means of accomplishing the result desired." The DLSE's interpretation of independent contractor classification is an even more rigorous standard than the

[32] US Department of Labor (2014).

[33] Faulman (2016); Ruckelshaus (2016).

[34] Gurrieri (2017).

DOL's. The standard is not *whether* the control is exercised by the company, but whether there is a *right* to control the worker, even if it is not exercised.

4.2.3   Industries Which Rely on the Independent Contractor Model

In recent years, personal transportation, home services, and other "on-demand" businesses have been the subject of litigation regarding independent contractor misclassification. Company's offering ride-share services such as Uber and Lyft, cleaning services such as Handy and Homejoy, delivery services such as Postmates, TryCaviar, and Amazon Prime Now have all been involved in misclassification litigation.[35]

Some traditional delivery services also rely on a business model utilizing independent contractors. FedEx Ground, for example, used independent contractors at one time and has been the subject of frequent litigation across the country.[36] Companies with similar operating models may also be vulnerable to misclassification claims. For example, the port drayage industry (the movement of cargo containers at US ports) has been experiencing a significant issue with misclassification litigation.[37] A 2014 report by the National Employment Law Project (NELP) found that "49,000 of the nation's 75,000 port truck drivers are misclassified as independent contractors." Similarly, the NELP report found that in California alone, trucking companies are likely liable for nearly one billion dollars in wage and hour violations annually.[38] Misclassification litigation in these industries appears to have been driven by the legal issues raised by the gig economy.

On the other side of the spectrum, many small businesses offering personal care services, such as hair salons, rely on contractors to manage fluctuations in customer demand, appointments, and services. This industry has operated with this independent contractor model for many years without issue. However, there is growing awareness that the current model may not be compliant with today's legal standards or in the best interests of all beauty service professionals.

4.2.4   Inconsistent Court Decisions

A powerful illustration of how variable enforcement is throughout the country can be seen in a review of the FedEx Ground litigation. Throughout the country, FedEx Ground has been hit with lawsuits alleging that it improperly classified its drivers as

---

[35] Leberstein (2012).

[36] Wood (2015).

[37] Leberstein (2012).

[38] Smith, Marvy, and Zerolnick (2014).

independent contractors. As of 2016, litigation has been filed in at least 20 states across the USA.[39] Some of the cases against FedEx Ground have been going on for many years and involve practices that have since been discontinued. For example, in 2011, FedEx Ground stopped working directly with independent contractors and now contracts with other businesses that employ drivers.[40] Interestingly, this change may have reduced the company's risk of independent contractor misclassification in one sense, but may increase risk related to other employment violations as a joint employer (joint employer concepts discussed below).

The court rulings in the FedEx Ground cases involve complex analyses, and some have been overturned. FedEx Ground drivers in some states (i.e., New Hampshire, Illinois, Kansas, Kentucky, California, and Oregon) have been found to be employees. However, FedEx counsel claimed in 2014 that more than 100 state and federal rulings have confirmed independent contractor status for their drivers.[41]

4.2.5 High-Profile Gig Economy Cases: Lyft and Uber

The two most well-known ride-sharing companies, Lyft and Uber, have both faced legal challenges to their classification of drivers as independent contractors.[42] Litigation has been filed against both companies in many different states across the country (and internationally), all alleging that drivers for these ride-share companies are employees misclassified as independent contractors.[43] To justify classification of drivers as independent contractors, Uber has argued that it is merely a "neutral technology platform" that connects drivers with passengers.[44] Others disagree with this concept, stating that Uber is actually a transportation company that relies on its drivers to provide its riders with its essential services. In *O'Conner v. Uber Technologies*, the court stated that "Uber's drivers provide an 'indispensable service' to Uber" and that "Uber could not be 'Everyone's Private Driver' without the drivers."

In *Cotter v. Lyft*, the judge noted the challenges of applying a "twentieth-century" test used by the California courts to determine employment status, which is "not very helpful to address this twenty-first century problem." It concluded:

> Some factors point in one direction, some point in the other, and some are ambiguous. Perhaps Lyft drivers who work more than a certain number of hours should be employees

---

[39] Wiessner (2016).

[40] Wiessner (2016).

[41] Kwidzinski and Trimarchi (2014).

[42] Kaufmann (2015).

[43] In July 2016 The Mercury News reported that Uber faced more than 70 cases in US Federal Court alone and had resolved more than 60 others (this does not include state cases), and in the first half of 2016, Lyft faced six lawsuits. Examples of other counties in which Uber is facing litigation include the UK, France, and Brazil (Kendall, 2016).

[44] *Uber v. Berwick*.

while the others should be independent contractors. Or perhaps Lyft drivers should be considered a new category of worker altogether, requiring a different set of protections. But absent legislative intervention, California's outmoded test for classifying workers will apply in cases like this. And because the test provides nothing remotely close to a clear answer, it will often be for juries to decide. That is certainly true here.

Lyft and Uber have settled some high-value cases, while others have been dismissed or ordered to arbitration.[45] Lyft reached a $27 million settlement in 2017 with drivers in California.[46] Uber preliminarily reached a settlement in 2016 worth $100 million with drivers in California and Massachusetts; however, the Uber settlement was rejected by the judge.[47] Negotiations in this case are ongoing at the time of publication.[48] Drivers for both companies remain independent contractors, and, due to conflicting rulings in other cases, their status remains uncertain.[49]

Perhaps due to these highly publicized cases and increased government enforcement of independent contractor classifications, some companies using an independent contractor model have decided to reclassify their workers as employees.[50] Some well-known gig economy companies that have reclassified their workers include Honor, Instacart, Zirtual, Shyp, Hello Alfred, Munchery, Eden, and Luxe.[51] Other "on-demand" companies hiring employees rather than contractors include a shipping company called Parcel, a laundry service called FlyCleaners, and an office-cleaning service called Managed by Q.[52]

4.2.6 Alternatives to Current Independent Contractor Classification

To help improve compliance with classification issues, several states have passed laws that apply to certain industries and specifically define workers as independent contractors.[53.] At least ten states have now passed these "presumption" laws which provide definitive guidance on classification to employers in sectors with frequent confusion regarding using contractors (e.g., construction, beauty services, transportation).[54] For example, several states have adopted a three-pronged "ABC test." These ABC laws create the presumption that any individual performing services for a company is an employee and require a company to demonstrate that all

---

[45] Pepper Hamilton, LLP (2017); Rosenblatt (2016); Faulman (2016).

[46] *Cotter v. Lyft.*

[47] *O'Connor v. Uber Technologies, Inc. et al.*

[48] Bayles (2017).

[49] Pepper Hamilton, LLP (2017).

[50] Kapp (2016).

[51] Kamdar (2016); Kosoff (2015a, 2015b); Faulman (2016).

[52] Kessler (2015).

[53] Massey (2017).

[54] Leberstein and Ruckelshaus (2016).

three elements are met. The details of the three elements may vary, and some are limited to specific industries.[55] For example, the three factors as laid out in the Massachusetts (and other) state statutes are (A) that "the individual is free from direction and control," applicable both "under his contract for the performance of service and in fact," (B) that "the service is performed outside the usual course of business of the employer," and (C) that the "individual is customarily engaged in an independently established trade, occupation, profession, or business of the same nature as that involved in the service performed."[56] Some ABC Tests are limited to specific types of evaluations, such as unemployment compensation decisions, and may not apply in other contexts.[57] Other states may soon be passing similar laws in other industries, such as the home care industry.[58] For example, as of January 2017, 23 states have created specific employment tests that apply only to regulating ride-sharing companies.[59]

Other experts have called for the implementation of "portable" benefits to address the lack of employer benefits received by independent contractors. With this model, workers' benefits are not tied to any particular job or company, meaning that they could work for multiple companies simultaneously and switch employers frequently and retain their benefits.[60]

Alternatively, some experts in the field of labor and employment and company leaders have proposed the creation of a new legal classification for workers which is a cross between an "employee" and an "independent contractor."[61] This new category has been called, by some, the "independent worker."[62] Revisions to US labor and employment law has also been suggested to accommodate the new category. In theory, the independent worker would enjoy both flexibility and greater worker protections. However, other experts state that such a category is unnecessary[63], and data from the US GAO 2015 Report shows that 85% of independent contractors and self-employed are satisfied with their current classification and do not want a change.[64]

---

[55] For example, some New York and Maryland tests apply only to the construction or landscape industry (Deknate & Hoff-Downing, 2015).

[56] Deknate and Hoff-Downing (2015).

[57] National Employment Law Project (2017).

[58] Ruckelshaus (2016).

[59] National Employment Law Project (2017).

[60] Rolf, Clark, and Bryan (2016).

[61] Harris and Krueger (2015).

[62] Harris and Krueger (2015).

[63] Sachs (2015).

[64] US Government Accountability Office (2015).

4.2.7 What Data Are Required to Evaluate Whether Independent Contractors Are Classified Appropriately?

Given the variety of factors that may contribute to the classification of an independent contractor, it is not surprising that there are multiple methods available to assess these factors (see Table 4.1). Key factors in this evaluation across all agencies and courts include (1) the control the employer exerts over the execution of work, (2) the level of supervision and monitoring, and (3) whether the work performed by the worker is integral to the business operations of the company. Though there is general consensus that these factors are relevant, the weight that a court assigns to these key factors may vary.

It is not generally the role of a consulting or testifying expert to make the ultimate determination regarding whether a worker should be classified as an independent contractor or employee. Rather, the goal of the analysis should be to accurately measure and characterize the relevant factors so that decision-makers (e.g., company leadership, judges, jurors) can make an informed decision about the proper classification of workers.

A critical component of an evaluation of independent contractor status is a measure of the degree of control the company exerts over the worker. The way in which control manifests itself tends to be dependent upon the industry as well as the company. Operationalizing the concept of "control" often requires an in-depth understanding of the company's operations. Some forms of control are more evident, such as how and when the worker is paid. Other forms of control may be subtle or variable and thus require a more detailed inquiry. Similarly, supervision may be reflected in various printed policies but may also manifest in the nature and content of interaction between the worker and the company. Factors such the frequency and duration of interaction between the worker and the company are often relevant for characterizing the degree to which a worker is supervised. However, the nature of that interaction, such as who initiates contact and the specific information being shared, may provide even more useful information.

To collect relevant data in most organizations, we suggest a comprehensive approach that involves collecting and analyzing data from multiple perspectives and sources: (1) workers, (2) company leadership, (3) employer "points of contact," and (4) secondary sources of data. Collecting data from multiple sources is recommended for two reasons. First, a single source typically does not provide comprehensive information on this issue. That is, workers often lack insight into the company's business strategy. Similarly, company leadership may not have direct knowledge of workers' personal practices. Second, two different sources may perceive the same factor differently. Asking the same questions to multiple groups, for example, enables an assessment of the accuracy of self-reports and may identify areas of disconnect that can be addressed. The sources of data and the information typically gathered from each source are represented in Table 4.2.

Collecting data directly from workers can yield valuable information for assessing employment status. Workers have direct knowledge of their relationship with

Table 4.2 Sources of data collection for independent contractor evaluation

	Source	Information typically collected
1	Workers	Relationship with the employer, aspects of control, personal practices, work environment
2	Company leadership	Business strategy, operating model, company policies, role of workers in the company's business
3	Points of contact	Frequency and duration of interaction with workers, nature of interaction with workers
4	Secondary sources	Company policies and procedures

the company, including the frequency with which they interact with company employees, and the nature of those interactions. They can also report on the degree to which their work activities are controlled by the company and the ways in which this occurs. Workers can also provide information about their personal practices such as whether they concurrently work for other companies, whether they operate as an individual or another entity such as a limited liability corporation (LLC), and what investments they have made in their work (e.g., training, equipment). Workers are also able to provide information about their work environment such as the proportion of time they are in the company's facilities or whether they are using company equipment.

Although workers can provide much of this information through self-report, it is important to keep in mind that they are reporting their perceptions of some factors. For some of the relevant topics, such as relationship with the company or degree of control, it is possible that the worker can misperceive certain aspects of the issue. For example, an employee could report that the company controls their work schedule, when in reality the only control in place is that workers cannot be in the facility outside of business hours. This example highlights three important points: (1) It is important to understand the business operations in order to create appropriate questions to ask, (2) detailed data such as open ended responses or follow-up may be necessary to gain a full understanding of the work and its context, and (3) collecting data from multiple sources may be required to accurately characterize the relationship.

The second source of data useful in the analysis is company leadership. Leadership is likely to provide useful information regarding business strategy, the company's operating model, and how workers are intended to fit into these operations. This information is useful in determining the role of the worker in the business and the extent to which the worker is an integral part of business operations. This is the first factor listed by the DOL and was particularly relevant in the *Uber* litigation.

The third source of data is what we call the employer's "points of contact." These are company employees who directly interact most frequently with workers. Points of contact sometimes work in multiple departments, divisions, and locations within the company. For example, truck drivers may call the logistics department when they are seeking information about a particular delivery or the technology department if they are having problems with their scanner. The frequency and nature of the interactions may differ, making it important to gather information from as many points of contact as possible. The points of contact are able to provide information about the frequency, duration, and nature of the interaction with the workers along with company policies related to the workers. This information is typically useful because it provides an alternate perspective to the workers' perceptions of the same factors.

Additional data regarding policies and procedures can be gleaned from company documents and materials containing policies and procedures related to topics such as training, compensation, and work guidelines. Electronic data sources, such as communications distributed and collected from workers, may provide some measure of company control. Security video and facility entrance and exit swipe data may be useful for evaluating the work performed, its location, and timing. External sources can also be mined for useful information such as industry norms and standards regarding classification practices. Data collected from these sources can be compared to data collected from employees to determine the degree to which policies are reflected in actual practice.

Data collected from multiple sources can provide a substantial amount of information and a robust perspective on the factors relevant to an independent contractor classification. These data will enable the researcher to characterize many of these factors which can help business leaders determine whether to classify workers as employees or independent contractors or help the court determine whether existing independent contractor classifications are appropriate.

4.3 Joint Employment

Joint employment exists when an employee is "employed" by two or more employers, and both employers are jointly responsible (whether this is explicitly stated or not) to the employee for compliance with employment laws.[65] Joint employment is commonly seen in franchises, companies using staffing agencies, and companies which subcontract activities to vendors. Industries where these business models are common include construction, agricultural, janitorial, warehouse and logistics, staffing, and hospitality industries.[66]

The changing nature of work has also affected joint employment, as many employers today have alternative relationships with their workforce. As a result of these complex relationships, it can be difficult to define the "employer" when evaluating joint employment. Similar to the independent contractor context, there is a lack of clarity and consistency regarding whether an entity is an employer because the factors and interpretations vary by jurisdiction and agency.[67]

---

[65] US Department of Labor (2016b).

[66] US Department of Labor (2016b).

[67] Jonathan et al. (2017).

Fig. 4.1 Example of horizontal joint employment

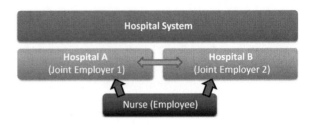

Currently, the DOL states that an employee can be formally employed by one employer (the primary employer) but also effectively employed by another employer (the secondary employer) if that secondary employer exercises sufficient control over the employee's work, among other factors.[68] This means, for example, that a business that uses a staffing agency to staff its store, but controls when, where, and how these individuals work, may be legally classified as a joint employer.

Being classified as a joint employer is significant because it makes both companies responsible for compliance with federal, state, and local labor and employment laws for the "jointly employed" employees.[69] Using a staffing agency as an example, this means that if any employment laws are not followed, such as providing proper meal and rest breaks, both companies may be liable for the violation, even though the workers were employees of the temporary agency through contract.[70] In addition, joint employer liability can involve the FLSA, the Family and Medical Leave Act (FMLA), the Americans with Disabilities Act (ADA), Title VII of the Civil Rights Act of 1964 (Title VII), and others.

Joint employment relationships for purposes of the FLSA have been broadly grouped into two categories by the DOL: horizontal and vertical. Each model is intended to describe a different form of joint employment relationship and each is described separately below.

4.3.1   Horizontal Joint Employment

When an employee has two (or more) technically separate but closely related or associated employers, it is considered a "horizontal joint employment relationship."[71] A common example of horizontal joint employment is when a nurse works for more than one hospital within the same hospital system during the workweek. If these hospitals are closely associated and coordinate regarding staffing and resources, they may be joint employers.[72] Figure 4.1 depicts this type of relationship. The two

---

[68] Dickinson et al. (2016).

[69] Jonathan et al. (2017).

[70] Dickinson et al. (2016).

[71] US Department of Labor (2016b).

[72] Bartlett and Young (2016).

entities may be technically separate but can be considered joint employers if they are under the same management and ownership, and/or share some other economic ties, are affiliated with or related to each other, jointly coordinate the scheduling of the employee's hours, and both benefit from that employee's work.[73]

Once a horizontal joint employment relationship is established, each of the employers is responsible for complying with all requirements of the FLSA, among other laws. For example, joint employers are responsible for ensuring compliance with minimum wage and meal and rest breaks.[74] This means that if the nurse in Fig. 4.1 works cumulatively more than 40 h for the two hospitals, he or she would be entitled to overtime pay from both.[75]

The DOL lists several factors which should be considered when evaluating a possible horizontal joint employer relationship, including any overlapping officers, directors, executives, or managers, and shared control over operations (e.g., hiring, firing, payroll, advertising, overhead costs), among others.[76]

4.3.2   Vertical Joint Employment

A more common type of joint employment relationship is called "vertical joint employment." A vertical joint employment relationship may exist when a company has contracted for workers who are directly employed by an intermediary company. In a vertical joint employment relationship, the worker is economically dependent on both employers: the intermediary employer (such as a staffing agency) and another employer who engages the intermediary to provide the workers.[77] The workers are employees of the staffing company but may also be joint employees of the company that engaged the staffing company.

Vertical joint employment is common in industries such as agriculture, construction, warehouse, logistics, and hotels.[78] For example, a national cable company may contract with a local business to provide installation services on behalf of the cable company. The installers interface with customers and install the cable company equipment using the cable company programs, but the installers are actually employed by the local installation company. If the installers at the local installation company are not compliant with time clock policies, for example, then both the national cable company and the local installation company could be liable for unpaid overtime. This relationship is depicted in Fig. 4.2.

---

[73] Weil (2016). We note that this Administrator's Interpretation was withdrawn by the US Department of Labor June 7, 2017. However, some of the information provided in the letter is still useful for understanding potential forms of joint employment.

[74] 29 CFR § 791.2 (a)

[75] Bartlett and Young (2016).

[76] US Department of Labor (2016b).

[77] Weil (2016).

[78] Weil (2016).

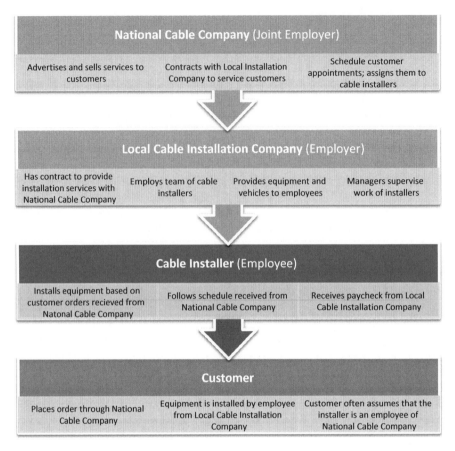

Fig. 4.2 Example of vertical joint employment

The DOL lays out several factors to consider when determining whether a vertical joint employment scenario exists.[79]

- Whether the potential employer directs, controls, or supervises the work performed
- Whether the potential employer controls employment conditions (including the power to hire and fire)
- The permanency and duration of the relationship
- Whether the work is repetitive and rote in nature
- Whether the work is integral to the business of the potential employer
- Whether the work is performed on the potential employer's premises
- Whether the potential employer performs administrative functions commonly performed by employers

---

[79] US Department of Labor (2016b).

In addition, the DOL also states that when evaluating a potential vertical joint employment relationship, the analysis must examine the "economic realities" of the relationships between the workers and each of the potential employers to determine whether the workers are economically dependent on both potential joint employers. If the employees are economically dependent on both, then both companies are likely employers of the workers.[80] This is in contrast to horizontal joint employment, where the relationship between the potential joint employers is the focus of a compliance evaluation.[81]

4.3.3 Issues for the Franchisee Model

The joint employer issue, and franchises in particular, has been an area of focus recently for the NLRB.[82] The NLRB's position has been that joint employment relationships are established when a company "possesse[s] and/or exercise[s] control over the labor relations policies" of its franchisees. Thus, merely "possessing" control over labor relations policies is sufficient to establish a joint employment relationship.[83]

In recent years there have been several high-profile cases against franchised fast food companies, including McDonald's and Domino's Pizza. [84] In March 2017, one court ruled that McDonald's was not a joint employer of employees from several of its franchises; however, the plaintiffs in this case stated that they would appeal the ruling.[85] Multiple other suits are still active. Similarly, while several cases against Domino's have settled, others are ongoing.[86] The outcomes of these high-profile cases may provide greater clarity regarding franchisor joint employer liability. Given how common the franchise model is, these decisions could have a major impact on fast food restaurant chains around the country. More than 80 percent of McDonald's restaurants around the globe are owned by franchisees, according to the company.[87] And while an NLRB ruling on this issue would not become law, it is significant in that it will likely be used for guidance by courts and lawmakers. It is difficult to predict how upcoming decisions made by the NLRB will impact the franchisor and franchisee relationship.

One noted issue in these cases has been the practice of providing technology and other operations tools to franchisees to help them run their business and to facilitate brand consistency. Though there are clear advantages to this practice in terms of

---

[80] US Department of Labor (2016b).

[81] US Department of Labor (2016b).

[82] NLRB Case No 32-RC-109684.

[83] Lipkin, LaRocca, and Lotito (2015).

[84] Casuga (2016).

[85] *Salazar et al. v. McDonald's Corp. et al.*

[86] New York State Office of the Attorney General (2016).

[87] "Company Overview" (2017).

business performance, these systems and tools may leave the franchisors vulnerable as joint employers due to the potential interpretation of "control" over the franchisee created by providing the franchise with the technology.[88] Legal experts acknowledge that the use of franchisor software by franchises is a significant challenge to compliance.[89] Another consideration is the extent to which the software is customizable by the franchisee.[90] These issues will likely be clarified as new rulings are issued.

4.3.4 What Data Should Be Collected to Evaluate Joint Employment?

Similar to an independent contractor analysis, there is no defined formula to determine whether a company is a joint employer due to inconsistent and changing interpretations of case law and enforcement practices. However, a comprehensive review across the different sources reveals some common themes that provide useful guidance. In many ways an evaluation of joint employment is similar to the evaluation recommended to study independent contractor status. Below, we describe some of the differences.

The factors relevant in an evaluation differ for horizontal and vertical joint employment, so the first step is to determine which model is being tested. Generally, data should be collected from both companies to determine the relationship between them and the role the employees play in the operations of either of the companies' businesses. Analyzing a potential joint employment relationship involves collecting and reviewing a significant amount of information from multiple sources to provide a comprehensive view of the work that employees perform and the relationship between them and the companies involved.

Employees are able to provide information about the nature of the work they are performing and the role each company plays in managing that work. The employee can provide insight into the degree to which tasks are supervised, who is providing that supervision, and the location of where work is performed. Employees may also be able to provide information regarding operational procedures. For example, an employee may know the extent to which two parties coordinate regarding work schedules and staffing. This information could be relevant to evaluating a horizontal joint employment relationship.

Because the economic relationship between entities is a major component of some joint employment analyses, reviewing financial records, legal documents regarding ownership, and operational procedures such as HR, inventory, and customer service may also provide key insight.

---

[88] Dubé (2016).

[89] Casuga (2016).

[90] Casuga (2016).

While the legal status of employees' relationships with franchisors and franchisee is not yet clear, the factors relevant to this unique relationship appear to be primarily focused at the management and operations level. It may therefore be useful to collect specific details regarding where programs and materials used at the franchise came from, such as the POS (point of sale) program, time clock/keeping system, and inventory software. Many franchisors require that their franchises use and maintain systems and materials purchased directly from the franchisor, so collecting this information may be fairly straightforward. Gathering specific information from leadership and/or managers regarding the flexibility given at the restaurant level to modify, customize, or adapt these programs to better fit individual needs may be important.

4.4   Other Non-employee Classifications

In addition to the working relationships already described, there are several other nonemployment relationships that have been subjected to legal scrutiny, including athletes at the minor league or collegiate levels, interns, and trainees. In each of these relationships, the individuals providing services are not employees and therefore are not entitled to minimum wage, overtime, or any other employee protections. In the following sections, we provide an overview of the issues involved in these classifications.

4.4.1   Minor League and Collegiate Athletes

Minor league or collegiate athletes, some of whom are also referred to as "amateurs," play a significant role in the US sports industry. Among this group are university student athletes, minor league players, and Olympic athletes. For some of these athletes, the governing body that oversees competition has strict criteria to define amateur status. The National Collegiate Athletic Association (NCAA), which oversees most college sports, for example, states the following:

> All incoming student athletes must be certified as amateurs. With global recruiting becoming more common, determining the amateur status of prospective student athletes can be challenging. All student athletes, including international students, are required to adhere to NCAA amateurism requirements to remain eligible for intercollegiate competition.

In general, amateurism requirements do not allow:

- Contracts with professional teams
- Salary for participating in athletics
- Prize money above actual and necessary expenses
- Play with professionals
- Tryouts, practice, or competition with a professional team

- Benefits from an agent or prospective agent
- Agreement to be represented by an agent
- Delayed initial full-time collegiate enrollment to participate in organized sports competition[91]

The classification of athletes has received recent media coverage, likely due to increased public awareness regarding various labor laws as well as recent public debate about the potential health consequences of engaging in some sports activities (e.g., concussions). Challenging standard practice, athletes from several organizations have filed litigation claiming that they should be legally classified as employees. Among these lawsuits are NCAA athletes and minor league baseball players in the USA and major junior hockey players in both the USA and Canada. Currently, these athletes are not considered employees and are therefore not subject to any of the same federal and state protections regarding working hours, compensation, or benefits that an employee would receive. It is common for athletes at this level to spend a substantial amount of time on team-related activities which would result in substantial costs for organizations if these athletes were classified as employees and thus entitled to minimum wage, overtime, and benefits.

In addition, if these players were considered employees, the NLRA would become applicable and therefore give the athletes the right to unionize, engage in collective bargaining, and challenge policies that control their behavior and activities.[92] Recent legal challenges regarding the classification of nonprofessional athletes have included lawsuits brought under the FLSA and to the NLRB.[93]

For some classifications, such as independent contractors and interns, the DOL has provided a list of relevant factors that can be used as a "test" to determine whether an individual meets the definition for a specific classification. One of the challenges to studying the employment status of these athletes is that there is no test specifically applicable to this group, making it difficult to determine which factors are relevant.

The primary issue in many of the recent lawsuits appears to be whether time spent on team activities (e.g., practice, workouts, travel, games) should be considered "work" under the FLSA.[94]

Another factor raised in this litigation is determining who *benefits* most from the relationship. Though athletes spend many hours on team activities for little or no direct compensation, some receive nonmonetary rewards such as training, development, or scholarships. Of course, the concept of receiving training, experience, and guidance from experienced professionals for little or no compensation with the hope of securing a professional job in the future is not new. Similar models (such as trainees and apprenticeships described later) have been in place throughout history.

---

[91] "Amateurism" (n.d.).

[92] Bahmani and Boggs (2016).

[93] For example, see *Dawson v. NCAA*.

[94] For example, see *Berger v. Nat'l Collegiate Athletic Ass'n*.

Another factor frequently raised in this area of litigation is the amount of money made by the teams and/or leagues based on the "work" performed by uncompensated or undercompensated players. Some amateur organizations, such as the NCAA, generate millions of dollars a year in revenue.[95] Meanwhile, many athletes do not. *Business Insider* investigated this issue and reported in 2016 that the 231 NCAA Division I schools with data available generated a total of $9.15 billion in revenue during the 2015 fiscal year from college athletics. That study reported that Texas A&M made the most with $192.6 million in revenue from college athletics, according to the article.[96] An example of the disparity in compensation between coaches and players was highlighted in a July 2016 article in the *Washington Post*, which reported that USA Olympic Swimming Executive Director Chuck Wielgus made $854,000, while the swimmers on the team made $42,000 per year. Similarly, the article stated that USA Olympics Triathlon CEO Rob Urbach makes $362,000 per year, while team triathletes compete receiving between $20,000 and $40,000 annually.[97]

A significant factor relevant to student athletes, and the analysis of classification of NCAA players in particular, is the fact that student athletes are sometimes required to miss classes to attend games.[98] This prioritization raises the question of whether players' relationships with their colleges are primarily educational and beneficial to the students or a financial benefit for the University.[99]

Recent examples of cases include *Berger et al. v. National Collegiate Athletic Association et al.*, in which track and field athletes at the University of Pennsylvania claimed that they should be employees because they did not meet many of the DOL's criteria for unpaid interns. In this case the trial court found that "there is not one set of immutable factors that applies to all interns in all situations, and there is certainly not one test that applies equally to interns and student athletes."

Instead of using the DOL's intern criteria in place at the time, the court applied the economic realities test to examine the relationship between the athletes and the University. This examination included several different factors that together represented the "totality of the circumstances," and the court found that these athletes were not employees under the FLSA. On appeal, the Seventh Circuit upheld the prior ruling, stating in part that "student-athletic 'play' is not 'work,' at least as the term is used in the FLSA."[100] In this decision, the court relied on the DOL's Field Operations Handbook (FOH), which specifies that student athletes are not employees.[101]

---

[95] "Revenue" (n.d.).

[96] Gaines (2016).

[97] Hobson (2016).

[98] Edelman (2014).

[99] For an excellent summary of this issue, the interested reader may review "Gaming the System: The Exemption of Professional Sports Teams from the Fair Labor Standards Act" by Charlotte S. Alexander and Nathaniel Grow (2015).

[100] See ruling in *Berger et al. v. National Collegiate Athletic Association et al.*, Appeal from the United States District Court for the Southern District of Indiana, Indianapolis Division. No. 14-cv-1710.

[101] US Department of Labor (2016c); § 10b24b.

The outcome of *Berger* and others has created a precedent which may be difficult for future NCAA athletes to overcome should they attempt to challenge their non-employment classification. To date, NCAA athletes have not been determined to be employees by any courts or federal agencies.[102]

Another notable case involved minor league baseball players.[103] In this case, a class of thousands of minor league baseball players filed a lawsuit against Major League Baseball (MLB) claiming that they should be employees and therefore should be paid minimum wage and overtime. The class of players was certified as a class in March 2017; however, the MLB was subsequently allowed to appeal the decision in June 2017.[104] The outcome of this case will likely provide important guidance moving forward.

Similarly, there is a pending lawsuit in Canada regarding hockey players in the Canadian Hockey League (CHL), which is a premier feeder league into the National Hockey League (NHL). The CHL consists of player's ages 16–20. The players participate in practices, workouts, and play upward of 70 games each 6-month regular season.[105] In exchange for their play, some of these junior league players live with host families, earn minimal pay (i.e., below minimum wage), and accrue a year of college scholarship money for every year they play in the league.[106] The players' have sued the league alleging that they should be considered employees and paid minimum wage.[107] Some of the specific issues evaluated in this case included whether the teams were profitable, the degree of control the team exercised over the players both on and off the ice, and the benefits received by players and the league. In 2017 the case was certified as a class action and remains pending. Though the case is in Canada, the labor laws in Canada are similar to those in the USA, and the outcome in these cases could have an impact on similar athletes in the USA.[108]

4.4.2   *Interns*

Many students choose to pursue internships as an opportunity to gain real-world work experience. Internships are typically a mix of performing some work for the employer's benefit and receiving valuable training and experience in exchange. Some internships also offer benefits such as academic credits or some compensation.

---

[102] Football players at Northwestern University also petitioned the NLRB to be employees under the NLRA and therefore able to unionize. A regional director for the NLRB concluded that the player were employees. This ruling was appealed and later dismissed on jurisdictional grounds.

[103] *Senne et al. v. Office of the Commissioner of Baseball*

[104] Rhodes (2017).

[105] Cohen (2015).

[106] Cohen (2015).

[107] For example, see *Walter v Western Hockey League*; *Berg v Ontario Hockey League*.

[108] For purposes of full disclosure, one of the authors of this chapter (Hanvey) served as a testifying expert in *Berg* and *Walter*.

This relationship can be mutually beneficial but also has the potential to be abused by companies that intentionally misclassify employees as "interns" to minimize or avoid compensating them.[109]

Unlike other non-employee relationships, the DOL has published specific criteria to evaluate whether a worker can be classified as an intern. Arguably, the most important factor is whether the intern or the employer is the primary beneficiary of the relationship. According to the DOL, to qualify as an unpaid internship, the following factors must be evaluated, but no single factor is determinative:[110]

1. The extent to which the intern and the employer clearly understand that there is no expectation of compensation. Any promise of compensation, express or implied, suggests that the intern is an employee—and vice versa.
2. The extent to which the internship provides training that would be similar to that which would be given in an educational environment, including the clinical and other hands-on training provided by educational institutions.
3. The extent to which the internship is tied to the intern's formal education program by integrated coursework or the receipt of academic credit.
4. The extent to which the internship accommodates the intern's academic commitments by corresponding to the academic calendar.
5. The extent to which the internship's duration is limited to the period in which the internship provides the intern with beneficial learning.
6. The extent to which the intern's work complements, rather than displaces, the work of paid employees while providing significant educational benefits to the intern.
7. The extent to which the intern and the employer understand that the internship is conducted without entitlement to a paid job at the conclusion of the internship.

If all the above factors are in place, an unpaid intern is not considered an employee for the purposes of the FLSA. However, if any of the factors are not met, the intern would be an employee and entitled to minimum wage and overtime.[111]

One case involving unpaid interns which received extensive coverage in the media is *Glatt v. Fox Searchlight Pictures, Inc.* The case started in February of 2010 when two former interns who had worked in various departments at Fox sued the company claiming that they were essentially being used as free labor to keep costs down. In June 2013, the district court judge ruled that Fox had misclassified the plaintiffs under the FLSA, stating that the plaintiffs' received little educational value from their internships. In the ruling the judge referenced the DOL Fact Sheet but rejected the "primary beneficiary test" (i.e., the intern being the primary beneficiary from the relationship) as being "subjective and unpredictable." Fox appealed the ruling to the Second Circuit.

In July 2015, the Second Circuit vacated the previous ruling, saying the interns were not employees and that a new primary beneficiary test should be applied to

---

[109] *See, e.g., Cooper v. LAC Basketball Club, Inc.* and *Schumann et al. v. Collier Anesthesia.*
[110] US Department of Labor (2018).
[111] Jackson (2016).

determine employee status. After rejecting the DOL's test, the court applied its own, more "employer friendly" seven factor, primary beneficiary test.[112] The appeals court remanded the case to district court to reach a decision using the new test. In January 2016, the Second Circuit amended its opinion. The court acknowledged that the relationship between interns and employers should not be analyzed in the same way as employer-employee relationships, noting that an intern enters the relationship "with the expectation of receiving educational or vocational benefits," while employees do not.

In July 2016, the plaintiffs asked the Judge to end the suit and asked that he approve payments of $3,500–$7,500 for the named plaintiffs. *Glatt* led to unpaid interns at other major media companies bringing similar class actions that challenged the previously common practice, including interns at NBCUniversal, Viacom, Warner Music Group, and Condé Nast.[113] Each company negotiated multimillion-dollar settlements with their former interns. These companies now compensate their interns or have abandoned their intern programs completely.[114]

4.4.3 Trainees

The Supreme Court has ruled that the FLSA definition of employment (to suffer or permit to work) does not mean that anyone who works "for their own advantage" on the premises of another is an employee.[115] This language is specifically relevant for individuals who are performing work for the purpose of learning a business, such as a trainee . While the accurate classification of a trainee depends upon all of the circumstances surrounding their work activities, the specific criteria to be evaluated is nearly identical to those used for interns prior to January 2018.[116]

4.4.4 What Data Are Needed to Evaluate the Status of These "Other" Categories of Employees?

The data needed to address each of these nonemployment relationships (e.g., amateur athlete, student, intern, trainee) is similar in some respects to independent contractors and joint employers but unique in other respects. To evaluate the status of

---

[112] Parlo and Shaulson (2015). The factors can be found at: https://law.justia.com/cases/federal/district-courts/new-york/nysdce/1:2011cv06784/385387/163/

[113] Raymond (2015).

[114] Miller (2016).

[115] *Walling v. Portland Terminal Co. See also,* US Department of Labor (n.d.b).

[116] The same factors apply to students. A detailed list can be found at http://webapps.dol.gov/elaws/whd/flsa/docs/trainees.asp. If all of the criteria used are applicable, the trainees are likely not employees.

interns and trainees, data can be collected from the interns/trainees themselves and from the company. Information regarding the skills, knowledge, and abilities being gained through the work can be gathered by directly from the intern/trainee. In addition, the intern/trainee's understanding regarding compensation and expectations regarding future employment can be self-reported by the intern/trainee. Information regarding the level of supervision by the organization can be collected from both the intern/trainee and from the organization. To determine who is benefiting from the work being performed, an evaluation of the work itself and the impact it has on the organization and others working at the facility is helpful.

Similarly, information can be gathered from the organization's leadership to assess the impact the work has on the organization's objectives. An evaluation of hiring data or interviews with hiring managers/HR can provide information regarding company staffing to determine whether the intern/trainee has displaced employee(s).

Information relevant to determining the employment status of athletes requires data from the players and the organization for which they play. The specific data needed to evaluate the classification of an athlete varies depending on the scenario, which organizations are involved, and the player's current classification (e.g., intern, trainee, student).

Data can be gathered directly from a sample of current players (former players may also be used to supplement the data collection) regarding the nature, frequency, and amount of time spent preparing, training, traveling, and competing in games. Information regarding issues that relate to perception and understanding of the non-employment relationship can be gathered from the players themselves. Data may include topics such as each player's expectation for employment after graduation, each player's understanding of the nature of his or her relationship with the organization, the benefit each player believes he/she is receiving from playing, and the extent to which the organization exerts control over the player both on and off the playing field. If the players have an on-site manager or "coach" from whom they receive direct instructions, he or she may also be a useful source of information.

The organization for which the athletes play can be analyzed to understand its role and relationship with the players. Information regarding other sports or programs and locations the organization runs can also be reviewed. Data can be collected regarding the level of supervision provided, the contracts executed by the players, the expectations communicated to the players, scheduling expectations, and the impact the athlete's playing has on the organization (i.e., does the organization benefit from the play).

Expectations from the organization regarding schedule, training time, and game times may also be found in hard copy or electronic materials generated by the organization and distributed to players. Review of this material can be informative. Compensation paid by the organization (either monetary or other form) may be collected through the organization's financial data or from the players. Data regarding the number of players who receive professional or other contracts which pay them to play can likely be collected from the organization or other external sources.

An external assessment of other programs and vocational programs offered in the same area of sport can be conducted by reviewing public industry and competitor data available online.

4.5 Recommended Data Collection Methods to Assess Employment Status

The foundations for the methods described in this section can be found in Chap. 2. In the following section, we discuss several components of these methods that are unique to an evaluation of employment status.

4.5.1 Time and Motion Observations

Observations involve systematically recording details about the tasks individuals perform. In the context of an employment classification study, the level of detail that can be collected using this method can be useful for evaluating a variety of relevant factors. For example, an observation captures the amount of time the worker spends interacting with the "points of contact" at the organization (whether they are from a company or a sports coach) as well as the frequency and medium (e.g., email, text, verbal). Further, the nature of interactions with the contacts can be documented. For example, whether a worker is asking for permission or simply providing a status update may be relevant to classification decisions. Evaluating the nature of the inter-actions is critical to assessing independent decision-making and control exerted by the organization. The absence of frequent interaction with the company can, in itself, be a useful finding.

Observations can also be conducted of employees working at the organization in the "points of contact" positions. As with the observation of the worker, capturing the employer side of any communication with workers can also be informative.

4.5.2 Structured Interviews

Collecting self-report data using an interview format enables information to be col-lected regarding a broad array of issues which may not be evident through observa-tions alone. An interview method allows the interviewer to ask for additional detail or clarification, as needed, to ensure that responses provide complete and useful information. Interviews with workers usually involve asking detailed questions about a range of issues, such as other sources of income the worker may have, train-ing he/she received, permission required from the organization to perform certain activities, activities which may be prohibited by the organization, individual decision-making, and the organization's policies regarding the method of executing work. It may also be possible to ask questions about frequency and time spent interacting with the company and with points of contact. Example scenarios and descriptions of typical procedures and activities can be useful ways to illustrate information. Another advantage of the interview format is that it can cover broad time period which can be beneficial in litigation in which a long period of time is relevant to the lawsuit.

A challenge in implementing this method is securing participation from workers. Given his or her non-employee status, he or she may not be willing to contribute the time and effort required to execute this method, and the company typically cannot require the worker to do so.

Interviews with employees, including leadership and points of contact at the relevant organization(s) are often necessary not only to collect key issues relevant to evaluating status but also to provide explanations and detail regarding the organization's operations and programs used at the company which may not be clear or evident to the workers. Evaluating employee status requires an understanding of the role the worker plays in the operations of each company's business. Interviewing multiple parties is preferable to ensure that information is comprehensive.

4.5.3   Survey

Another method which involves collecting self-report information is a survey. Similar to an interview, survey questions can be crafted to collect relevant information regarding a range of topics and can ask participants about a broad time period. However, because the survey completion is unlikely to be monitored, the survey must be designed to be as simple, clear, and short as possible. Therefore, the length of the survey should be limited, and closed-ended questions are frequently used. Although these data can be collected easily and quantitative, this method does not allow for any follow-up or clarification of responses if needed.

A survey administration typically requires less time and fewer resources than observations and interviews and can be administered to a larger group of people. The method therefore results in a larger and potentially more varied dataset. However, asking company leadership and subject matter experts to complete a survey may not be desirable due to the sensitive nature of some of the questions. In addition, because independent contractor participants are unlikely to be compensated for this time, response rates from this group may be low.

4.5.4   Hybrid Approach

Some studies benefit from using a "hybrid approach," which involves using multiple data collection methods. Given the range of participants and topics relevant to an employment relationship analysis, it may make sense to combine approaches.

For example, a study that includes observations of workers, and interviews with subject matter experts can result in a comprehensive dataset which includes information from multiple perspectives. The approach must be customized to fit each unique situation. The method(s) selected should be driven by the nature of the information being collected.

4.6 Conclusion

This chapter has provided an overview of some of the current legal landscape in the workplace related to employment status. While some of the issues presented are applicable to a relatively narrow range of people (e.g., amateur athletes, interns), others have broad implications which impact many different industries (e.g., independent contractor misclassification). Our goal was to introduce these concepts and provide suggestions on how to utilize well-established research methods to generate data and information relevant to these classification issues.

While the facts and guidelines presented in this chapter are current at the time of writing, we recognize that the landscape in employment law is always shifting. Because of this, we have suggested flexible research methods which collect data relevant to the key questions which are unlikely to change based on political or legal trends.

References

Alexander, C. S., & Grow, N. (2015). Gaming the system: The exemption of professional sports teams from the Fair Labor Standards Act. *UC Davis Law Review, 49*, 123–181. Retrieved from https://lawreview.law.ucdavis.edu/issues/49/1/Articles/49-1_Alexander_Grow.pdf

Amateurism. (n.d.). Retrieved from NCAA website: http://www.ncaa.org/amateurism

Bahmani, S., & Boggs, S. P. (2016, December 22). Reigniting the debate over student-athletes as employees. *Law360*. Retrieved from https://www.law360.com/articles/869195/reigniting-the-debate-over-student-athletes-as-employees

Bartlett, B., & Young, K. (2016, January 20). *WHD issues another momentous interpretation, mapping joint employer status on horizontal and vertical planes. [Web log post].* Retrieved from Seyfarth Shaw Wage and Hour Litigation Blog: http://www.wagehourlitigation.com/joint-employment/another-momentous-ai/

Bayles, C. (2017, March 23). Uber, drivers play 'Hopscotch,' and 9th Circ. Not amused. *Law360*. Retrieved from https://www.law360.com/articles/905384/uber-drivers-play-hopscotch-and-9th-circ-not-amused

Carre, F. (2015). *(In)dependent contractor misclassification* (Briefing Paper No. 403). Retrieved from The Economic Policy Institute website: http://www.epi.org/publication/independent-contractor-misclassification/

Casuga, J. B. (2016, November 30). Franchise technology may tip scales in joint employer cases. *Bloomberg Labor & Employment*. Retrieved from https://www.bna.com/franchise-technology-may-n73014447847/

Cohen, J. (2015, March 13). The fight to keep junior hockey players from getting paid. Washington's junior hockey teams are turning to the government as a way to get out of paying players who are mobilizing against them. *Vice*. Retrieved from https://sports.vice.com/en_us/article/the-fight-to-keep-junior-hockey-players-from-getting-paid

Company Overview and Segment Information. (2017). Retrieved from http://corporate.mcdonalds.com/mcd/investors/company-overview/company-overview-segment-information.html

Deknate, A., & Hoff-Downing, L. (2015). ABC on the books and in the courts: An analysis of recent independent contractor and misclassification statutes. *University of Pennsylvania Journal of Law and Social Change*, 18(1).

Dickinson, J. G., De Haro, H. D., Gottlieb, B., Doyle, J. D., Hewitt, D. J., Matura, M., et al. (2016). *"Independent contractors" and contingent workers under the NLRA: Whose employees are they anyway?* Presented at the annual labor and employment law conference of american bar association section of labor and employment law, Chicago, IL.

Dishman, L. (2017, January 5). How the gig economy will change in 2017. *Fast Company*. Retrieved from https://www.fastcompany.com/3066905/how-the-gig-economy-will-change-in-2017

Dubé, L. E. (2016, October 14). McDonald's labor board deal may speed joint employer ruling. *Bloomberg Labor & Employment*. Retrieved from https://www.bna.com/mcdonalds-labor-board-n57982078619/

Edelman, M. (2014, January 30). 21 reasons why student-athletes are employees and should be allowed to unionize. *Forbes*. Retrieved from https://www.forbes.com/sites/marcedelman/2014/01/30/21-reasons-why-student-athletes-are-employees-and-should-be-allowed-to-unionize/#3baa33fe8d05

Farrell, D., & Greig, F. (2016). *The online platform economy. Has growth peaked?* Retrieved from JP Morgan Chase & Co. website: https://www.jpmorganchase.com/corporate/institute/document/jpmc-institute-online-platform-econ-brief.pdf

Faulman, S. (2016, April). *Worker vulnerability in the "gig economy"*. Paper presented at the annual conference of the american bar association. Washington, DC. Retrieved from http://www.americanbar.org/content/dam/aba/events/labor_law/2016/04/tech/papers/gig_economy_faulman.authcheckdam.pdf

Fox, K. (2017, June 8). Gig economy, independent contractors, and new york law. *The National Law Review*. Retrieved from https://www.natlawreview.com/article/gig-economy-independent-contractors-and-new-york-law

Gaines, C. (2016, October 14). The difference in how much money schools make off of college sports is jarring, and it is the biggest obstacle to paying athletes. *Business Insider*. Retrieved from http://www.businessinsider.com/ncaa-schools-college-sports-revenue-2016-10

Gurrieri, V. (2017, June 7). DOL Yanks Obama-Era Joint Employer, classification guidance. *Law360*. Retrieved from https://www.law360.com/employment/articles/932130

Habans, R. (2016). *Is California's gig economy growing? Exploring Trends in Independent Contracting*. Retrieved from UCLA Institute for Research on Labor and Employment website: http://irle.ucla.edu/old/publications/documents/Habans_IndependentContractor.pdf

Harris, S. D., & Krueger, A. B. (2015, December). *A proposal for modernizing labor laws for twenty-first-century work: The "independent worker"* (Discussion Paper 2015-10). Retrieved from the Hamilton Project website: http://www.hamiltonproject.org/assets/files/modernizing_labor_laws_for_twenty_first_century_work_krueger_harris.pdf

Hathaway, I. & Muro, M. (2016, October 13). Tracking the gig economy: New numbers. *The Brookings Institution*. Retrieved from https://www.brookings.edu/research/tracking-the-gig-economy-new-numbers/

Hobson, W. (2016, July 30). Olympic executives cash in on a 'Movement' that keeps athletes poor. *The Washington Post*. Retrieved from https://www.washingtonpost.com/sports/olympics/olympic-executives-cash-in-on-a-movement-that-keeps-athletes-poor/2016/07/30/ed18c206-5346-11e6-88eb-7dda4e2f2aec_story.html?utm_term=.cad26a7c0990

Jackson, C. D. (2016, November). *Who is an employer? Expansive considerations of coverage*. Presentation at the annual labor and employment law section conference of the american bar association. Chicago, IL. Retrieved from https://www.americanbar.org/content/dam/aba/events/labor_law/2016/11/annual/papers/57d.authcheckdam.pdf

Jonathan, M. L., McRee, E. B., Armistead, K. T., Werntz, A., Woods, A., & Couzo, V. (2017, March 28). Joint employment relationships: Best practices and risks. *Law360*. Retrieved from https://www.law360.com/articles/906291/joint-employment-relationships-best-practices-and-risks

Kamdar, A. (2016, February 19). Why some gig economy startups are reclassifying workers as employees. *OnLabor Workers, Unions, Politics*. Retrieved from https://onlabor.org/2016/02/19/why-some-gig-economy-startups-are-reclassifying-workers-as-employees/

Kapp, D. (2016, May). Uber's worst nightmare. *San Francisco Magazine*. Retrieved from https://modernluxury.com/san-francisco/story/ubers-worst-nightmare

Katz, L. F., & Krueger, A. B. (2016). *The rise and nature of alternative work arrangements in the United States, 1995–2015*. Retrieved from https://krueger.princeton.edu/sites/default/files/akrueger/files/katz_krueger_cws_-_april_26_2016.pdf

Kaufmann, A. (2015, November). *Current implications of the fissured workplace: A compendium of significant litigation and NLRB developments*. Presented at the annual section of labor and employment law conference of the american bar association. Chicago, IL.

Kendall, M. (2016, July 4). Uber battling more than 70 lawsuits in federal courts. *The Mercury News*. Retrieved from http://www.mercurynews.com/2016/07/04/uber-battling-more-than-70-lawsuits-in-federal-courts/

Kessler, S. (2015, February 17). The gig economy won't last because it's being sued to death. *Fast Company*. Retrieved from https://www.fastcompany.com/3042248/the-gig-economy-wont-last-because-its-being-sued-to-death

Kosoff, M. (2015a, June 22). $2 billion grocery delivery startup Instacart is reclassifying some of its workers as employees. *Business Insider*. Retrieved from http://www.businessinsider.com/why-instacart-is-reclassifing-some-of-its-workers-as-employees-2015-6

Kosoff, M. (2015b, July 19). Uber's nightmare scenario: Here's what a huge, expensive pain it would be to turn thousands of drivers into employees. *Business Insider*. Retrieved from http://www.businessinsider.com/what-it-would-take-for-uber-to-reclassify-all-its-drivers-2015-7

Kwidzinski, A., & Trimarchi, M. (2014, September 11). Rulings raise issues for employers of independent contractors. Bloomberg *HR & Payroll Resource Center*. Retrieved from https://www.bna.com/rulings-raise-issues-n17179894760/

Leberstein, S. (2012, August). *Independent contractor misclassification imposes huge costs on workers and federal and state treasuries*. Retrieved from National Employment Law Project website: http://nelp.org/content/uploads/2015/03/IndependentContractorCosts1.pdf

Leberstein, S., & Ruckelshaus, C. (2016, May). *Independent contractor vs. Employee: Why independent contractor misclassification matters and what we can do to stop it*. Retrieved from National Employment Law Project website: http://www.nelp.org/content/uploads/Policy-Brief-Independent-Contractor-vs-Employee.pdf

Lipkin, H. A., LaRocca, D. R., & Lotito, M. J. (2015, January 21). Expert analysis: NLRB joint employer redefinition threatens franchises. *Law360*. Retrieved from https://www.law360.com/articles/613307/nlrb-joint-employer-redefinition-threatens-franchises

Lolito, M. J. & Schuman, I. (2017, January 6). *Department of labor's exit memorandum calls for changes to address gig economy employment [web log post]*. Retrieved from Littler News & Analysis: https://www.littler.com/publication-press/publication/department-labors-exit-memorandum-calls-changes-address-gig-economy

Manyika, J., Lund, S., Bughin, J., Robinson, K. Mischke, J., & Mahajan, D. (2016, October). Independent work: Choice, necessity, and the gig economy. *McKinsey Global Institute*. Retrieved from https://www.mckinsey.com/global-themes/employment-and-growth/independent-work-choice-necessity-and-the-gig-economy

Massey, H. J. (2017, March 10). *Independent contractor standards uncertain despite new administration. [Web log post]*. Retrieved from Seyfarth Shaw Wage and Hour Litigation Blog: http://www.wagehourlitigation.com/independent-contractors/independent-contractor-standards-uncertain-despite-new-administration/

Miller, D. (2016, July 12). Fox unpaid intern case is drawing to a close with proposed settlement. *Los Angeles Times*. Retrieved from http://www.latimes.com/entertainment/envelope/cotown/la-et-ct-fox-interns-legal-case-20160712-snap-story.html

National Employment Law Project. (2017, January). *State legislatures and agencies can better protect on-demand and other contingent workers in their labor laws [policy brief]*. Retrieved from http://www.nelp.org/publication/the-on-demand-economy-state-labor-protections

New York State Office of the Attorney General. (2016). *A.G. Schneiderman announces lawsuit seeking to hold domino's and its franchisees liable for systemic wage theft [press release]*. Retrieved from https://ag.ny.gov/press-release/ag-schneiderman-announces-lawsuit-seeking-hold-dominos-and-its-franchisees-liable

Parlo, C. A. & Shaulson, S. S. (2015, July 7). *Second circuit establishes new test for unpaid intern claims*. Retrieved from Morgan Lewis Lawflash: https://www.morganlewis.com/pubs/second-circuit-establishes-new-test-for-unpaid-intern-claims

Pepper Hamilton, LLP. (2017). March 2017 independent contractor misclassification and compliance news update. *JDSupra*. Retrieved from http://www.jdsupra.com/legalnews/march-2017-independent-contractor-18490/

Perez, T. E. (2017). *Department of labor: Memorandum to the American people [cabinet exit memo]*. Retrieved from https://www.dol.gov/sites/default/files/dol-exit-memo.pdf

Raymond, N. (2015, June 10). Warner Music to pay $4.2 million to end intern wage lawsuit. *Reuters*. Retrieved from https://www.reuters.com/article/us-warnermusic-lawsuit-interns/warner-music-to-pay-4-2-million-to-end-intern-wage-lawsuit-idUSKBN0OQ2KC20150610

Reibstein, R. (2015). *2015 White Paper "Independent contractor misclassification: How companies can minimize the risk". [Web log post]*. Retrieved from Independent Contractor Misclassification and Compliance: https://independentcontractorcompliance.com/legal-resources/white-paper/

Revenue. (n.d.). Retrieved from NCAA website: http://www.ncaa.org/about/resources/finances/revenue

Rhodes, A. (2017, June 14). 9th circ. OKs MLB appeal in minor leaguer wage action. *Law360*. Retrieved from https://www.law360.com/articles/934647

Rolf, D., Clark, S., & Bryan, C. (2016). *Portable benefits in the 21st century. Future of work initiative*. Retrieved from the Aspen Institute website: https://dorutodpt4twd.cloudfront.net/content/uploads/2016/07/Portable_Benefits_final2.pdf

Rosenblatt, J. (2016, June 23). Lyft's $27 million accord with drivers wins court approval. *Bloomberg Technology*. Retrieved from https://www.bloomberg.com/news/articles/2016-06-23/lyft-s-27-million-settlement-with-drivers-wins-court-approval

Ruckelshaus, C. (2016, May). *Independent contractor vs. employee: Why misclassification matters and what we can do to stop it* (Policy Brief). Retrieved from National Employment Law Project website: http://www.nelp.org/publication/independent-contractor-vs-employee/

Sachs, B. (2015, December 8). Do we need an "independent worker" category? *OnLabor Workers, Unions, Politics*. Retrieved from https://onlabor.org/2015/12/08/do-we-need-an-independent-worker-category/

Smith, R., Marvy, P. A., & Zerolnick, J. (2014, February). *The big rig overhaul restoring middle-class jobs at American's ports through labor law enforcement*. Retrieved from https://changetowinn.app.box.com/s/2kgbbx5e4f9wok50gl5z

Steinmetz, K. (2015, June 17). Why the California ruling on Uber should frighten the sharing economy. *Time Magazine*. Retrieved from http://time.com/3924941/uber-california-labor-commission-ruling/

Steinmetz, K. (2016, June 30). The gig economy: TIME survey explores historic shift. Exclusive survey: The future of work in America. *Time Magazine*. Retrieved from http://time.com/4388733/gig-economy-uber-lyft-employment-survey/

The 'On-Demand Economy' Is Reshaping Companies And Careers. (2015, January 4). *The Economist*. Retrieved from http://www.businessinsider.com/the-on-demand-economy-is-reshaping-companies-and-careers-2015-1

Twenty Trends that Will Shape the Next Decade. (2010, October). *Intuit 2020 Report.* Retrieved from https://http-download.intuit.com/http.intuit/CMO/intuit/futureofsmallbusiness/intuit_2020_report.pdf

U.S. Department of Labor. (2011). *Labor secretary, IRS commissioner sign memorandum of understanding to improve agencies' coordination on employee misclassification compliance and education (Release Number: 11-1373-NAT) [News Release].* Retrieved from https://www.dol.gov/opa/media/press/whd/WHD20111373.htm

U.S. Department of Labor. (2014). *Fact sheet #13: Am I an employee? Employment relationship under the Fair Labor Standards Act (FLSA).* Retrieved from https://www.dol.gov/whd/regs/compliance/whdfs13.pdf

U.S. Department of Labor. (2016a). *Fiscal year 2017 Department of Labor Budget in Brief.* Retrieved from http://www.dol.gov/sites/default/files/documents/general/budget/FY2017BIB_0.pdf

U.S. Department of Labor. (2016b). Fact sheet #35: Joint employment under the Fair Labor Standards Act (FLSA) and Migrant and Seasonal Agricultural Worker Protection Act (MSPA). Retrieved from https://www.dol.gov/whd/regs/compliance/whdfs35.htm

U.S. Department of Labor. (2016c). FLSA coverage: employment relationship, statutory exclusions, geographical limits. In *Field operations handbook.* Retrieved from https://www.dol.gov/whd/FOH/FOH_Ch10.pdf

U.S. Department of Labor. (2018). *Fact sheet #71: Internship programs under the Fair Labor Standards Act.* Retrieved from https://www.dol.gov/whd/regs/compliance/whdfs71.htm

U.S. Department of Labor. (n.d.-a). *Misclassification of employees as independent contractors.* Retrieved from https://www.dol.gov/whd/workers/misclassification/

U.S. Department of Labor. (n.d.-b). *Fair Labor Standards Act advisor: School-to-Work.* Retrieved from http://webapps.dol.gov/elaws/whd/flsa/scope/ee15astw.asp

U.S. Government Accountability Office. (2015). *Contingent workforce: Size, characteristics, earnings, and benefits (GAO-15-168R).* Retrieved from https://www.gao.gov/assets/670/669766.pdf

U.S. Government Accountability Office. (2016). *Employment arrangements: Improved outreach could help ensure proper worker classification (GAO-06-656).* Retrieved from http://www.gao.gov/new.items/d06656.pdf

Weil, D. (2016). *Joint employment under the Fair Labor Standards Act and Migrant and Seasonal Agricultural Worker Privacy Act* (Administrator's Interpretation 2016-1). Retrieved from U.S. Department of Labor website. [This Administrator's Interpretation was withdrawn by the U.S. Department of Labor June 7, 2017].

Weil, D. (2017). Lots of employees get misclassified as contractors. Here's why it matters. *Harvard Business Review.* Retrieved from https://hbr.org/2017/07/lots-of-employees-get-misclassified-as-contractors-heres-why-it-matters

Wiessner, D. (2016, June 16). FedEx to settle driver lawsuits in 20 states for $240 million. *Reuters.* Retrieved from http://www.reuters.com/article/us-fedex-settlement-idUSKCN0Z229Q

Wood, R. W. (2015, June 16). FedEx settles independent contractor mislabeling case for $228 million. *Forbes.* Retrieved from http://www.forbes.com/sites/robertwood/2015/06/16/fedex-settles-driver-mislabeling-case-for-228-million/#48256e315f5a

Court Cases

Berg v Ontario Hockey League, Court File No. CV-14-514423, Ontario Superior Court (Canada).

Berger v. Nat'l Collegiate Athletic Ass'n, Case No.:14-cv-1710, Appeal from the United States District Court for the Southern District of Indiana, Indianapolis Division (2016).

Borello & Sons, Inc. v. Dept. of Indus. Relations, 48 Cal. 3d 341, 350 (1989).

Cooper v. LAC Basketball Club, Inc., Case No. 2:14-cv-04445 (C.D. Cal. June 10, 2014).

Cotter et al. v. Lyft, Inc., Case No. 13-cv-04065-VC. (N.D. Cal. 2016).

Dawson v. NCAA, Case No. 0:17-cv-15973 (N.D. Cal. 2017).

Glatt et al. v. Fox Searchlight Pictures Inc., Case No. 1:11-cv-06784, (S.D. N.Y. 2015).

NLRB Case No 32-RC-109684.

O'Connor, et al., v Uber Technologies, Inc., et al., Case No. 13-cv-03826-EMC (N.D. Cal.).

Salazar et. al., v. McDonald's Corp. et al, Case No.: 3:2014cv02096, (N.D. Cal. 2014).

Schumann et al v. Collier Anesthesia, P.A. et al, Case No. 2:2012cv00347 (M.D. Fla. 2017).

Senne et al v. Office of the Commissioner of Baseball, et al, Case No. 3:2014cv00608, (N.D. Cal. 2014).

Uber v. Berwick, Labor Comm'n Case No. 11-46739 EK (June 3, 2015), Super. Ct. Case No. CGC-15-546378.

Walling v. Portland Terminal Co., Case No.: 330 U.S. 148 (1947).

Walter v. Western Hockey League, et al., Court File No. 1401-11912, Court of Queen's Bench of Alberta (Canada).

Chapter 5
Off the Clock Work

Chester Hanvey

5.1 Introduction

An increasingly common wage and hour issue involves allegations of employees working "off the clock." Employees are said to be "on the clock" between the time they clock in and the time they clock out, that is, the time for which employees are being paid. In contrast, employees are not being paid either before or after their shifts, during which time they are said to be off the clock. When employees are performing compensable work during a time for which they are not being paid, they are working off the clock. Employees may choose to initiate litigation to recover unpaid wages and overtime for the uncompensated time.

Off the clock work can occur in a variety of ways. Some of the more frequent allegations include employees starting work before clocking in, clocking out before finishing work, performing work from home but not reporting the time (e.g., work-related phone calls or emails), donning or doffing required uniforms or equipment before or after shifts, time shaving (i.e., paying employees for fewer hours than they worked), or improper time clock "rounding" practices. Employers can be liable for significant damages for not paying employees for the total amount of time worked.

Off the clock claims are only applicable to non-exempt "hourly" employees, as exempt employees are paid the same salary regardless of the number of hours they work. The Fair Labor Standards Act (FLSA) requires that non-exempt employees are paid at the overtime rate (e.g., 1.5 times the regular rate of pay) for all hours worked over 40 in a workweek.[1] The FLSA also requires employees to be paid a minimum wage for all hours worked, currently $7.25 per/h at the federal level. Thus, an employee working off the clock triggers an FLSA violation in two situations: (1) the employee is not paid overtime when the unpaid time exceeds 40 h in workweek, or (2) the employee is paid less than minimum wage when the unpaid

---

[1] 29 U.S.C. §§ 206–207 (2012).

© Springer International Publishing AG, part of Springer Nature 2018
C. Hanvey, *Wage and Hour Law*, https://doi.org/10.1007/978-3-319-74612-8_5

hours result in the employee's hourly rate falling below the minimum amount. As an example, assume an employee is paid the exact minimum wage of $7.25 per/h. If that employee works even 1 min of unpaid time, adding that minute to their hours worked and diving by the paid amount will result in an hourly rate below the minimum wage.

Many states have more stringent requirements related to overtime and minimum wage. In some states, including Alaska, California, and Nevada, overtime may be required not only for all hours worked in excess of 40 per workweek but also for all hours worked in excess of 8 h in a workday.[2] In addition, many states and even some cities have minimum wage requirements higher than the federal minimum wage. As a result, local, rather than federal, violations are more apt to occur, and damages for off the clock work can accrue more rapidly in certain jurisdictions.

Litigation regarding off the clock work often involves understanding not only *what* activities performed by employees but also *when* the work is performed.[3] At the highest possible level, the evaluation of an off the clock claim requires a comparison of the amount of time worked to the amount of paid time. While this is a simple task conceptually, it is rarely simple in practice primarily because time worked off the clock is generally not recorded separately from the work time recorded for payroll purposes. As a result, it often becomes the job of an expert retained in these cases to collect reliable data to retrospectively "recreate" the actual time worked so that it can be compared to paid time. In some instances, this can be accomplished using existing electronic data such as phone records, email records, register data, computer activity data, or security badge entries. In other instances, electronic data is either unavailable or insufficient to answer relevant legal questions, and collecting data from other sources is necessary. Observations and self-report approaches may be applicable for this purpose.

5.2 Potential Causes for Off the Clock Work

There are several potential causes for off the clock work that are frequently alleged by plaintiffs in litigation. Plaintiffs often point to company policies that restrict overtime usage as a factor that causes employees to work off the clock. For example, some companies prohibit employees from working overtime without prior approval as a strategy to control labor costs. As a result, plaintiffs often claim they are "forced" to work off the clock in certain situations, such as when they have an excessive workload or customer demands require them to work beyond their scheduled shift. Plaintiffs may report that they are required to perform these tasks but feel pressure not to report this time because it was not pre-approved.

---

[2] Alaska Stat. §§ 23.10.050–23.10.150 (2016); Cal. Lab. Code § 510 (2016); Nev. Rev. Stat. § 608.018 (2016).

[3] There are various other legal questions in these cases such as whether the employer had knowledge of employees performing work off the clock. These types of questions are not typically addressed through a systematic study.

Another frequently alleged cause of off the clock work is unrealistic performance targets. If employees are evaluated based on performance targets (e.g., sales goals) that cannot reasonably be achieved within the employee's scheduled workweek, they may claim that working off the clock is required to meet company expectations.

A third potential cause of off the clock work is reclassification of employees from exempt to non-exempt. In an effort to comply with FLSA exemption regulations, or to avoid litigation, many employers have chosen to reclassify formerly exempt managers as non-exempt.[4] While the risk of misclassification litigation is eliminated by reclassification, the risk of other wage and hour violations, such as off the clock work, can increase. Exempt managers typically work more than 40 h per workweek but may be asked to work no more than 40 h after reclassification to avoid overtime costs. Unless the workload is decreased after reclassification, it may not be possible for the reclassified managers to accomplish the same tasks they performed prior to reclassification within 40 h. Some managers may be tempted to work off the clock to keep productivity up while staying within the 40 h expectation.

It is worth noting that although these policies are commonly alleged to cause off the clock work, the presence of these policies is not an evidence that employees have worked off the clock. Most companies, for example, have an interest in limiting overtime usage and may require pre-approval for that purpose. It does not follow that employees in all of these companies are working off the clock. Similarly, most companies in the retail industry set challenging sales targets for employees to increase motivation and job performance, and it's not uncommon for some employees to find these targets unreasonable. Again, one cannot conclude that all companies that establish sales targets for non-exempt employees are violating the FLSA. Whether violations have actually occurred is a question best answered through an analysis of the data. Methods for collecting and analyzing these data are described in a later section.

5.3   Compensable Work

The terms "hours worked" and "compensable time" are defined by the US Department of Labor as the time an employee must be on duty, on the employer's premises, at any other prescribed place of work, or any additional time the employee is allowed (i.e., suffered or permitted) to work. That is, if an employer knows that work is performed, the time should be counted toward hours worked, even if the work was not requested by the employee or it was performed away from company premises.[5] Thus, a critical component when studying off the clock work is identifying which employee activities should be considered "work." Though somewhat obvious, this component is sometimes overlooked and can be a source of substantial debate.

---

[4] Chap. 3 discussed issues in relation to classification of employees as exempt or nonexempt from the FLSA.

[5] Kearns (2002).

When evaluating the amount of time working off the clock, one must differentiate between compensable work activities and non-compensable activities. However, employees often perform activities that do not clearly fall into either category. A manager talking with an employee before a shift about a personal issue could be considered part of her responsibility as a manager (i.e., building rapport with staff) or could be considered a non-work task, similar to any other conversation that occurs outside of the workplace. Classifying activities as compensable or non-compensable often benefits from the input of a legal expert, either an attorney involved in the case or an external legal expert. Similar to classifying tasks as exempt or non-exempt (see Chap. 3), the ultimate decision is largely within the court's domain. As a practical matter, however, tasks must be classified in some manner to analyze and present study results. Depending on the methods used, study results can be updated fairly easily if the court finds the classification of any activities to be improper. Regardless of who makes classification decisions, it is important for the expert to capture enough detail about the tasks performed to allow those decisions to be made or reviewed. Knowing that an employee "made a phone call," for example, lacks some important detail that would aid in task classification. Additional information such as who the employee called (e.g., co-worker or spouse), the content of the call (e.g., issues in the store, arranging a ride home), or even which phone was used (e.g., company phone, personal phone) may play a role in the classification of a task as compensable or non-compensable.

5.4 Measurement Precision

In Chap. 2, I discussed some trade-offs to consider when determining the precision with which time measurements will be captured. Recording time measurements in larger intervals (e.g., 10 s) is less precise but often preferred in situations such as evaluations of FLSA exemption status because larger intervals enable observers to record more detail about the tasks performed. In addition, when observations cover a long period of time (e.g., full shift), slightly reduced measurement precision is unlikely to have any meaningful impact on overall study results.

Studies of off the clock work, on the other hand, typically require precise time measurement. Because the period of time at issue is rarely more than a few minutes, it is feasible (and often preferable) to record time to the nearest second. Less precise measurements have the potential to substantively impact study results when the total observation time is short. Also, the range of tasks being considered in an off-the clock case is typically a greatly reduced subset of all the tasks an employee may perform. Thus, it may be feasible to generate a predefined list of tasks that will be observed in this context. In some situations, the observed tasks may be performed in a known sequence and can be pre-populated into a data recording tool, thus eliminating the need for the observer to record any task descriptions, allowing them to focus all of their attention on time measurements.

In many off the clock studies, the time that an employee clocks in or clocks out is recorded as part of the observation. In some cases, it may be possible to cross-check observation data with timekeeping data to verify its accuracy. This requires the observer to synchronize his or her clock to the timekeeping system. However, because many timekeeping systems record data to the nearest minute, comparisons may also need to be performed to the nearest minute. Regardless, a comparison to external data demonstrates the validity of the data collection and can strengthen the value of the study.

5.5 Common Types of Off the Clock Work

There are a variety of ways in which off the clock work can occur. Broadly, off the clock work either occurs before the employee clocks in or after the employee clocks out. In the following sections, I highlight some commonly alleged off the clock work claims. I also discuss methodological options for evaluating each type of claim. The underlying principles for data collection methods are provided in Chap. 2, and issues related to data analysis are discussed further in Chap. 8.

5.5.1 Call Centers

In recent years, a variety of call centers have faced allegations related to compensating employees while they boot up their computers prior to starting their shift. In addition to many well-known companies within the telecommunications industry such as AT&T,[6] Comcast,[7] and Charter Communications,[8] companies operating call centers in other industries have faced similar litigation such as pharmaceuticals,[9] heath care,[10] staffing,[11] banking,[12] and energy.[13] Call centers function in a highly structured manner and use sophisticated software to precisely record employee activities throughout the day such as when they are on a calls and when they are available to receive calls. It is not uncommon for companies that operate call centers to schedule their employees' day to the minute and record the degree to which they adhere to that schedule. In fact, many call centers use this scheduling data as key performance indicator.

---

[6] See, e.g., Lamarr et al. v. Illinois Bell Telephone Co. et al.

[7] See, e.g., Faust et al. v. Comcast Cable Communications Management LLC.

[8] See, e.g., Davenport v. Charter Communications, LLC.

[9] See, e.g., Williams v. AmerisourceBergen Drug Corporation.

[10] See, e.g., Brown et al. v. Permanente Medical Group Inc.

[11] See, e.g., Holmes v. Kelly Services USA LLC et al.

[12] See, e.g., Sheffield v. BB&T et al.

[13] See, e.g., Volney-Parris v. Southern California Edison Company.

There have been a number of lawsuits against call centers alleging that employees are not compensated for time spent logging into their computers and loading necessary applications before they are clocked in. Plaintiffs allege that this occurs either because employees must log into their computers before their scheduled start time to ensure they are available to take calls when their shift starts or because they use an application on their computer to clock in which cannot be accessed until the computer is booted up.

There are a few potential approaches to studying this issue. Observations and work simulations are both useful methods in this circumstance. Electronic data may also be useful in some situations, and the use of these sources of data is discussed at the end of this chapter. For all approaches, the goal is to determine how much time it takes the computer to boot up before the employee clocks in, and to the extent possible, to account for the various factors that influence this boot up time (e.g., whether the computer is powered down or waiting on the restart screen when the employee arrives or the specific applications and the order in which they are loaded).

The observational approach has the advantage of collecting data from actual employee behaviors, thus eliminating any concerns about the degree to which simulations accurately replicate the employee's environment. Observers can be strategically positioned to observe employee activities once they arrive in the facility and record the tasks performed and the duration of those tasks up until the employee is clocked in. Observations can be challenging when the facility is large. Because all activities performed before employees arrive at their desk are potentially relevant, the observer may need to identify the employee upon entrance into the facility and follow him through the facility. The observer must also be physically positioned to clearly see the employee's computer screen and accurately record the sequence of tasks performed. Properly executed observations provide compelling information about the tasks employees perform prior to clock-in and the amount of time spent on them.

Alternatively, work simulations[14] have the advantage of generating a significant amount of data within a relatively short period of time. In addition, a variety of different scenarios can be replicated as desired, as opposed to waiting for them to naturally occur in an observation. The ability to collect multiple measurements also minimizes sampling error. It is important when conducting simulations to replicate the actual employee environment as closely as possible. For instance, using computers with comparable processing speed and memory, on the same network, loading the same applications in the same order all contributes to a higher-fidelity simulation. Conducting a simulation on multiple computers and in multiple call center locations (when applicable) adds to the robustness of the simulated data.

Simulations can be conducted with assistance from an employee who is knowledgeable about the login procedures, such as a supervisor or trainer. The employee performing the test should be knowledgeable about the process employees use to start their shift and be able to identify when something unusual happens that

---

[14] Work simulations are a common technique in other areas of human resources such as validation of personal selection procedures. *See* Whetzel et al. (2012) for additional information about work simulations.

impacts the results (e.g., software update, failed login). The employee can perform the steps an employee would follow to login, and each step in the process can be timed. The process can be repeated as many times as necessary to obtain a sufficient amount of data.

5.5.2 Working Remotely

One of the advantages of the widespread use of smartphones and other mobile technology is the flexibility it offers employees to accomplish work from a variety of locations. Advancements in technology, however, can also increase risk that non-exempt employees will perform work-related tasks outside of the workplace and off the clock. This includes tasks such as making or receiving work-related calls, reading and responding to work-related emails, reviewing reports, preparing work schedules, or other tasks that can be accomplished remotely.

Evaluating the occurrences of these activities can be challenging because observation is not feasible and these events may occur irregularly. However, there are two primary strategies that can be used in the context. First, an analysis of electronic data (e.g., phone and email records) may be useful. If the employee is using a company phone, for example, call logs can be used to determine when certain work-related activities occurred and the duration of those activities. These data can be compared to time records to see whether the activities occurred when the employee was off the clock. While this can provide some useful information, the data may be limited. For instance, electronic data will not reveal the content of the phone calls. Other sources of electronic data such as email records would include the content of each message. However, a somewhat lengthy process review is required to determine whether each message is work-related. Records of email communication are also limited in that the amount of time reading or composing emails is generally not known.

An alternative approach to evaluating the occurrence of these activities is through self-report. Although notable limitations to self-report exist in this context, there are times where this is the best approach to obtain reliable estimates of these activities. Many of the limitations are discussed in Chap. 2, but the most problematic in this situation is the tendency of employees to overestimate absolute time spent performing work tasks. In litigation involving off the clock work, estimates of absolute time are almost always necessary. Therefore, features to minimize, if not eliminate this bias, should be built into the methodology to the extent possible. Chapter 2 describes a technique known as the "events history calendar" along with a variety of studies that have demonstrated the effectiveness of these types of exercises for improving recall accuracy. This approach involves linking a memorable event from the relevant time period to the less memorable event that addresses a relevant legal question. When possible, self-report data can also be compared to external data to assess its accuracy. For example, if an employee's self-reports align with their phone and/or email data, confidence in the accuracy of the self-report is substantially increased.

5.5.3 Security "Bag Checking"

Many companies, especially within the retail industry, require employees to have their belongings inspected before leaving the premises as a strategy to mitigate internal theft. Legal questions sometime arise, however, regarding whether these policies require employees to work off the clock. Plaintiffs have alleged that "bag checks" are mandatory and the employee is therefore under the control of the employer until the bag check is complete, thus making time waiting for and submitting to a bag check compensable. Bag check policies have been challenged legally at several well-known retail companies in recent years including Amazon,[15] CVS,[16] Nordstrom,[17] Macy's,[18] Apple,[19] Converse,[20] and Nike.[21]

There are typically three broad research questions in cases involving bag checks: (1) How often do employees submit to bag checks? (2) Are the bag checks performed on the clock or off the clock? (3) What is the duration of the bag checks? Observation is typically the preferred method for answering these questions. Through observation, the sequence of events leading up to the bag check, time waiting for the bag check and the bag check itself, can be documented and timed. Both video and live observational approaches are applicable here. Video has the advantage of collecting a large amount of data in a short period of time, and videos can be re-watched by multiple observers to maximize timing accuracy and reliability. Live observers have the advantage of capturing contextual information not observable through video. In several bag check lawsuits, observation data demonstrated that bag checks occurred inconsistently, and when they did occur, they lasted for only a few seconds. The evidence was influential in judges' decisions to not certify a class or decertify an existing class.[22]

5.5.4 Donning and Doffing

Another potential off the clock activity that has received attention in the court system is "donning and doffing" (i.e., putting on and taking off) uniforms and personal protective equipment (PPE) that are "integral" to the employees' principal work activity.[23] These allegations are concentrated in jobs requiring employees to wear protective equipment to perform their work. Food processing,[24]

---

[15] *Integrity Staffing Solutions v. Busk.*

[16] *Murphy v. Caremark CVS Corp. et al.*

[17] *Ogiamien et al. v. Nordstrom Inc.*

[18] *Narez v. Macy's West Stores Inc.*

[19] *Frlekin et al. v. Apple Inc.*

[20] *Chavez v. Converse Inc. et al.*

[21] *Rodriguez v. Nike Retail Services Inc. et al.*

[22] See, for example, *Murphy v. Caremark CVS Corp. et al.*

[23] See 29 C.F.R. §785 et seq.

[24] One well-known case involving donning and doffing against Tyson foods is highlighted at the end of Chap. 8.

law enforcement,[25] and manufacturing[26] are a few industries that have faced lawsuits in which employees claimed they were not compensated for time spent donning and doffing required PPE.

The first question is whether the PPE worn by employees is integral to the job, thus making time donning and doffing that PPE compensable. In many cases, this issue is debated by attorneys and decided prior to involving an expert. The key question for experts is the amount of time employees spend donning and doffing uniforms and PPE. This can be measured using observational approaches or work simulations. Observations provide information regarding how long these activities actually take whereas work simulations provide information about how much time is required to complete the activities (two slightly different questions). The speed at which employees don or doff their PPE depends on various factors and may differ from person to person. As an example, an employee who arrives early for his shift may perform the task more slowly because there is little urgency, whereas an employee who arrives late is likely to perform the task as quickly as possible. In other words, observation results are influenced by factors other than the task being performed.

Observations can be conducted using live observers or video cameras. Privacy is an issue when using either approach. Jobs where PPE is donned over the top of one's clothes and done in open view are more conducive to an observational approach. An additional advantage, beyond those described in the previous section, to live observations in this context is the ability to capture information about unusual events. For example, if an employee is interrupted during the process or there is something wrong with the equipment, a live observer is more likely to be able to capture that information and interpret the data accordingly.

Work simulations involve an employee demonstrating the process of donning and doffing PPE for an observer to measure the time. This can be repeated as many times as necessary to obtain a sufficient sample size. This approach provides information about how much time is required to perform the task, as the employee conducting the simulation can focus their attention primarily on the simulation and perform the task efficiently. These data provide a useful estimate for how quickly the process could be completed by a motivated employee. The more employees included in this process, the more robust the data. This approach may be preferred when data cannot be collected directly from incumbents.

5.5.5   Time Clock Rounding

Another allegation involving off the clock work is related to company policies with respect to "rounding" time entries. Many companies have time clock policies that round all time entries to the nearest 15 min. If an employee clocks in at 8:07 am, his paid time will begin at 8:00 am. In other words, he would be paid 7 min more than

---

[25] *Martin v. City of Richmond.*

[26] *Sandifer v. U.S. Steel Corp.*

he actually worked. However, if they instead clock in at 8:08 am, his paid time will begin at 8:15 am, and he would be paid 7 min less than he actually worked. Time clock rounding is a common practice in many industries such as healthcare.

Time rounding policies are generally considered legal, provided that the policy does not systematically round time in the employer's favor, thus underpaying employees. In other words, the policy must be both neutral in theory and in practice. In theory, rounding polices are almost always neutral because the same number of minutes would round up to 8:00 am, for example, as the number of minutes that would round down to 8:00 am. The question for experts in this case is how rounding policy has affected employees *in practice*. Plaintiffs often argue that because employees are expected to be at work at their scheduled start time (typically right at the start of an hour), they are much more likely to arrive a few minutes early than a few minutes late. If this is true, the time system would round time in the employer's favor more frequently, which may be ruled to be a violation.

Experts in these cases usually rely on electronic data to reach conclusions about the neutrality of the policy. Some time clock systems maintain the actual entry and the rounded entry, which simplifies the analysis. If only the actual entry is available, it becomes relatively straightforward to re-create the rounding rules to determine the impact of the policy. However, it would not be possible to create the actual time entries based on data showing the rounded entries. At a minimum, the actual time entries are needed to conduct analysis of electronic data.

In Chap. 8, I discuss a variety of issues related to data analysis. In particular, data quality is an important consideration before conducting the analyses. Without reliable data, results are undermined regardless of how well the analyses are conducted. Assuming the data are acceptable, analysis can indicate the frequency that time was rounded in the employee's favor, the employer's favor, or not rounded at all. The analysis can also determine the total net impact of the policy over time, that is, the amount of time that was rounded in the employer's favor and the employee's favor and the difference between the two.

One final consideration is whether the actual clock-in time should be considered the beginning of compensable work time. In a structured work environment such as an assembly line, it may not be feasible for an employee to start working before the assembly line begins running. In such a case, it may be more appropriate to use the time the employee is known to begin working (e.g., when the assembly line begins) in the analysis, rather than their actual clock-in time.

5.6 Strategies to Prevent Off the Clock Work

The frequency and high costs associated with allegations of off the clock work leave many companies searching for strategies to prevent its occurrence, ensure all employees are paid for all time worked, and minimize litigation risk. While eliminating risk of litigation entirely is not possible, this section contains some strategies that can reduce this risk. In most companies, the interests of management and employees are aligned on this issue: employees are paid for all time they work. The recommendations below work toward that goal. Not all recommendations are feasible in all companies, but the more effort dedicated to reducing off the clock work, the greater the expected impact.

Early in the chapter, I discussed some company policies that are often cited by plaintiffs in litigation as causes of off the clock work. One of these was an inflexible prohibition on overtime usage without prior approval. Though the desire to reduce payroll usage is reasonable and ubiquitous, this can often be accomplished in a way that also minimizes legal risk. Adding flexibility to such a policy would help avoid employee perceptions of being pressured to avoid reporting time worked. For example, the policy could include an acknowledgment that infrequent situations occur wherein prior approval is not possible and employees will be paid for all time worked in these situations, whether pre-approved or not. Such a policy is likely to reduce perceptions that all time cannot be reported.

Training employees and managers on wage and hour compliance is also a way to mitigate risk. Some employees believe they are being a "team player" by not reporting all of their hours. This practice, however, can have serious financial consequences for the company if litigation arises. Employees should know that they are expected to report all hours worked, and managers should be vigilant in making sure that this occurs. Employees can be trained to avoid using personal devices for work-related activities when off the clock, and some companies may have the ability to block remote employee access to company email. Managers should also be trained to avoid reaching out to non-exempt employees when they are off the clock when possible and when not possible, to ensure that they record the time as worked time. Managers can also periodically perform random time record audits to look for evidence of off the clock work. As an example, some employees self-report their start time and record the same start time each day or always round their time entries to the start of an hour. It is unlikely that the employee actually started working at the exact time each day and could result in the employee working off the clock.

A common strategy for companies to influence employee behavior is by measuring it. Adding wage and hour compliance as a performance metric, for instance, will formally communicate to employees the importance of not working off the clock.[27] When performance is tied to compensation, this becomes a primary driver of employee motivation.[28] Companies that discipline employees for not meeting sales targets, but provide no repercussions for employees working off the clock, may increase the risk of employees working off the clock, as employees are likely to pursue goals they perceive to be most beneficial. Employees who work off the clock without reporting time can receive feedback in the form of a progressive disciplinary plan to further reinforce this message. Regardless of whether a policy was violated, litigation risk can be reduced by paying employees for the time they actually worked.

---

[27] *See* Martocchio (2011).

[28] Milkovich and Wigdor (1991).

Another fairly typical practice is to require employees to review their time entries each week and verify that they included all hours worked by physically or digitally signing the time sheet. Plaintiff attorneys usually dispute the validity of these signatures in litigation, but they are still valuable to have, especially in combination with some of the other measures discussed to minimize off the clock work.

Finally, some employers recognize that employees regularly perform a small amount of compensable work prior to clocking in or after clocking out. To ensure these employees are paid properly and to minimize litigation risk, additional time can be added to each employee's recorded time each time to cover the additional work. As an example, an employer whose employees don and doff PPE that is believed to be compensable might add time to each employee's timecard on every day they wear PPE. Observational data and/or simulations are useful for determining the appropriate amount of time to add.

5.7 Conclusion

This chapter describes the legal context for off the clock work. There are a variety of scenarios in which off the clock tends to occur and a variety of causes that are frequently alleged in litigation. Methods such as observations, work simulations, and analysis of electronic data are useful for evaluating whether off the clock work has occurred and, if it has, quantifying the amount. In addition, several strategies were proposed to minimize risk of employees working off the clock.

References

Kearns, E. C. (2002). *"Off-the-clock" time-when is it compensable?* Boston: Epstein Becker & Green.
Martocchio, J. J. (2011). Strategic reward and compensation plans. In S. Zedeck (Ed.), *APA handbook of industrial and organizational psychology* (pp. 343–372). Washington, DC: American Psychological Association.
Milkovich, G. T., & Wigdor, A. K. (1991). *Pay for performance*. Washington, DC: National Academy Press.
Whetzel, D. L., McDaniel, M. A., & Pollack, J. M. (2012). Work simulations. In M. Wilson, W. Bennet, S. Gibson, & G. Alliger (Eds.), *The handbook of work analysis: The methods, systems, applications and science of work measurement in organizations*. New York: Routledge.

Statutes and Regulations

29 U.S.C. §§ 206–207 (2012).
See 29 C.F.R. §785 et seq.
Alaska Stat. §§ 23.10.050–23.10.150 (2016).

Cal. Lab. Code § 510 (2016).
Nev. Rev. Stat. § 608.018 (2016).

Court Cases

Brown et al. v. Permanente Medical Group Inc., No. 3:2016cv05272 (N.D. Cal.).
Chavez v. Converse Inc. et al., No. 5:15-cv-03746 (N.D. Cal.).
Davenport v. Charter Communications, LLC, No. 4:12-cv-00007 (E.D. Mo.).
Faust et al. v. Comcast Cable Communications Management LLC, No. 1:10-cv-02336 (D. Md.).
Frlekin et al. v. Apple Inc., No. 3:2013cv03451 (N.D. Cal.).
Holmes v. Kelly Services USA LLC et al., No. 2:2016cv13164 (E.D. Mich.).
Integrity Staffing Solutions v. Busk, 574 U.S. ___ (2014).
Lamarr et al. v. Illinois Bell Telephone Co. et al., No. 1:15-cv-08660 (N.D. Ill.).
Martin v. City of Richmond, 504 F. Supp.2d 766 (N.D. Cal. 2007).
Murphy v. Caremark CVS Corp. et al., No. BC464785 (Cal. Super. Los Angeles).
Narez v. Macy's West Stores Inc., No. 5:16-cv-00936 (N.D. Cal.).
Ogiamien et al. v. Nordstrom Inc., No. 2:13-cv-05639 (C.D. Cal.).
Rodriguez v. Nike Retail Services Inc. et al., No. 5:14-cv-01508 (N.D. Cal.).
Sandifer v. U.S. Steel Corp., 571 U.S. ____ (2014).
Sheffield v. BB&T et al. No. 7:16-cv-00332 (E.D.N.C.).
Volney-Parris v. Southern California Edison Company, No. BC493038 (Cal. Super. Los Angeles).
Williams v. AmerisourceBergen Drug Corporation, No. 1:17-cv-06071 (N.D. Ill.).

Chapter 6
Meal and Rest Breaks

Chester Hanvey

6.1 Introduction

Allowing employees to take short breaks during their workday is a common employment practice in many industries and is generally considered to increase the efficiency of employees. While providing breaks to employees is not federally mandated, state statutes and regulations in many states do require employers to provide their employees with meal and rest breaks. Specific break requirements, however, vary from state to state. Whereas some states do not mandate that employers provide any meal or rest breaks to employees, other states require that employers provide up to an hour of break time to employees who work an 8-h shift. Employers can provide meal or rest breaks of any length to employees, provided that they meet the minimum requirements within their state. That is, the break requirements specify a minimum break length, but employers may offer longer breaks if they choose. Similarly, employers in states with no break requirements may provide breaks of any length to employees.

Meal and rest break protections only apply to non-exempt (hourly) employees. Exempt employees[1] or non-employee workers such as independent contractors[2] are not covered by meal or rest break requirements. Although workers in these classifications often take breaks, they are not legally required. Therefore, litigation related to meal or rest break compliance is focused exclusively on non-exempt employees. Litigation arises when employees allege that they did not receive the meal and/or rest breaks to which they were legally entitled, the break they received was shorter than the minimum break required, or the break was not taken within a required win-

The original version of this chapter was revised. A correction to this chapter can be found at https://doi.org/10.1007/978-3-319-74612-8_10

[1] Issues related to classification of employees as exempt or non-exempt are discussed in Chap. 3.

[2] Issues related to classification of workers as employees or independent contractors are discussed in Chap. 4.

C. Hanvey, *Wage and Hour Law*, https://doi.org/10.1007/978-3-319-74612-8_6

dow of time. Breaks may also be considered non-compliant when employees are interrupted to perform work tasks during their breaks or have certain activities restricted during their break, thus preventing them from being relieved of all duties. Costs associated with violating meal and rest break requirements can be substantial, with one recent case resulting in a $90 million verdict.[3]

Most other topics covered in this book are primarily based on federal regulations. Because meal and rest break requirements occur at the state level and differ from state to state, it is challenging to adequately describe all meal and rest break requirements for all employees. In addition to differences across states, the applicability of meal and rest break requirements may depend on a variety of other factors such as sector (private or public), industry, employee shift length, nature of the work, age of the worker, number of employees, or other special circumstances (e.g., meal break waivers) for an employer. Due to the many variations in meal and rest break requirements, this chapter is focused on providing a general framework for evaluating meal and rest break compliance that will be applicable in most circumstances. To help provide some legal context for those evaluations, a broad overview of meal and rest break requirements across states is provided in the following sections.

A proper analysis of meal and rest break compliance requires knowledge of several legal components including which employees are covered, which shifts are eligible for meal or rest breaks, the minimum length of a compliant break, and potential exceptions to the general requirements. Often, it is wise to consult with an attorney as part of this process to confirm the proper interpretation of meal and rest break requirements.

6.2   Meal Breaks

Employers in many states are required to provide meal breaks to non-exempt employees. During meal breaks, the employee is not required or permitted to perform any work-related tasks and is free to leave the premises.[4] A summary of the minimum meal break duration by state is contained in Table 6.1. The table is useful as a quick reference for general meal and rest break length for most private sector employees who work a full shift (e.g., 8 h). However, longer shifts may require addition breaks, and shorter shifts may require fewer or no breaks. For instance, many states only mandate meal breaks for employees who work a minimum shift, which is often either 5 or 6 consecutive hours.[5] In addition, some states also require that a second meal break be provided for longer shifts.

Though requirements vary from state to state, the most common minimum meal break length is 30 min per workday. Though the Fair Labor Standards Act (FLSA) does not require employer to provide meal breaks to employees, FLSA regulations

---

[3] *Augustus v. ABM Security Services, Inc.*

[4] Department of Labor Standards Enforcement (2012).

[5] US Department of Labor (2017a).

Table 6.1 Minimum meal and rest break requirements by state[a]

State	Meal break length[b]	Rest break length[c]
California	30 min	Two 10-min breaks
Colorado	30 min	Two 10-min breaks
Connecticut	30 min	–
Delaware	30 min	–
Illinois	20 min	Two 15-min breaks (hotel attendants only)
Kentucky	"Reasonable" period. Ordinarily 30 min	Two 10-min breaks
Maine	30 min	–
Maryland	15–30 min (depending on shift length)	–
Massachusetts	30 min	–
Minnesota	"Sufficient" time	Two "adequate" rest periods
Nebraska	30 min	–
Nevada	30 min	Two 10-min breaks
New Hampshire	30 min	–
New York	30–60 min (depending on industry and shift length or time)	–
North Dakota	30 min	–
Oregon	30 min	Two 10-min breaks
Rhode Island	20–30 min (depending on shift length)	–
Tennessee	30 min	–
Vermont	"Reasonable opportunities" for breaks	"Reasonable opportunities" for breaks
Washington	30 min	Two 10-min breaks
West Virginia	20 min	–

[a]States with no minimum meal or rest break requirements are not included in the table. The information in the table is based on information compiled by the US Department of Labor, dated January 1, 2017
[b]US Department of Labor (2017a)
[c]US Department of Labor (2017b)

state that time spent taking meal breaks should not be counted toward an employee's hours worked.[6] This means that the length of meal breaks must be recoded for payroll purposes, and it is common practice for employees to clock out at the beginning of their meal break and clock back in at the end of their break. The significance of this from an analysis perspective is that electronic time clock data can usually be used to assess some aspects of meal break compliance.

---

[6] 29 C.F.R. §785.19.

6.2.1 On-Duty Meal Periods

A unique type of meal break policy that is permissible in some states is known as on-duty meal periods. Unlike a typical meal period in which an employee is off the clock and relieved of all duty, an employee taking an on-duty meal period is not relieved of all duty during their break. Rather, the break is taken on the clock, meaning the employee is paid during this time and may be required to perform work during this time. An employee who eats lunch at their desk while continuing to work is an example. On-duty meal period policies were adopted in many companies after managers (e.g., retail, food service) were reclassified to non-exempt either because of litigation or in an effort to avoid litigation over FLSA exemption status. Despite their non-exempt classification, these managers may still have responsibility for the overall operations of the facility, making it challenging in some settings to take a 30-min, off-duty meal break.

Several states allow on-duty meal breaks including California, Colorado, and New Hampshire[7] provided that certain conditions are met. The primary issue when evaluating the legality of an on-duty meal break is whether the "nature of the work" prevents the employee from being relived of all duties. California's Department of Labor Standards Enforcement (DLSE) provides several examples of employees for whom an on-duty meal break may apply, including a sole worker in an all-night convenience store or a coffee kiosk, or a security guard stationed alone at a remote site.[8] The agency also issued a 2002 opinion letter that provided several criteria relevant to an evaluation on an on-duty meal period: type of work, availability of other employees to fill-in during the break, consequences to the employer if the employee is relived of all duties, the ability to minimize these consequences, and the extent to which the work product would be damaged as a result of an off-duty meal break.[9]

An evaluation of on-duty meal break polices requires an understanding of the entire work environment including staffing levels, timing and predictability of events, and consequences of performing tasks at a later time. One approach is to start by identifying the tasks an employee performs and determining whether those tasks could be performed by others in the employee's absence and the consequences for the task not being performed immediately. The next step would be to assess the frequency with which employees are required to perform those tasks to help assess whether it would be feasible for an employee to take a 30-min off-duty break or whether the nature of the work prevents such a break.[10]

---

[7] US Department of Labor (2017a).

[8] Department of Labor Standards Enforcement (2012).

[9] Department of Labor Standards Enforcement (2002).

[10] *See* Hanvey and Arnold (2012) for a detailed example of a methodology to evaluate the issue.

6.3 Rest Breaks

In addition to meal breaks, employers in many states are required to provide rest breaks to non-exempt employees. Similar to meal breaks, employees are not permitted to perform any work-related tasks during rest breaks. The minimum rest break lengths by state are provided in Table 6.1. Many states require employers to provide two 10-min rest breaks during a shift, although the minimum length varies by state and is influenced by other factors such as shift length and industry.

Unlike meal breaks, rest break time is compensable and must be counted toward an employee's hours worked under the FLSA.[11] As a result, rest breaks are not typically recorded in time clock systems because the length of rest breaks taken is not necessary for payroll purposes. More commonly, rest break compliance is documented separately from time clock data. For example, employees may be required to sign weekly time sheets to confirm that they received their full rest breaks. Therefore, electronic data indicating the length of rest breaks are rarely available, requiring other methods to evaluate compliance. Data collection methods such as self-report or observational approaches are often used to evaluate rest break compliance. In addition, employees may be required to remain on the employer's premises during rest periods because they are paid during this time.[12]

6.4 Factors That Impact Meal and Rest Break Compliance

There are many factors that cause a meal or rest break to be non-compliant. Although not all are applicable in all situations, I have highlighted several of the most common factors that are considered when evaluating meal or rest break compliance in the following sections.

6.4.1 Types of Non-compliant Meal and Rest Breaks

There are three primary reasons for why a meal or rest break is non-compliant: (1) break was not taken, (2) break was shorter than the minimum requirement, or (3) break was taken too close to the start or end of the shift. Analysis of compliance involves determining the number of meal and rest periods to which an employee is entitled each shift and comparing that to the number of minimum length meal and rest periods the employee took. For meal break compliance, an extra step may be required in certain states to determine whether the break was taken within a permissible window of time. In California, meal breaks generally must begin "before the

---

[11] 29 C.F.R. §785.18.

[12] Department of Labor Standards Enforcement (2017).

end of the employee's fifth hour of work."[13] That is, a 30-min meal break that begins 5 h and 15 min after the shift began would not be non-complaint in most situations.[14]

It has been my experience that the timing of the meal breaks accounts for the majority of non-compliant meal breaks. This may be due to relatively limited awareness among managers and employees of these requirements. Compared to the fairly widespread awareness that minimum meal breaks are required, managers and employees tend to have less awareness regarding requirements that breaks are taken within a specific time window. If this is indeed the case, it also presents an opportunity in many companies to educate employees and managers on this aspect of meal break compliance.

6.4.2 Interrupted Breaks

A related issue occurs when an employee is interrupted during their break to perform a work-related task. A compliant break generally requires the employee to be relieved of all job responsibilities for the duration of the break. However, employees are sometimes interrupted during their breaks to perform a work-related task. For instance, they may be asked a work-related question by a co-worker or manager, and they may answer a work-related phone call or respond to a sudden customer rush by helping some customers before returning to their break. These situations are especially likely to occur when the employee remains on the premises during their break. When employees are interrupted, it can turn an otherwise compliant meal or rest break into a non-complaint break, thereby introducing legal risk for the company. An examination of the frequency with which employees' breaks are interrupted can be an important component of an evaluation of meal and break compliance. Often this is not reflected in electronic time records, so this evaluation typically involves additional data collection such as self-report or observation.

6.4.3 Auto-Deduct Meal Periods

A specific meal break policy that has been subject to litigation involves automatically deducting ("auto-deduct") meal break time from employees' hour worked. Under this policy, employees do not clock out at the start of their meal period or back in at the end of their meal period. Instead, employees are expected to take a legally compliant meal period, and the amount of time associated with a compliant meal break (e.g., 30 min) is automatically deducted from their work hours each day. Legal challenges may arise when the policy or time clock system does not allow

---

[13] Department of Labor Standards Enforcement (2012).

[14] Note that the "fifth hour" ends 5 h into the shift.

employees to report their actual meal break duration when it differs from the default or the policies to make those adjustments are not followed. The healthcare industry in particular has faced numerous challenges to these policies[15] as many hospital workers have claimed that patient demands prevented them from taking a full meal break, even though the full meal break time was deducted from their hours worked. The primary research question here is whether employee actual meal break behavior is consistent with the meal break data.[16] An assessment of the degree to which employees are taking compliant breaks will not be reflected in electronic data and therefore requires additional data collection.

6.4.4 Relieved of All Duty

Generally, employees must be "relieved of all duty"[17] during meal and rest breaks. Recently, questions about what it means to be relieved of all duty has been addressed by the courts. In *Augustus v. ABM Security Services, Inc.*, the California Supreme Court addressed the issue of whether a policy that requires employees to be on-call during rest breaks qualifies as being relived of all duty. The case involved thousands of security guards assigned to sites throughout California who were required to keep their radios and pagers on during rest breaks in the event a situation arose that required an immediate response. The case was eventually appealed to the California Supreme Court which ruled the requirement for employees to "be at the ready" during their rest break is inconsistent with the requirement to be relieved of all duty and therefore violated rest break requirements. The plaintiffs were awarded $90 million in damages. This case illustrates that the threshold to be duty free can be extremely high. Studies that fail to account for this factor may miss important data that could help determine whether breaks are compliant.

6.4.5 Obligation to "Provide" Meal and Rest Breaks

An important component to meal and rest break compliance is the obligation of an employer to "provide" a meal or rest break. Suppose that a manager instructs an employee to take a break but the employee refuses do so. Has the employer met their obligation in this situation or have they committed a violation because no

---

[15] *See, e.g.*, *Frye v. Baptist Memorial Hospital, Inc.;* White v. Baptist Memorial Health Care Corp; *Camesi et al. v. University of Pittsburgh Medical Center et al.*; *Quickley v. University of Maryland Medical System Corp.*

[16] Legal questions such as whether the policy allows employees to report the actual break time when it differs from the automatic time are not typically addressed through data collection or statistical analysis.

[17] *See, e.g.*, Department of Labor Standards Enforcement (2012).

break was taken? This was one of the primary issues addressed in *Brinker v. Superior Court*. The ruling in the case shifted the way meal and rest break requirements are interpreted by clarifying several aspects of California's meal and rest break requirements. Most notably, the court stated that an employer's obligation to "provide" meal and rest breaks means that they must simply make breaks available to employees, as opposed to ensuring that breaks are taken.[18] In the example above, the employer's actions would likely be considered compliant under *Brinker* because they made a break available to the employee, but the employee chose not to take it. However, companies may still run into legal trouble if, for example, employees do not know what breaks they are entitled to or if they are pressured to forgo their breaks. In these situations, employers may not meet their obligation to provide breaks consistent with *Brinker*.

The impact of this interpretation from a methodological perspective is that whether a break was taken does not completely answer the question of whether the employer violated meal or rest break requirements. In addition to knowing whether a break was taken, the reason that breaks were not taken may be a critical component in an evaluation. An employee who typically does not take lunch breaks because they want more work hours to make more income would be interpreted differently from an employee who does not take breaks because the store is understaffed and they need to help out. In some cases, self-report data may be necessary to collect this information.

6.5   Methods to Evaluate Compliance

Evaluating meal and rest break compliance may involve several different approaches, including analysis of existing time clock data or other sources of electronic data, designing and administering self-report surveys to collect information from employees about meal and rest break compliance, or conducting observational studies to determine the length of breaks actually taken and whether compensable work was performed during breaks. Each of these methods is discussed below.[19]

6.5.1   Analysis of Electronic Data

Because employees typically clock out for meal breaks, electronic time clock data is often a useful source of information and may serve as the primary basis for an evaluation of meal break compliance. Analysis of time clock data typically involves working with a large volume of data. Datasets are often structured such that one row represents a single clocking event for an employee on a particular day. That is, an

---

[18] *See* Banks and Arnold (2008) for a more in-depth review of this decision.

[19] The foundation for self-report and observational approaches is discussed in Chap. 2.

employee who clocks out for their meal break would have four time entries per day (in for day, out for lunch, in from lunch, out for day). When a class of employees is involved and the recovery period extends several years, the dataset can quickly reach millions of rows. After removing nonrelevant employees and time periods from the dataset, the number of hours worked by each employee on each day can be calculated by taking the difference between the end of shift and start of shift and removing the length of the meal break. This may require the data to be manipulated such that all clocking events for an employee in a single shift appear within the same row. Based on the hours worked, the number of meal and rest breaks for which the employee is eligible can be determined. This is where involvement from an attorney is often useful to confirm understanding for the thresholds that define the number of meal and rest breaks to which employees is entitled. The number of compliant meal breaks taken according to time clock data (i.e., minimum length and within the appropriate time window) can then be counted and used to determine the number of non-compliant meal breaks. This information is applicable for class certification purposes and liability purposes as the pervasiveness of non-compliant breaks and the proportion of employees impacted may be important factors in class certification decisions, and the frequency of non-compliant breaks is an important factor in findings of liability. Damages can generally be calculated by applying the applicable pay rates, penalties, and interest to instances of non-compliant meal breaks.

While an analysis of electronic data can provide valuable information, there may also be limitations. Before analyzing time clock data, it is important to determine whether the data represent an accurate measure of actual employee behavior. For example, evidence that employees routinely took shorten meal breaks but waited until 30 min had passed before clocking back in (thus giving the false impression of a compliant break) would undermine the value of analysis based on the time clock data. Similarly, evidence may suggest that employees who self-report time (rather than using an electronic time clock system) round off their time entries rather than reporting the actual time they began and stopped working. If this practice is common, it may be difficult to tell from time clock data alone whether breaks are compliant. Similarly, electronic data do not provide information about whether employees were interrupted during their meal breaks. Unless the employee clocked back in when they were interrupted to perform a work task, the electronic data will not correctly represent the length of the break. Therefore, an important first step is assessing the quality of the data. Topics related to data analysis, assessing data quality, and identifying and eliminating erroneous data are discussed in Chap. 8.

6.5.2 Self-Report Approaches

There are some circumstances in which self-report approaches are the preferred method. For example, electronic time records may be unavailable or, as discussed in the previous section, may be unreliable for a number of reasons. Also, electronic data is typically not available for evaluations of rest break compliance. In each of these instances, an alternative data collection method is needed, which is often either a self-report approach or an observational approach.

Self-report approaches offer at least two advantages over observations in this context. First, self-report is the only way in many circumstances to gather reliable data about the *reasons* that breaks were not taken which can be an important component of compliance. Second, self-report is retrospective which means data can be collected about an employee's work experience in the past. In the context of a class action, lawsuit, that may be a factor that favors a self-report approach.

Most often, self-report data to assess meal or rest break compliance is collected in the form of a survey. Surveys in this context can be relatively short, especially when compared to an FLSA exemption questionnaire (see Chap. 3) that may take over an hour to complete. In contrast, a meal and rest break compliance survey can be designed to require 10–20 min to complete. A self-report survey in this context is usually designed to estimate (1) how often does the employee work shifts long enough to be eligible for a meal break or rest break, (2) how often do they take a meal or rest break, (3) how long are the meal breaks or rest breaks, (4) how often are meal or rest breaks interrupted for work-related tasks, and (5) if the meal or rest break is not taken, the reason why it is not taken.

Some of the more frequently disputed aspects of this type of survey are the instructions given to the participants and the wording of the survey questions. Although many of the best practices regarding these aspects of a survey are covered in Chap. 2, a few items are worth noting here. In comparison to self-report tools designed to assess FLSA exemptions or employment status, it is much easier for participants to purposely distort data to impact the outcome in a lawsuit in one direction or the other. Instructions should be carefully crafted to minimize this possibility. For example, emphasizing that the survey sponsor is a neutral third party can help minimize "socially desirable" responses. Another strategy to maximize data quality is to embed questions about meal and rest break compliance within a broader survey that covers additional work-related topics. This will make it less obvious to the employee that the survey is related to meal and rest break compliance, thus increasing honesty related the topics of interest. The degree to which this is an issue will vary, but it is worth considering in most cases.

To increase the accuracy of participants' memory, exercises such as the event history calendar may be useful in this context. In addition, research has demonstrated that employees tend to overreport the amount of time they spend working. In this context, this could impact whether a shift is eligible for a meal break or a rest break. Because this survey would only be relevant for hourly employees, self-reports of total work hours could be cross-checked with time records to evaluate accuracy. See Chap. 2 for additional information about both of these potential biases and limitations.

6.5.3 Observation Approaches

In some situations, observation data will provide the most accurate data for evaluating meal or rest break compliance. Observation data has the advantage of not relying on employees' ability to accurately recall and report their experiences. Observation data is collected by an objective third party and is more difficult for an employee to purposely distort.

Both video observation and live observation can provide useful data in this context. The decision between two forms of observation depends on several factors. In most evaluations, either form of observation will provide data regarding several key activities: when the employee stops working, when the employee clocks out, what the employee does during their break (i.e., work-related tasks), when the employee clocks back in, and when the employee resumes working. The physical layout in some workplaces may allow all of that information to be captured by a small number of stationary cameras. The physical layout of other workplaces may not allow some of these key activities to be captured which could limit the conclusions that can be reached based on the study.

Another consideration is the tradeoff between the amount of data and the detail within the data. Video observation can generate more data at less cost than live observations. However, that often comes at the expense of the detail that a live observer can gather but cannot be captured in a video observation. As an example, the person to whom an employee is talking during their break and the content of the conversation could impact whether the break is considered interrupted. This information would be difficult to capture using a video approach. On the other hand, video data can be coded relatively inexpensively when compared to the cost of a trained observer travelling to the workplace to collect live data. Video observations also have the advantage of more precise timing as the same video can be re-watched multiple times to ensure accuracy. Though observations of all sorts provide rich and compelling data, video footage can be retained and shown in court as evidence. The ability to produce video or still shots may add to the compelling nature of observations in a trial and can be very persuasive.

6.6 Conclusion

This chapter highlighted the requirements for employers to provide meal and rest breaks to non-exempt employees in many states. These requirements may represent a source of legal risk as compliance can be challenging in some situations. There are many forms of non-compliant breaks, and the methods required to evaluate compliance depend on the type of break, work environment and the availability of electronic data related to breaks. The most common strategies for evaluating meal and rest break compliance include analysis of electronic data, self-report surveys, and observational methods.

References

Banks, C. G., & Arnold, E. B. (2008). California employers get a break with Brinker (but what does it really mean?). *HR Advisor: Legal and Practical Guidance*, 19–23.

Department of Labor Standards Enforcement. (2002). *Opinion letter 2002.09.04 Re: On-duty meal periods*. Retrieved from https://www.dir.ca.gov/dlse/opinions/2002-09-04.pdf

Department of Labor Standards Enforcement. (2012). *Meal periods*. Retrieved from https://www.dir.ca.gov/dlse/faq_mealperiods.htm

Department of Labor Standards Enforcement. (2017). Rest periods/lactation accommodation. Retrieved from https://www.dir.ca.gov/dlse/FAQ_RestPeriods.htm

Hanvey, C. M., & Arnold, E. B. (2012). Nature of the work: On-duty meal periods. *HR Advisor: Legal and Practical Guidance*, 20–28.

U.S. Department of Labor. (2017a). *Minimum length of meal period required under state law for adult employees in private sector*. Retrieved from http://www.dol.gov/whd/state/meal.htm

U.S. Department of Labor. (2017b). *Minimum paid rest period requirements under state law for adult employees in private sector*. Retrieved from http://www.dol.gov/whd/state/rest.htm

Statutes and Regulations

29 C.F.R. §785.18 (2017).

29 C.F.R. §785.19 (2017).

Court Cases

Augustus v. ABM Security Services, Inc., 2016 Cal. LEXIS 9627 (Dec. 22, 2016).

Brinker Rest. Corp. v. Superior Court, 2012 Cal. LEXIS 3994 (Apr. 12, 2012).

Camesi, et al., v. University of Pittsburgh Medical Center, et al., No. 15–1865 (3d. Cir.).

Frye v. Baptist Memorial Hospital, Inc., 2012 U.S. App. LEXIS 17791 (6th Cir. 2012).

Quickley v. University of Maryland Medical System Corp., No. 1:12-cv-00321-CCB (D. Md.).

White v. Baptist Memorial Health Care Corp., 2012 U.S. App. LEXIS 22752 (6th Cir. Nov. 6, 2012).

Chapter 7
Suitable Seating

Elizabeth Arnold and Chester Hanvey

In this chapter, we explore issues related to recent litigation in California known as "suitable seating."[1] We note that this topic is not directly related to either "wages" or "hours." However, the issue is generally considered to fall within the wage and hour category for at least two reasons. First, the topic is directly related to employee protections in the workplace, the same goal as other wage and hour requirements. In addition, the relevant factors and the approaches to measure those factors have significant overlap with other wage and hour matters.

7.1 Background on Suitable Seating

In the last decade, employers in California have seen a new wave of litigation related to whether employers are legally required to provide seats for their employees while working. The basis for this litigation is language in the California Wage Orders[2] which states that employees must be provided suitable seats under certain circumstances. Specifically, the Wage Orders state, in part, that:[3]

- *All working employees shall be provided with suitable seats when the nature of the work reasonably permits the use of seats.*
- *When employees are not engaged in the active duties of their employment and the nature of the work requires standing, an adequate number of suitable seats shall be placed in reasonable proximity to the work area, and employees shall be*

---

[1] We borrow much of the content for this chapter from a white paper we previously published on this topic (Arnold and Hanvey, 2017).

[2] The Wage Orders are California state laws which regulate wages, hours, and working conditions in certain industries or occupations.

[3] As explained in greater detail later, similar language is included in 14 of the 17 individual Wage Orders.

© Springer International Publishing AG, part of Springer Nature 2018
C. Hanvey, *Wage and Hour Law*, https://doi.org/10.1007/978-3-319-74612-8_7

permitted to use such seats when it does not interfere with the performance of their duties.[4]

These provisions have existed in the Wage Orders for decades[5] but were not enforced by the state and rarely even discussed until recently. Enforcement of these provisions began to change in 2004 when the State of California enacted the Private Attorneys General Act (PAGA).[6] Among other things, PAGA empowers individual employees to sue their employers on behalf of themselves, other employees, and the state for any violation of the California Labor Code.[7]

In this chapter, we provide an overview of suitable seating regulations, PAGA, and notable suitable seating litigation. In later sections, we propose data collection methods to assess compliance with the suitable seating regulations.

7.2 History of Suitable Seating Regulations

Until 2004, an agency within California's Department of Industrial Relations called the Industrial Welfare Commission (IWC) was responsible for setting orders to regulate the wages, hours of work, and working conditions of California employees[8]. The IWC issued 17 wage orders (called "IWC Orders," or "Wage Orders"),[9] each applicable to a specific industry or occupation. Every private employer in California is covered by one industry or occupation Wage Order and must comply with the applicable regulations. Fourteen of the Wage Orders contain nearly identical language regulating suitable seating.[10] The IWC was defunded in 2004 and no longer exists;[11] however, the Wage Orders it produced remain in effect and are now enforced by California's Division of Labor Standards Enforcement (DLSE).[12]

Using PAGA, an employee can seek up to one year of civil penalties and attorney fees for violating any of the Wage Orders, including a civil penalty of $100 for each impacted employee per pay period for the initial violation and $200 for each impacted employee per pay period after that.[13] Each pay period in which a violation occurs is typically considered to be a violation, making potential penalties for employers under PAGA significant. Penalties resulting from the litigation are divided between the state and the "aggrieved" employees.[14]

---

[4] IWC Wage Order 4-2001, Sec. 14.

[5] Department of Industrial Relations (2017a).

[6] James (2014).

[7] Private Attorneys General Act (2004).

[8] Department of Industrial Relations (2017b).

[9] Department of Industrial Relations (2017c)

[10] Koonin (2014).

[11] Department of Industrial Relations (2017d).

[12] Department of Industrial Relations (2017b).

[13] Private Attorneys General Act (2004).

[14] Private Attorneys General Act (2004).

7.3   Notable Suitable Seating Litigation

One of the first suitable seating lawsuits was filed in 2005 and involved guest service agents at the San Francisco Hilton.[15] Following that case, there was a string of similar lawsuits in the retail industry in California. In 2010, the Second Court of Appeals made a significant ruling in *Bright v. 99 Cents Only Stores*. This case involved a cashier who claimed that she and other employees should have been provided seats while working. The trial court dismissed the plaintiff's complaint, but the Second District Court of Appeals reversed this ruling and permitted employees to pursue monetary penalties under PAGA for violations of the Wage Orders.[16] This decision opened the door to allow employees to pursue civil monetary penalties under PAGA when employers violate Wage Orders and therefore had a significant impact on the legal landscape.[17]

Bright and other early cases fueled a wave of litigation, which included well-known retail brands such as Home Depot[18], Walgreens[19], Rite Aid[20], Costco[21], Walmart[22], Kmart[23], and Blockbuster Video[24]. As of fall 2017, more than 60 class and representative PAGA actions alleging violations of the suitable seating Wage Order have been filed against California employers, the majority of which remain pending.[25]

7.3.1   California Supreme Court Clarifies Requirements

One of the challenges that employers and the court system have encountered in evaluating this regulation was the lack of detail in the Wage Orders about when suitable seating was required. On April 4, 2016, the California Supreme Court issued a much-anticipated ruling that clarified many important aspects of the suitable seating requirements.[26] The ruling was issued in response to two suitable seating lawsuits: Kilby v. CVS Pharmacy and Henderson v. JPMorgan Chase Bank. In both cases, the trial court rulings were appealed by plaintiffs to the ninth Circuit Court of Appeals.

---

[15] *Hamilton v. San Francisco Hilton.*
[16] Ryan and Drous (2011).
[17] Ryan and Drous (2011).
[18] *Home Depot USA v. Superior Court.*
[19] *Zamora v. Walgreen Co.*
[20] *Hall v. Rite Aid Corp.*
[21] *Justice v. Costco Wholesale Corp.*
[22] *Brown et al. v. Wal-Mart Stores Inc.*
[23] *Garvey v. Kmart Corp.*
[24] *Currie-White v. Blockbuster Inc.*
[25] Wohl and Herald (2016).
[26] *Kilby v. CVS Pharmacy.*

Table 7.1 Relevant factors in a Totality of the Circumstances suitable seating evaluation

No.	Factor	Description
1	Job duties	Tasks and activities actually performed by employees, as well as the location within the workplace where the work is performed
2	Task frequency and duration	Frequency and duration of tasks performance at specific locations within the workplace
3	Impact of seating on job performance and work quality	The extent to which the presence of a seat interferes with an employee's ability to perform her or his work safely and effectively
4	Impact of seating on "customer service" duties	The extent to which the presence of a seat interferes with an employee's ability to provide quality customer service. Although related to the previous factor, this primary responsibility of retail employees was specifically mentioned in the ruling
5	Physical layout of the workplace	The physical layout of the workplace is a relevant factor, especially when the layout impacts the employee's job duties
6	Employer's business judgment	In particular, an employer may use business judgment to define the duties expected of her or his employees. However, the court also notes that business judgment is an objective standard that does not include an employer's mere preference

To address the issues in these pending cases, the ninth Circuit requested clarification from the California Supreme Court on the proper interpretation of three aspects of the suitable seating requirement, including the proper interpretation of "nature of the work" and "reasonably permits."

This Supreme Court ruling provided guidance to employers on how to interpret the suitable seating provisions within the Wage Orders. Specifically, the Supreme Court outlined several factors that, in totality, should be used to determine whether an employer has a legal obligation to provide seats for employees. That is, no single factor is dispositive in evaluating whether seats must be provided. Multiple factors should be considered in aggregate to make a reasonable assessment. This is evident from the court's repeated references to the "totality of the circumstances" as the standard for evaluating suitable seating requirements.

A review of the ruling reveals six key factors relevant to a totality of the circumstances inquiry. These factors are summarized in Table 7.1. The court noted that an analysis of these factors is not a rigid quantitative inquiry but a "qualitative" assessment of all relevant factors.[27] In later sections, we discuss methodological approaches to operationalize and measure each of these factors.

The court stated that seating requirements must be determined for specific job duties performed at a specific physical location within the workplace and not by an assessment of the various activities an employee may perform throughout the

---

[27] *Kilby v. CVS Pharmacy* (p. 18).

workday. To determine the nature of the work, one must "examine subsets of an employee's total tasks and duties by location, such as those performed at a cash register or a teller window, and consider whether it is feasible for an employee to perform each set of location-specific tasks while seated."[28] This clarification is significant for researchers because it requires an examination of the work performed by employees at specific physical locations within the workplace. For example, even if a checker spends much of their workday stocking shelves (work for which seating is less feasible), an employer may still be required to provide a seat for that employee when they work at the register based on the nature of the work performed at that location, provided that the amount of time working at the register is not "negligible."[29] In addition to the tasks performed by employees, the duration of those tasks and the frequency with which they are performed are cited repeatedly throughout the ruling as relevant factors.

Another factor relevant to the totality of the circumstances inquiry is the impact of seating on employee job performance. The extent to which the presence of a seat interferes with an employee's ability to perform work effectively is an important consideration when evaluating whether the nature of the work reasonably permits a seat. Whether it is feasible to add a seat without impacting job performance is based on (1) whether providing a seat would unduly interfere with other standing tasks, (2) whether the frequency of transition from sitting to standing may interfere with the work, and (3) whether seated work would impact the quality and effectiveness of overall job performance.[30] Although related to the previous factor, an employee's job responsibly to provide customers with quality service was specifically mentioned in the ruling. This factor is of particular relevance to employers in the retail industry, where customer service is often a primary duty of customer-facing employees.

The court also identified secondary factors which are relevant for an evaluation. Among them is the physical layout of the workplace. To the extent the physical layout helps determine an employee's job duties, this factor should be included in the analysis. Finally, the employer's "business judgment" as to whether the employee should stand and the physical layout of the workplace should both be given some weight in the determination. However, the court added, this cannot be based on "mere preference…The standard is an objective one."[31] The business decision must be based on evidence related to the impact seating has on the performance of the employees and ultimately the business overall.

Beyond providing clarification regarding the language of the Wage Orders related to suitable seating, the ruling also stated that it is the employer's responsibility to justify why seats are *not* provided. Specifically, when the nature of the work is

---

[28] *Kilby v. CVS Pharmacy* (p. 16).

[29] *Kilby v. CVS Pharmacy* (p. 16).

[30] Wohl and Herald (2016).

[31] *Kilby v. CVS Pharmacy* (p. 21).

considered, the court stated that, "… if an employer argues there is no suitable seat available, the burden is on the employer to prove unavailability."[32]

7.3.2 Implications of the California Supreme Court Ruling

At the time this chapter was written, no suitable seating cases have been litigated since the California Supreme Court's ruling. Thus, the ruling currently serves as the primary authoritative source for how to properly evaluate suitable seating requirements. While the Supreme Court's ruling contained substantial guidance on defining and evaluating suitable seating, it did not provide a definitive formula which employers can follow to assess "the nature of the work" or to determine whether that nature reasonably permitted seats.

The court stated that determining whether seating is necessary requires a qualitative assessment based on the "totality of the circumstances…The weight given to any relevant factor will depend upon the attendant circumstances."[33] No simple test was provided, and even with increased clarity, there is still uncertainty regarding implementing the information from the ruling as some of the language appears to be subject to interpretation.[34]

Employers should be aware that the ruling states that employers cannot rely on job titles, job descriptions, or an employee's abilities in deciding whether to provide seating. Instead, employers must conduct a thorough analysis which includes reviewing different aspects of the workplace and the work performed by employees. While employers have many factors to consider when making this qualitative assessment, the ruling states that employers must at least conduct a reasonable evaluation before deciding not to provide seating for a particular task.[35]

The assessment described by the court suggests that a comprehensive study of all tasks performed by employees is required. This should include a careful evaluation of job tasks performed at each physical location to determine whether it is feasible to provide seats to employees at those locations. In addition, documenting rationale that supports a decision not to provide seats to employees is likely to prove valuable.[36] In many cases, employers may benefit from engaging in this assessment before litigation arises.

---

[32] *Kilby v. CVS Pharmacy* (p. 2).

[33] *Kilby v. CVS Pharmacy* (p. 20).

[34] Palmer and Colón (2016).

[35] Brown (2016).

[36] Brown (2016).

7.4 Approaches to Collecting Relevant Data

While the Supreme Court ruling has provided additional information regarding the factors which should be considered in an evaluation regarding suitable seating, some uncertainty remains regarding how to properly measure and evaluate these factors. In this section, we propose an approach to operationalizing and measuring each relevant factor.[37] The proposed approach applies three commonly used methods in other employment contexts to provide reliable data that directly address the relevant factors in this context.

7.4.1 Time and Motion Observations

The foundations for time and motion observations are described in Chap. 2. In this chapter, we focus our discussion on features of an observational study that are specific to the suitable seating context.

Observational methods are well suited for collecting detailed data showing the tasks employees perform, the frequency with which those tasks are performed, and the duration of those tasks. In addition, the specific location at which each task is performed can be recorded and analyzed. For example, an observational study could provide objective data to determine which tasks employees perform at a location, the frequency with which employees perform tasks at the check stand, the duration of those tasks, when (i.e., time of day) employees are at each location, and how much time employees spend at each location. Data such as the frequency, duration, and nature of customer interactions can also be collected and analyzed in an observation study. These data are likely to be relevant to the totality of the circumstances inquiry. Two examples of observation records are included in Table 7.2.

In some circumstances, the use of video technology may be useful to supplement live observation data. If not already present, video cameras can be strategically positioned to capture all events that take place at a specific location (e.g., the check stand). The recordings can then be coded and analyzed to evaluate the frequency and duration of many different tasks. Video observations have the advantage of capturing a large volume of data across different employees and time periods at a potentially lower cost than live observations. Video observations tend to be most useful for capturing information about repetitive tasks that are clearly visible, such as physical tasks that are performed at a particular location in the store.

Observation studies can also be specifically designed to capture information regarding the physical demands (i.e., movements) associated with individual work tasks. For example, data can be collected to show the frequency with which

---

[37] We note that these approaches have not been subjected to legal scrutiny in the context of suitable seating. However, the methods are commonly used to address other wage and hour dispute and directly assess factors relevant to this issue.

Table 7.2 Portions of two sample observation records

Task start	Task end	Duration	Task	Location
Example 1				
11:14:20	11:15:40	0:01:20	Make change for cashier at register	Register
11:15:40	11:16:20	0:00:40	Ask employee to assist on register	Register
11:16:20	11:19:10	0:02:50	Approve cash checking for customer	Register
11:19:10	11:22:10	0:03:00	Gather and review safety information for training	Office
11:22:10	11:23:40	0:01:30	Review staff work schedule	Office
11:23:40	11:25:20	0:01:40	Compose email to district manager	Office
11:25:20	11:33:40	0:08:20	Train service manager on how to track holiday shipments online	Office
11:33:40	11:35:10	0:01:30	Email store supervisor to request more information about inventory report	Office
11:35:10	11:38:00	0:02:50	Talk with employee which employees have the copies of the keys to the safe	Office
11:38:00	11:40:10	0:02:10	Check off which employees have arrived on work schedules	Office
11:40:10	11:41:40	0:01:30	Place extra keys in safe	Office
Example 2				
16:14:50	16:15:20	0:00:30	Help cashier with questions about customer transaction	Register
16:15:20	16:16:00	0:00:40	Check lotto ticket for customer to see if he won	Register
16:16:00	16:39:20	0:23:20	Process customer transactions at register	Register
16:39:20	16:39:50	0:00:30	Direct employee to re-stocked specific products	Sales floor
16:39:50	16:42:00	0:02:10	Compose and send email to warehouse to find out if special order item is available	Office

employees are required to reach across the check stand or to the end of the belt to assist a customer with a purchase; activities that may be more difficult to perform while seated. These data can help to address the degree to which work at a specific location can be performed effectively and safely while seated.

7.4.2   Work Simulations

Work simulations are carefully designed exercises that replicate the actual employee work environment. Work simulations are a well-recognized technique commonly used in several employment contexts, such as assessing a job applicant's ability to perform job-related tasks or evaluating the validity of a personnel selection procedure.[38]

---

[38] *See, e.g.*, Whetzel et al. (2012) for discussion of work simulations.

Work simulations may also provide useful data in the context of suitable seating. Specifically, simulations can be designed to assess the impact of seating on employee performance and productivity, factors relevant to the totality of the circumstances inquiry. For instance, different versions of the work environment can be created that differ only on key factors, such as seating, and job performance in terms of employee productivity and efficiency can be measured and compared. These data can also be compared to existing benchmarks, such as electronic register data from different time periods or locations, to provide additional points of comparison and evaluate the validity of the simulations.

Work simulations can be designed in a number of ways, depending on the employer and the work environment. In some circumstance, for example, "mock" customer purchases can be simulated using real registers after hours when a store is closed. Actual employees can be asked to participate in the test, and actors or real customers could be used to replicate purchase transactions. During the testing period, the employee would be observed and measured to determine how his or her work performance is impacted by sitting down. Depending on the environment, work performance may be measured through efficiency and quantity of items scanned, accuracy of the transaction, or other relevant metrics. Additional relevant data can also be collected during the test, such as the number of times the employee had to stand during his or her time at the register to perform a particular task for a customer.

An alternative to conducting simulations during off-hours is to modify the work environment when stores are operating. This could be done in the absence of litigation or at stores not likely to be involved in active litigation (e.g., outside California). Data can then be collected from actual customers, and their perceptions of the customer service they received from seated employees could be gathered. Many companies in the retail industry already have existing processes for collecting customer feedback, such as invitations to participate in satisfaction surveys online after a purchase. These types of processes could also be leveraged to collect actual data regarding customer perception and the actual impact of modifications to the environment, such as the cashier being seated during the sales transaction.

7.4.3 Subject Matter Expert Interviews

A common approach for collecting information about various aspects of the work environment is conducting interviews with employees who have direct knowledge of the relevant topic, called subject matter experts (SMEs). Information collected from qualified SMEs is widely accepted as a valid source of data in organizational research.[39] In the context of suitable seating, SMEs can serve as a valuable resource for collecting data relevant to certain factors in the totality of the circumstances inquiry.

---

[39] *See, e.g.*, Gael (1988).

Another noted component of this evaluation is the extent to which physical features in stores may impact the tasks performed by employees. As an example, some stores have self-checkout stands that will likely impact not only the amount of time employees spend interacting with customers but also the nature of those interactions.

One approach to collecting information relevant to this evaluation is to conduct interviews with SMEs who have specific knowledge regarding the variety of store features and types and how those impact the tasks employees perform. In many companies, the appropriate SMEs work in positions such as local or regional management, operations, or facility design. In addition SME input can be useful in identifying which specific aspects of the work employees perform may be impacted by different store features. This information can then be used to isolate relevant pieces of an observation record, for example.

Each employer has a perspective on how providing seats to employees may impact the business. Some employers are particularly concerned about the impact it may have on employees' performance, such as reduced productivity and efficiency. Others may be more concerned that having customer-facing employees seated while they serve customers will negatively impact on customer satisfaction. Interviews can be conducted with company leadership to determine their specific areas of concern and to identify how to characterize their "business judgment" regarding the impact of providing seating to employees.

7.4.4 Literature Review and External Sources of Data

A significant amount of research has been conducted on the topic of "customer service," both generally and specific to various industries.[40] Given the desire of many businesses to grow and improve their customer service levels, different perspectives about how best to accomplish this can be found in academic, industry, and mainstream news and publications. It may be useful to investigate these publications for existing standards or "industry norms" around "reasonable level of customer service" expectations.

Research by different government agencies and other research institutions on topics such as workplace safety[41] may also be relevant. A review of these studies may be useful in identifying some notable advantages and disadvantages of standing, sitting, and moving between the two. Accident and injury rates for different industries and workplace configurations are also available from other

---

[40] For example, see extensive research published in the following journals: *Journal of Consumer Satisfaction, Dissatisfaction and Complaining Behavior*, *Journal of Customer Behaviour*, *Journal of Service Theory and Practice*, *Journal of Service Management*, *Journal of Service Research*, *Journal of Services Marketing*, *Journal of Strategic Marketing*, *Psychology and Marketing*, *Journal of Bank Marketing*, and *Journal of Retailing*.

[41] *See, e.g.*, Occupational Safety and Health Administration (2014).

government sources, such as the Center for Disease Control, Occupational Health and Safety Administration, Bureau of Labor Statistics, and may provide useful data to analyze.

7.4.5 Additional Considerations Regarding Physical Layout

Information regarding the physical layout of the workplace can be integrated into the data collection methods described above. This process may be expedited through the collection and review of existing blueprints, diagrams, and/or schematics. These materials can provide useful data regarding the variety of physical layouts at stores.

Supplementing data collection with photos or video can also provide valuable information. These visual references can capture the work being performed as well as the physical store layout and can be valuable resources throughout the project. These photos and videos are fairly easily obtained using current wearable technology (e.g., phone cameras, Go-Pro video cameras).[42] Photos can also be a compelling aspect of a written report that describes the assessment process and the rationale behind decisions. Existing store video collected for internal and external theft purposes may be useful to review; however, in our experience the quality of the video is sometimes insufficient.

Evaluating physical worksites can be an extensive task for employers who have multiple locations around the state, particularly if each location is unique. Some employers with multiple locations have at least some consistent patterns or "styles" of locations, driven by the age of the location, the local market needs, or special features. Sampling from each type or variety of type will contribute to a comprehensive evaluation.

7.5 Conclusion

In this chapter, we have provided an overview and background of the recent wave of litigation related to suitable seating. The California Supreme Court's 2016 ruling regarding suitable seating requirements provided clarity regarding the factors that should be considered when evaluating an employer's compliance. The ruling describes specific factors which appear to be relevant to a totality of the circumstances inquiry. Scientifically sound methodological approaches that will generate valid and reliable data to allow an objective evaluation of these relevant factors were also presented. Companies with operations in California should conduct a thorough assessment to determine what action, if any, they should take to ensure compliance with the suitable seating language in the Wage Orders.

---

[42] Note: to the extent notices of videotaping already exist in the store, taking videos should not present any legal issues; however, we advise consulting counsel before taking any electronic images of customers.

References

Arnold, E. B., & Hanvey, C. M. (2017). *Suitable Seating: Totality of the Circumstances Inquiry [white paper]*. Emeryville, CA: Berkeley Research Group.

Brown, J. (2016, April 27). A new perspective on seated work for Calif. *Law360*. Retrieved from https://www.law360.com/articles/788186/a-new-perspective-on-seated-work-for-calif-employers

Department of Industrial Relations. (2017a). *Industrial Welfare Commission wage orders – History*. Retrieved from https://www.dir.ca.gov/iwc/wageorderindustriesprior.htm

Department of Industrial Relations. (2017b). *Industrial Welfare Commission (IWC)*. Retrieved from http://www.dir.ca.gov/iwc/

Department of Industrial Relations. (2017c). *DLSE - Glossary*. Retrieved from http://www.dir.ca.gov/dlse/Glossary.asp

Department of Industrial Relations. (2017d). *Effective July 1, 2004 the Industrial Welfare Commission will no longer be in operation*. Retrieved from https://www.dir.ca.gov/IWC/IWC_Defunded.html

Gael, S. (1988). *The job analysis handbook for business, industry, and government*. New York: Willey.

James, B. (2014, August 1). Workers warn Calif. High Court on seating class actions. *Law360*. Retrieved from https://www.law360.com/articles/563484/workers-warn-calif-high-court-on-seating-class-actions

Koonin, M. A. (2014, March). California Supreme Court to weigh in on suitable seating issues. *Employment Law Alerts* [Web log post]. Sedgwick LLP. Retrieved from http://www.sedgwicklaw.com/insights/publications/2014/03/california-supreme-court-to-weigh-in-on-suitable-s

Occupational Safety and Health Administration. (2014). *OSHA guidelines for retail grocery stores (OSHA 3192-05N, 2004)*. Retrieved from https://www.osha.gov/Publications/osha3192.pdf

Palmer, C. G., & Colón, J. A. (2016, April 8). The California Supreme Court finally weighs in on suitable seating. *The National Law Review*. Retrieved from http://www.natlawreview.com/article/california-supreme-court-finally-weighs-suitable-seating

Ryan, T. F., & Drous, E. (2011, February). Employees can now sue for suitable seating (among other things): Bright v. 99 cents only stores and home depot U.S.A. v. Superior Court (Harris). *Morrison & Forester Employment Law Commentary, 23*(2), 1–3. Retrieved from https://media2.mofo.com/documents/110222-employment-law-commentary.pdf

Whetzel, D. L., McDaniel, M. A., & Pollack, J. M. (2012). Work simulations. In M. Wilson, W. Bennet, S. Gibson, & G. Alliger (Eds.), *The handbook of work analysis: The methods, systems, applications and science of work measurement in organizations*. New York: Routledge.

Wohl, J. D., & Herald, R. A. (2016, April 8). California Supreme Court rules for first time on requirement of suitable seating for working employees. *Paul Hastings*. Retrieved from https://www.paulhastings.com/publications-items/details/?id=9e23e969-2334-6428-811c-ff00004cbded

Statutes and Regulations

IWC Wage Order 4-2001, Sec. 14.

Private Attorneys General Act (2004). Cal. Lab. Code § 2698, et seq. Retrieved from: http://leginfo.legislature.ca.gov/faces/codes_displayText.xhtml?lawCode=LAB&division=2.&title=&part=13

Court Cases

Bright v. 99 Cents Only Stores, Inc., 189 Cal. App. 4th 1472 (2010).
Brown et al. v. Wal-Mart Stores Inc., No 12-17623 (9th Cir.).
Garvey v. Kmart Corp. No. 3:11-cv-02575 (N.D. Cal.).
Hall v. Rite Aid Corp., 226 Cal.App.4th 278.
Hamilton v. San Francisco Hilton, Case No.04-431310 (S.F. Sup. Ct. 2005).
Home Depot USA v. Superior Court, 191 Cal. App. 4th 210 (2010).
Justice v. Costco Wholesale Corp. et al., No 2:11-cv-06563 (C.D. Cal.).
Kilby v. CVS Pharmacy, 368 P.3d 554, 63 Cal. 4th 1 (2016).
Zamora v. Walgreen Co., Case No. 2:11-cv-07664 (C.D. Cal.).

Chapter 8
Sampling and Statistics

Chester Hanvey

In this chapter, I address several issues related to statistical sampling and statistical analysis when used as evidence in wage and hour litigation. Though these concepts are involved to some degree in studies that proactively evaluate compliance, they typically become significantly higher stakes when used in litigation. Sampling and statistical analysis are commonly used in a variety of legal contexts including antitrust, employment discrimination, toxic torts, and voting rights cases.[1] Properly designed and executed statistical analysis is generally considered admissible in litigation under the Federal Rules of Evidence as most sampling and analysis methods meet the "scientific knowledge" requirement in *Daubert v. Merrell Dow Pharmaceuticals*,[2] a case which guides the admissibility of expert evidence in litigation.

This chapter focusses on aspects of sampling and statistical analysis that are most frequently applied to address wage and hour disputes. This typically includes descriptive statistics to summarize data collected from a sample or estimates of population characteristics ("parameters") based on data from a sample. Though these types of analyses are conceptually simple, disputes over sampling and statistical analysis are common and often play a major role in a court's decisions to certify a class or determine liability. Disputes tend to be unrelated to the accuracy of the calculations but rather the reliability of the underlying data, the representativeness of the sample from which the data were collected, or the proper interpretation of statistical analysis results. I discuss each of these issues in the following sections.

The original version of this chapter was revised. A correction to this chapter can be found at https://doi.org/10.1007/978-3-319-74612-8_10

[1] *see, generally,* Gastwirth (2000), DeGroot et al. (1986), and Fienberg (1989).

[2] Kaye and Freedman (2011).

© Springer International Publishing AG, part of Springer Nature 2018
C. Hanvey, *Wage and Hour Law*, https://doi.org/10.1007/978-3-319-74612-8_8

Table 8.1 Research questions applicable to each stage of the lawsuit

Stage	Key legal question[a]	Examples of research questions
Class certification	Are the claims of the putative class members similar enough to be resolved on a class-wide basis?	• What proportion of putative class members were misclassified as exempt? • To what degree do class members vary on the percent of time spent performing exempt tasks? • What proportion of class members worked off the clock? • To what degree do class members vary on the frequency of non-compliant meal breaks? • To what degree does the company exert similar control over independent contractors?
Merits/liability	Did the defendant violate a wage and hour law?	• Were class members misclassified as exempt? • Were class members misclassified as independent contractors? • Did class members receive compliant meal breaks? • Did class members work off the clock?
Damages	What amount of monetary recovery will fairly compensate class members?	• What amount of wages did employees lose as a result of being misclassified as exempt? • What amount of wages did employees lose as a result of being misclassified as independent contractors? • What penalties are employees owed for not receiving compliant meal breaks? • What amount of wages did employees lose by working off the clock?

[a]There are numerous legal questions at each stage. This table provides examples of legal questions that are typically addressed by experts

8.1   Stages of a Class Action Lawsuit

Most wage and hour lawsuits are brought as class or collective action.[3] A wage and hour class action typically proceeds through three broad phases: class certification, liability/merits, and damages. The legal questions at each stage differ in meaningful ways, and accordingly, the data and analyses required to answer these questions often differ. Examples of research questions at each phase are included in Table 8.1

At the class certification stage, the goal of the analyses is to characterize the degree of variability between putative class members to allow the court to determine whether the claims of class members can be resolved on a class-wide basis. If the

---

[3]For simplicity, the term "class action" is used for the remainder of this chapter to refer to both types of multi-plaintiff actions. See Chap. 1 for more detail.

class is certified, the next question becomes whether the defendant violated the law (i.e., liability/merits). The analyses at this stage are less focused on differences between class members and more focused on describing the work experiences of class members generally as its already been determined that their claims are similar. If the court finds in favor of plaintiffs on liability/merits (i.e., defendant violated the law), the third phase is to quantify the "damages" class members suffered as a result of the violations. This may include unpaid wages, unpaid overtime, meal break penalties, interest or a variety of other state-specific penalties such as inaccurate wage statement penalties, or penalties for failing to provide all wages at the time of termination for former employees.

8.2 Sampling

Nearly all data collection exercises to evaluate wage and hour compliance involve some form of sampling. The ultimate goal of data collection is typically to provide the court useful information about legally relevant factors (e.g., average amount of off the clock work per workweek) for members of the class or proposed class. However, collecting data from all class members or putative class members, called a "census," is rarely feasible[4] as a class may include up to tens of thousands of employees. Aside from being time and cost prohibitive, many class members may be unavailable or unwilling to participate in a study or otherwise provide data. Most classes also include a mix of former and current employees who may be unable or unwilling to participate in a study for a variety of reasons. For example, former employees cannot be observed on the job and may be difficult to locate for participation using other methods (e.g., self-report).

Therefore, a sampling approach is usually required. Sampling refers to a process of selecting elements (e.g., employees) from a population (e.g., all class members) in a way that allows an accurate description of some aspect of the population.[5] There are a variety of textbooks that provide a discussion of the many issues involved in sampling.[6] In this chapter, I will discuss the aspects that are frequently disputed in wage and hour litigation.

8.2.1 Population and Sampling Frame

Two important concepts in sampling are the population and the sampling frame. The population consists of all "elements" whose characteristics the sample is intended to represent.[7] The sampling frame is the group from which the sample is selected.

---

[4] Kaye and Freedman (2011).

[5] *See* Diamond (2011); Babbie (1990).

[6] *See, e.g.*, Thompson (2012).

[7] Diamond (2011).

Ideally, the population and sampling frame would be identical, but imperfect overlap between the two groups occurs in many cases. Typically, the population consists of all class members or putative class members, which is defined by plaintiffs filing the lawsuit. This is not always clearly defined, so to the extent possible, the researcher needs to understand who is included within the class in order to determine the appropriate representation in the sample. In addition, the time period of the lawsuit should also be defined because it impacts which, if any, former employees are included.

In many situations, all class members cannot be included in the sampling frame, making reasonable compromises necessary.[8] For example, certain members of the class may be inaccessible and therefore cannot be included in the study.[9] In other instances, it is prudent to collect data only from current employees (e.g., observational study), even if former employees are included on the class. Consistent with job analysis practice, data should be collected from persons who are most knowledgeable about the job and best situated to provide accurate job data (see Chap. 2). Because of potential problems with former employee data, such as memory decay and motivated distortion, it often makes sense to collect data from current employees. In this circumstance, it may be necessary to define the sampling frame as all current employees in the job title. The impact of this decision is that the sample is representative of current employees, and results are relevant to former employees because they were current employers in the same position at some point during the class period. Unless significant changes to the job have occurred during the class period, former employees are likely to have performed the job in a manner similar to those currently in the job.[10] Therefore, current employees usually provide the best estimates of work performed for former employees during a time when they were also employees in the job title.

8.2.2 Sampling Strategies

The ultimate goal in sample selection is typically to obtain a sample that is "representative" of the population. Data collected from a representative sample is desirable because sample data can be used to make useful estimates of population characteristics.[11] Representative samples also provide "unbiased" estimates of population parameters, meaning that the results will not systematically over- or underestimate population parameters. Although data from a representative sample may produce a value (e.g., percent of time performing exempt tasks) that is higher or

---

[8] Diamond (2011).

[9] Diamond (2011).

[10] This does not mean that former and current employees are similar for purposes of addressing class certification decisions. It means that the pattern of variability within current employees is likely similar to what would be found for former employees.

[11] See Diamond (2011); Kaye and Freedman (2011); Babbie (1990).

lower than the corresponding population value, the expected sample value is equal to the population value, and results from the sample will not be systematically biased in either direction.

The manner in which the sample is selected is often closely scrutinized in wage and hour litigation, and substantial thought and care is devoted to the sample selection process. The accuracy of the information collected from a sample depends not only on how the data were collected but on how the sample was selected.[12] There are two broad categories of sampling strategies: probability sampling and non-probability sampling. Non-probability sampling is subject to a variety of sampling biases and is less common in wage and hour litigation.[13] Probability sampling is the preferred method in most situations because it offers two important advantages.[14] First, probability samples generally result in a sample that is more representative because this approach avoids many of the biases associated with some non-probability methods. Second, probability sampling allows a researcher to use probability theory to quantify the degree of uncertainly in estimates of population parameters. This is particularly important when the results are used in litigation because the degree of uncertainty in the estimate may determine whether a study is admissible.

When using a probability sampling technique, each element within the sampling frame has a known, nonzero probability of being included in the sample.[15] Random selection is a key component in probability sampling and is typically accomplished by assigning a random number to each element,[16] sorting by the random number, and selecting those at the top of the list. There are multiple forms of probability samples that range in complexity from simple random samples to complex multistage sampling designs.[17] In a simple random sample, for example, all elements in the sampling frame have an identical probability of being selected.[18] For example, if the population consists of 100 employees and a sample of 30 is selected, each population member will have an identical 30% probability of being selected.

A simple random sampling procedure ensures that, within the limits of chance, a sample will be representative of the population from which it was drawn. However, this procedure does not guarantee that any one sample will be representative. Due to chance (i.e., sampling error), some samples will over-select certain features and

---

[12] Kaye and Freedman (2011).

[13] *See* Thompson (2012) for further discussion of non-probability samples.

[14] *See* Babbie (1990).

[15] Diamond (2011). It is common in job analysis to exclude employees from the sample if they have not been the position for a period of time long enough to learn the job fully or who are known to not be performing the job adequately (e.g., undergoing disciplinary action).

[16] Random number generators are available in most statistical analysis software, including Microsoft Excel.

[17] Diamond (2011).

[18] Kaye and Freedman (2011).

under-select others.[19] A common method to minimize this form of sampling error is to use a stratified random sampling procedure. This approach involves identifying key characteristics of the population that may impact the results, dividing the population into mutually exclusive groups ("strata") based on these characteristics, and randomly selecting samples from within these strata.[20] For example, assume that we want to estimate the average height of all students at a high school based on a sample of 200 students. Fifty percent of students at the school are female and 50% are male. If we select a simple random sample, it's possible that, due to chance, we will get a sample with more females than males (or vice versa). Because females are shorter than males on average, the sample is likely to underestimate the height of the entire population. In a stratified random sampling approach, we would split the population into two subpopulations (females and males) and randomly select a sample from within those groups. In this example, we would ensure that the sample consists of 50% females and 50% males to match the population by randomly sampling 100 females and 100 males.

In wage and hour cases and job analysis, stratified random sampling procedures are used to ensure that certain employee characteristics that may impact the study results are appropriately represented in the sample. Depending on the issue being studied, this may include factors such as job title, employment status (i.e., active or terminated), location type, location sales volume, or tenure in position. Factors included in the sampling plan differ by organization and can be identified during the preliminary phase of the project.

8.2.3   Representativeness

As described in the previous section, the term "representative" has a specific meaning within the scientific community. However, the same term sometimes has a slightly different meaning when used within the court system. For example, procedures designed to collect "representative testimony" are often proposed by plaintiffs in support of their position to certify a class. This approach is so common that simply using the term "representative" in the context of sampling is sometimes interpreted to be supportive of class certification. Defense attorneys may try to avoid using the term, and plaintiffs' attorneys may argue that any use of the term by defense experts supports certification of a class.

This perspective seems to be based on differences in the use of the term across disciplines. Within the court system, representative testimony is used in Fair Labor Standards Act (FLSA) cases to increase efficiency of the judicial process by eliminating redundant testimony from plaintiffs with similar circumstances.[21]

---

[19] Larger samples and samples from homogeneous populations are less susceptible to sampling error (Kaye & Freedman, 2011; Babbie, 1990).

[20] Diamond (2011); Babbie (1990).

[21] Finberg and Thoreen (2007).

The inherent assumption in this approach is that there is similarity between class members who share certain characteristics. Thus, the testimony from one class member can be used to "represent" other class members who would have provided similar testimony. No such assumption is made by a social scientist who selects a representative sample. Whether class members have similar work experiences is an empirical question that can be answered based on the data that are collected. The choice of sampling method should not be interpreted to mean that the researcher is acknowledging any degree of similarity between putative class members, only that the resulting sample will not over- or under-select certain types of putative class members.

8.2.4   Sample Size

How big should the sample be? More often than not, this is one of the first questions asked when preparing a sampling plan.[22] However, as Kaye and Freedman (2011) put it, "there is no easy answer to this sensible question." Generally speaking, "more is better" because, all else being equal, increasing the sample size reduces error and increases precision of estimates.[23] Larger samples also tend to be more representative of the population. A sample that comprises 90% of the population is likely to be more representative than a sample that comprises 5% of the population. Despite the universal desire for more data, practical constraints such as cost, time, or access to individuals limit the amount of data that can be collected. Logistically, a sample cannot be selected without first determining the size of the sample.[24] Therefore, specifying the desired sample size is a critical first step in most sampling plans.

There are a variety of factors that influence the desired sample size including the level of error that is tolerable, the nature of the issue, or the degree of variability within the population. [25] An overarching consideration is the intended use of the study results. Many studies are conducted for the purpose of estimating population parameters based on data from a sample. Other studies are conducted for the purpose of measuring the degree of variability within a group. The approach to determining an appropriate sample size differs in these two scenarios.

To select a sample used to estimate population parameters, a common method is to calculate the sample size that will be required to make population estimates within a specified degree of precision. That is, the mathematical formulas used to calculate confidence intervals (more on this later in the chapter) after data are collected can be "flipped" to calculate the sample size needed to generate an estimate

---

[22] Thompson (2012).

[23] Kaye and Freedman (2011).

[24] In some situations, samples are supplemented at a later time; however a sample size still must be specified to select the initial sample.

[25] Surprisingly, population size usually has little impact on the degree of precision of estimates or the required sample size (Kaye & Freedman, 2011).

within a specific confidence interval. That is, rather than calculating the confidence interval based on the known sample size, the sample size can be calculated based on a desired confidence interval. Using this approach, one must specify three variables in order to calculate sample size: (1) desired confidence interval width, (2) estimated amount of variability in the sample, and (3) confidence level.[26] This approach has the advantage of being based on a widely accepted formula, which lowers the perceived subjectivity of this process. However, subjectivity is still required to arrive at sample size. Of the three components that must be specified to calculate sample size, two (confidence interval width and amount of variability)[27] must be estimated, and experts often disagree on the correct values that should be used. The width of the confidence reflects the amount of uncertainty in estimates after data are collected. Ultimately, it is up to the court to decide what amount of uncertainty is tolerable.[28] As a practical matter, an expert must use professional judgment to specify a reasonable confidence interval. The amount of variability within the sample may also be disputed. The more variability within the sample, the larger the sample must be to obtain estimates at a given degree of precision.[29] One approach when estimating a proportion (e.g., proportion of employees misclassified) is to assume the maximum possible variability (0.50) and calculate the sample size based on that assumption.[30] This guarantees that the sample will provide an estimate at least as precise of the value specified. However, the resulting sample size will be relatively large which may be impractical in some circumstances. When estimating a population average, there is no "maximum possible" variability. Instead, the sample variability can be estimated either by using variability found in a pilot study, using existing data, or using an existing proxy to estimate the degree of variability that will be found in the sample.

Alternatively, many studies are conducted to estimate the degree of variability between putative class members, not to estimate population parameters. These studies are most likely to be conducted to address questions related to the certification of a class. In this circumstance, the sample size may be based on the number of data points needed to generate a representative sample, not to estimate population parameters. This also requires professional judgment as there are not widely agreed-upon standards for the proper sample size. One useful source of guidance is research based on the central limit theorem, which has demonstrated measures of central tendency (such as the average) become normally distributed for samples of 30 or

---

[26] Most textbooks on statistical analysis and sampling (e.g., Thompson, 2012) contain formulas and steps for calculating confidence intervals in a variety of scenarios.

[27] Most experts apply a 95% confidence interval; however there may be some situations where a 90% or a 99% confidence interval is used (Kaye & Freedman, 2011).

[28] As an example, the California Supreme Court in *Duran v US Bank* (described later in the chapter) found that a relative confidence interval of 43% (confidence interval/average) contained too much uncertainty and the analyses were not accepted.

[29] Kaye and Freedman (2011).

[30] When estimating a proportion, the maximum possible variability occurs when the estimate is 0.50. That is, 50% of the group fall into one category and 50% fall into the other category.

more, regardless of whether the population values are normally distributed.[31] Using this research as a rule of thumb, a minimum sample size of 30 is often used in wage and hour litigation, especially when data collection involves methods that collect large amounts of detailed data from each employee such as observations or structured interviews.

There are some rare situations where the researcher is unable to specify the sample size in advance because there are significant restrictions on access to putative class members or their willingness to participate in a study. That is, the researcher may need to simply "take what they can get." When a sample is obtained in this manner, there are significant limitations on the inferences that can be made from sample data. However, if collected appropriately, those data can still provide valuable information about the experiences of the individuals included in the sample but will be less useful for describing the experiences of other individuals. Potentially useful applications for data collected in this manner are to evaluate the validity of information collected from other sources and to determine if there are meaningful differences between the members of the sample.

8.3 Impact of Non-responses

A concern for researchers arises when some of those selected into the sample do not participate. This frequently occurs when collecting self-report data, for example, as it is extremely rare to achieve a 100% participation rate in surveys.[32] Even when a perfectly selected random sample is drawn, non-responses may compromise randomness of the sample and the ability to make accurate estimates about the population. If the pattern of non-responders is random, valid inferences about the population can still be drawn based on data from the sample.[33] Evaluating whether non-response bias is likely to have impacted the results requires the researcher to determine, to the extent possible, the degree to which non-respondents differ from the respondents in the responses they would have provided if they were present in the sample.[34] The presence of non-respondents does not ensure that study results will be biased,[35] only that the sample is susceptible to bias. The higher the response rate, the less likely non-respondents will bias the results.

---

[31] *See, e.g.*, Brase and Brase (2011); Howell (2010).

[32] Krosnick and Presser (2010); Stetz, Beaubien, Keeney & Lyons (2008).

[33] Diamond (2011).

[34] Diamond (2011).

[35] Krosnick and Presser (2010).

8.4 Extrapolation and Confidence Intervals

Many legal questions in wage and hour class actions require information about the entire population of class members. To address these questions, experts often use extrapolation to estimate one of two population parameters: population average (or mean) or population proportion. For example, extrapolation may be used to estimate the average amount of time the class members spend working off the clock each workweek. Alternatively, extrapolation could be used to estimate the proportion of class members who are misclassified as exempt.

Estimating population parameters based on sample data is imperfect, as the estimates are unlikely to be exactly equal to population parameters due to sampling error. [36] The exact amount of the error is unknown because data are only available for the sample; however confidence intervals are often reported to quantify the likely magnitude of this error.[37] Statistics calculated from the sample, called the "point estimate," are considered the best estimate of the population parameters, assuming that data are collected from a representative sample and not impacted by non-response bias or other forms of systematic error.[38] The upper bound of the confidence limit is obtained by adding the confidence interval to point estimate, and the lower bound of the confidence limit is obtained by subtracting the confidence interval from the point estimate.[39] Confidence intervals are typically expressed as the point estimate "plus or minus" some value.

Smaller confidence intervals are generally preferable because they reflect less uncertainty in the estimate. The width of a confidence interval is based on three factors: sample size, variability within the sample, and the desired confidence level.[40] All things being equal, larger samples are associated with smaller confidence intervals. This is because estimates based on more data points have less uncertainty than estimates based on fewer data.[41] All things being equal, less variability within the sample is associated with smaller confidence intervals. If all employees in a sample report the same (or very similar) experiences, one would expect less uncertainty in the extrapolation when compared to a sample that reports highly diverse experiences. Finally, the desired confidence level also impacts the width of the confidence interval. While the first two factors are based on the data provided by the sample, the confidence level is determined by the researcher. By far the most common confidence level used by scientists is 95%,[42] although occasionally 90% or 99% confidence intervals are used.[43] The 95% confidence interval roughly corresponds to two

[36] Kaye and Freedman (2011); Babbie (1990).

[37] Kaye and Freedman (2011).

[38] Kaye and Freedman (2011); Howell (2010).

[39] Howell (2010).

[40] Diamond (2011).

[41] Kaye and Freedman (2011).

[42] Diamond (2011).

[43] Kaye and Freedman (2011).

standard error units and is often used interchangeably with the term "margin of error."[44] Most statistics textbooks contain a discussion of confidence intervals including the theoretical basis, basic calculation formulas, adjustments for small samples, adjustments for small populations, and use of one- or two-tailed intervals.[45] Disputes regarding confidence intervals in wage and hour litigation tend not to be related to the mathematical accuracy of the calculations but rather the interpretation of the results. Therefore, I focus the discussion below on conceptual issues related to applying confidence intervals to address legal questions in wage and hour cases.

8.4.1 Implications of Variability on Confidence Interval Interpretation

The interpretation of confidence interval width is sometimes misunderstood. For example, small confidence intervals have been interpreted by plaintiffs arguing in support of class certification to indicate a high degree of similarity between putative class members. However, remember that a confidence interval reflects the precision with which we can estimate the population average (or proportion). The degree of variability within the sample is only one of the three factors that influence the width of a confidence interval. To illustrate this point, imagine data were collected from the entire population rather than a sample. In that situation, the confidence interval would be zero, because there is no uncertainly in our estimate of population parameters (we have data from the entire population). This will be true regardless of the degree of variability within the population. In other words, the ability to estimate the average, regardless of the degree of precision with which this can be done, reveals nothing about the amount of variability within the population. A sample with extremely high variability can yield a very small confidence interval if the sample is large enough.

The issue of variability is more problematic in the legal context when some of the class members in the sample don't have any recovery (e.g., not misclassified). When this occurs, the proportion of the sample with no recovery is sometimes used as an estimate of the proportion of the entire class has no recovery. For example, suppose there is a class of 1000 employees who claim they were required to work off the clock. To evaluate this claim prior to class certification, a random sample of 100 is selected to provide data about the amount of time they worked off the clock each workweek. Data show that 40 of the 100 class members in the sample worked off the clock and the other 60 never worked off the clock. An expert in this case would be able to estimate that because 40% of the sample worked off the clock, 40% of the entire class (or 400 class members) have also worked off the clock. However, it is

---

[44] Kaye and Freedman (2011).

[45] *See. e.g.*, Thompson (2012); Howell (2010); Witte and Witte (2010).

not possible, based on data from the sample, to determine *which* of the 900 class members who were not sampled worked off the clock and which did not. Instead there is a 40% probability that each of the 900 non-sampled class members worked off the clock. When the percent of class members in the sample with no recovery approaches 50%, the representative sampling approach is only capable of calculating a 50% likelihood that any non-sampled class member has liability, which would literally be equivalent to determining liability by flipping a coin.

8.4.2   Group vs Individual

Another point to consider is the utility of extrapolated results when variability within the sample is high. When estimating the average, it is important to understand what information a confidence interval provides about the population versus individuals within the population. The average is single number that is used to summarize a group of numbers (or data from many class members). In other words, it provides information about the group overall but limited information about any individual within that group. As an example, suppose that a group of students takes a multiple-choice test. Half of the students receive a perfect score (100% correct), and half of the students do not get any answers correct (0%). The average score for that group of students is 50%, and if a large enough sample was taken, the confidence interval around that point estimate may be very narrow. However, knowing that the point estimate is 50% and that there is a small confidence interval around that estimate is not helpful for describing the performance of any of the students. In fact, that result would be quite misleading. No student in the sample scored anywhere close to 50%. If this average were applied to others outside the sample (as is often done in wage and hour litigation), the error associated with that procedure would be extremely large. Though mathematically correct, the results are not very meaningful in this example.

Situations like this, though not nearly as extreme, occur in wage and hour class actions. This can be problematic because certain legal questions, such as exemption classifications or damages, are made on an individual basis. The mean and confidence interval do not provide much information relevant to that inquiry, especially when variability within the sample is high.

8.5   Assessing Variability

A critical question in class certification decisions is the degree of variability between putative class members on relevant factors. At the class certification stage, the analyses must address whether the degree of variability is such that the claims of the putative class members are capable of being resolved on a class-wide basis. For example, do employees perform the same set of tasks? Do they spent the same amount of time on the tasks they perform? Do they perform a similar set of activities before they clock in or after they clock out? Do they take meal breaks with the same frequency?

A comparison of any group of employees will reveal *some* variability, so the question is whether the amount of variability is so great that class treatment becomes inappropriate or whether differences between employees are trivial. This question can be partly answered using statistics but also relies on professional judgment. A variety of descriptive statistics are available to address variability (e.g., range, standard deviation, coefficient of variation), and these are typically calculated to quantify the degree of variability within a group. However, there is not widespread agreement about which statistic is most appropriate.[46] Perhaps more challenging is that these statistics lack defined thresholds that would be required to draw objective conclusions about variability.[47] As a result, experts, enforcement agencies, attorneys, and judges have used various methods and thresholds to arrive at conclusions about whether individuals are similar enough to certify a class. Experts often rely on additional information beyond statistics to reach conclusions about the degree of variability including shape of the frequency distribution, the proportion of individuals for whom violations exist (e.g., misclassified, denied meal breaks, worked off the clock), variation in factors that impact the results (e.g., regions, sales volume), differences in the sequence of tasks performed, and unique features of the job that apply to some individuals such as special roles or assignment or unique features of certain locations (e.g., operating hours, unique policies, or procedures). Each of these may play a role in the court's decision to certify a class. Expert opinions regarding the degree of variability between putative class members tend to be strongest when they are supported by multiple types of reliable data.

8.6 Data Quality Issues

One of the first steps in a statistical analysis is to assess the quality of the data being relied upon. In this regard, an assessment of data quality is listed as an ethical responsibility for anyone conducting statistical analyses by the American Statistical Association.[48] In litigation, experts often have an additional responsibility to base their opinions on reliable data.[49] The value of the results from any statistical analysis is dependent on the quality of the underlying data[50] leading one author to comment "most statistics books assume you are using good data, just as a cookbook assumes

---

[46] Kaye and Freedman (2011).

[47] Some recent strategies have been proposed for establishing objective thresholds including rules of thumb for the coefficient of variation (Murphy, 2014) and repeated measure strategies (Hanvey, 2014). No strategy has yet been widely accepted and applied.

[48] American Statistical Association (2016).

[49] Allen et al. (2011).

[50] Kaye and Freedman (2011).

you are not buying rancid meat and rotten vegetables."[51] In wage and hour litigation, disputes frequently arise over the quality of the data used in statistical analyses.[52]

When a researcher analyzes data they have collected themselves, they have detailed knowledge about the study design and the degree to which the data are reliable and valid. However, many times a statistician[53] relies on data from an external source. For example, a survey expert may collect self-report data, and a statistician may analyze the data,[54] or a statistician may analyze existing electronic data such as time clock, payroll, or register data. It is these situations, where performing an assessment of the underlying data quality is particularly important. Without this assessment, the statistician has no way of knowing whether the data upon which their conclusions are based are meaningful.

Some authors have noted that certain data sources are inherently more reliable than others. Allen et al. (2011) state that data quality is based, in part, on common-sense indicators of accuracy and bias. They provide a list of data sources in rough order of "presumptive validity" that are commonly used for damage calculations in litigation. The top of the list includes official government publications and databases such as those produced by the Bureau of Labor Statistics. Data from these sources require less assessment of their quality. The middle of the range includes survey data prepared by a survey expert following survey design standards. An assessment of the degree to which the survey was properly designed and executed is a critical component of an assessment of data quality. At the low end of the range are studies that estimate damages specifically for the purpose of litigation. Studies of this sort are not typically found in wage and hour cases. However, plaintiffs regularly self-report critical components in litigation either through declarations or depositions. These components may include number of hours worked per workweek, time worked off the clock, or frequency of missed meal or rest breaks. An important consideration before conducting any analysis using these data is the degree to which these estimates are accurate, as the presumptive validity of these reports is low.

An additional question to consider when working with existing data is what the data were intended to measure. Some analyses involve data from a reliable source, but the data were intended for a purpose other than addressing legal questions. For example, suppose employees allege they worked off the clock at the beginning of their shift. Employees at this company are required to swipe a security badge to enter the building. To determine the amount of uncompensated time, the swipe data is compared to the time clock data, and discrepancies for each employee on each workday are calculated. Though both sources of data (swipe data and time clock data) are considered reliable for their intended purpose, the results of the analysis may not provide meaningful information about the amount of time employees have

---

[51] Wheelan (2013) (p. 111).

[52] Kaye and Freedman (2011); Allen et al. (2011).

[53] I use the term "statistician" in this chapter to refer to any person performing statistical analysis, regardless of their educational or professional background.

[54] *See* Kaye and Freedman (2011).

worked off the clock. One reason could be whether the clocks in both systems were synchronized. In many organizations, the security and time clock systems are operated by two different vendors, and the clocks may not match. One or both systems may not be centralized, so the amount of discrepancy between the two system's clocks differ in each facility. Therefore, calculating an adjusted time for one of the systems to synchronize them may be very challenging and potentially impossible depending on the class period.

A more fundamental issue is whether the data actually address relevant legal questions. The results of the analysis tell the court how much time elapsed between employees entering the building and clocking in. This is different from the legal question: How much compensable work do employees perform before clocking in? In this example, electronic data alone may not be able to answer this question because they reveal nothing about what the employee actually does after entering the building. Although employees may perform compensable activities during this period of time, they may also eat breakfast, talk to co-workers about personal matters, put their personal belongings away, make personal phone calls, or any number of activities that are typically not compensable. Despite the quality of the underlying data in this example, the results of the analysis may be of limited utility because of what the data measure and more importantly do not measure.

Ultimately, the validity of data is a matter of professional judgment.[55] An evaluation of data quality is most effective before the data are analyzed. Although the type of data will largely dictate the steps in the evaluation, it is good practice in most situations to review relevant data fields to evaluate the degree to which data are missing or erroneous. For example, datasets sometimes contain duplicate data, data that are not properly aligned, dates in the future, more than 24 h in a day, or highly implausible data (e.g., employees working 18-h shifts every day). It is often a valuable exercise to identify these types of issues within the data. Experts in litigation have a general obligation to rely on data that are as accurate as possible and free of erroneous information.[56] When possible, the data can also be cross-checked with other data to assess the quality.[57] For example, time records can be cross-checked with payroll data to determine whether they are consistent.

The presence of erroneous data raises two questions. The first is whether they provide evidence that the entire dataset is flawed and therefore should not be relied upon. For example, if a significant portion of the data are found to be erroneous, it may be difficult to justify relying on remaining data from that same dataset. Assuming the dataset is not fatally flawed, the second question is how to conduct the analysis such that these data do not introduce error into the results. In many cases, erroneous data found within company electronic data can be resolved through consultation with the company that produced the data.[58] For example, manual time

---

[55] Allen et al. (2011).

[56] Allen et al. (2011).

[57] Allen et al. (2011).

[58] In many organizations, an IT or HRIS employee will be the most knowledgeable about the details of the data.

clock edits may be retained in a separate database which can be incorporated to replace erroneous records. Many payroll systems provide datasets with many similarly labelled fields which require a conversation to understand the appropriate fields for analysis. Even after attempting to get clarity on the data, erroneous data may still remain in the dataset. Typically, these data will be removed before conducting analyses.

The consequences of relying on unreliable or inaccurate data increase when those data are extrapolated to a larger group. Attempting to extrapolate unreliable sample data to a population will magnify errors and result in inaccurate conclusions about the population. The smaller the sample or the larger the population, the greater impact data errors in the sample will have.

8.7   Calculating Damages

Statistical analysis is commonly used to calculate estimates of financial damages for wage and hour violations. That is, an analysis is required to determine the amount of money each class member is owed as compensation for the organization's violations (e.g., back overtime pay, unpaid meal break premiums). Damage calculations are typically required if plaintiffs prevail in the merits of the case, but they may also be calculated at earlier stages by plaintiffs to demonstrate to the court that the case is manageable as a class action.[59] Defendants may also conduct a similar analysis called an "exposure analysis" early in the litigation to estimate potential damages or assist in settlement negotiations.

Typically, the statistical analysis to calculate damages in wage and hour cases is not overly complex, as it rarely involves advanced statistical modeling, for example. Instead, one of the primary challenges is working with datasets that may be extremely large or are not in a format conducive to analysis. It is not uncommon for a time clock database to include tens of millions of rows, for example. In some cases, separate datasets are generated for each employee, requiring hundreds of datasets to be combined before the analyses can begin. This step becomes especially time-consuming when the datasets do not contain identical fields or use different formats (numeric in some datasets and character in others) or lengths.

Working with large datasets requires an analysis program that is capable of handling large volumes of data such as SAS, SPSS, R, or STATA. Each of these programs is capable of handling large volumes of data and can work with data in a variety of formats. Large datasets also require quality checking throughout the analysis process. Manual quality checking is not very feasible, so part of the analysis should include checking the data and results throughout the analysis process. If a formula is written to calculate the number of overtime hours worked per workweek, for example, the resulting values can be inspected to assess whether they fall within a reasonable range. Extremely high or low values may indicate an error in the

---

[59] Allen et al. (2011).

calculation and likely warrant a further attention being paid to the formula and underlying data.

Statistical analysis conducted for purposes of damages generally has a more "relaxed standard of proof" when compared to analyses used to determine liability.[60] However, the outcome of a damages analysis will have a direct financial impact on all parties involved in the litigation. The relaxed standard refers to the amount of uncertainly that is tolerable as a result of the available data[61] and not in the quality of the analyses performed.

8.7.1 Damages Based on Representative Sampling

In many cases, an approach called "representative sampling" is proposed to estimate damages. This approach typically follows a consistent pattern. First, a sample of class members is selected, data are collected from the sample, and inferences about the entire class are made based on data collected from the sample. Issues related the sampling and extrapolation were addressed in prior sections. In this section, I will focus on how the approach is typically applied for calculating damages.

When calculating damages, many experts perform an analysis that assumes the sample average (e.g., unpaid hours each workweek) for all non-sampled class members and calculates damages based on that assumption. For example, suppose a class consists of 500 employees who allege they were misclassified as exempt and not paid overtime. Damages on this claim are based on the number of overtime hours worked by each class member. A sample of 50 class members is selected, and each class member reports the number of overtime hours they personally worked per workweek. The class members in the sample report an average of 10 h of overtime per workweek. To calculate damages for the remaining 450 class members, the analysis assumes that each of them worked 10 h of overtime each workweek (based on the sample average). Practically, we know that this assumption is unlikely to be accurate for most, if not all, of the class members. Because courts are generally willing to tolerate a reasonable degree of uncertainty, the question becomes how much uncertainly is included in these estimates. The confidence interval will answer this question at the group level, but not at the individual level. In other words, the confidence interval may be useful for estimating the average and therefore the total damages for the entire class, but not the amount of error associated with any one class member. One way to address this is to analyze the degree of variability within the sample. In the prior example, assume that all 50 class members in the sample reported working between 9 and 11 h per workweek. This situation is likely to produce relatively small errors on an individual level after extrapolation. However, what if individuals in the sample reported anywhere between 1 h and 30 h of

---

[60] "[B]roadly speaking, the law tolerates more uncertainty with respect to damages than to the existence of liability" *Duran v US Bank (p. 38)*.

[61] *See Duran v. US Bank*; *Bruckman v. Parliament Escrow Corp. (1987)*.

overtime per workweek? The non-sampled class members are likely to reflect a similar pattern of variability, and therefore applying an average of 10 h to each of them will result in large errors at an individual level. The direction and magnitude of the error for each individual cannot be known using this approach.

8.8   Documenting the Analyses

An issue that comes up regularly when statistical analyses are used in litigation is how the analyses are documented and "produced." Experts are typically required to produce all files upon which they relied for review by both parties. When a statistical analysis is performed, the production usually includes data and analysis files. Issues related to file production are unique to litigation, and the amount of time and resources required may not be anticipated by those without prior exposure to this process.

It is not uncommon for disputes to arise over experts' file production. In many cases, there are specific legal requirements that define an expert's obligation to provide information responsive to a production request. However, this may differ by jurisdiction or can be impacted by informal agreements between the parties. Therefore, production is generally performed in collaboration with the attorney who retained the expert to ensure that obligations with respect to file production are met. In this section, I describe some of the professional standards which may be helpful in determining what information should be documented and produced.

Experts in wage and hour case often rely on a statistical analysis program to analyze electronic data. The more sophisticated computer programs require the user to write programming code to conduct the analysis. It is standard practice to save this code in its native format. In addition to the analysis files, it is standard practice to retain and produce the original "raw" data in their native format. The contents of the analysis files and raw data files will allow anyone with access to the analysis program to rerun, modify, or inspect the analyses. Inspection of the analysis code also allows another expert to identify potential errors in the analysis and all assumptions that were included in the analysis.

Disputes sometimes occur when files are produced in non-native format. For example, a database may be printed as a table in a pdf document. This may technically fulfill the requirements of an imprecisely worded subpoena but is not useful for purposes of evaluating the work performed by the expert. In other situations, experts may perform analyses within excel files but overwrite formulas within the cells before producing the files. This is another area that can lead to disputes regarding the adequacy of production. An additional issue may arise when analyses are performed within a program such as excel because it may be difficult or impossible to retrace all the steps in the analysis. Unlike programs such as SAS, SPSS, or R, excel allows the user to manipulate, move, copy and paste, or combine data without any record of the specific actions that were performed. This can make it difficult if not impossible to replicate the analyses.

8.9 Key Litigation Involving Sampling and Statistics

Issues related to sampling and statistical analysis are involved to some degree in nearly all wage and hour class actions. However, recent rulings from the California Supreme Court and the US Supreme Court have directly addressed the use of sampling and statistical analysis in wage and hour cases. These cases are regularly cited by attorneys and have a substantial impact on the work performed by experts working in this area. These cases are summarized below.

8.9.1 Duran v US Bank

The *Duran* case was a class action in California in which loan officers at US Bank alleged they were misclassified as exempt. US Bank argued that the employees met the criteria for the outside salesperson exemption. The final class included 260 current and former employees who worked for the company between 1997 and 2005. The trial court found in favor of plaintiffs and awarded the class a verdict of $15 million. The case was appealed up to the California Supreme Court ("the court") which issued a ruling on May 29, 2014.

The primary issue addressed by the court was the trial court's reliance on a representative sampling procedure to assess liability. The trial court allowed a sample of 21 class members to provide testimony in trial and, based on that testimony, found the *entire* class of 260 current and former employees to be misclassified. An overview of the procedure used by the trial court is provided below.

Representative Sampling Plan Used by the Trial Court The trial court selected 20 random class members to provide testimony. Then the two named plaintiffs were added to the sample, called the "representative witness group" (RWG). The trial court then excluded one person from the RWG, because his work activities differed from a "true" employee in the loan officer role. After the sample had been selected, the class definition was revised, and class members were given a second opportunity to opt out of the class. Nine class members, including four from the RWG, elected to opt out of the class at that point. New class members were randomly selected to replace the members of the RWG who had been excluded or opted out. Each member of the RWG provided testimony regarding their experience, except for one who failed to appear for his testimony. The final RWG therefore consisted of 21 class members, and the court ruled that the entire class was misclassified based on the testimony provided by this group.

The court noted several deficiencies in the process used by the trial court, which it described as "profoundly flawed."[62] Below, I discuss the issues raised by the court that are related to sampling and statistical analysis.

---

[62] *Duran v. US Bank* (p. 2).

Sample Size The sample of 21 was too small to provide reliable information about the larger group. This lead to an "intolerably" large margin of error. The data from the sample enabled a statistics expert to estimate that the average number of overtime hours worked per workweek by the class was 11.86 h, with a margin of error of 5.14 h. The 43% relative margin of error (margin of error divided by the average) reflected more uncertainly than the court was comfortable with. In addition, the data from the sample allowed the same statistics expert to determine that at least 87% of the class members were misclassified. The court noted that using these calculations, up to 13% of the class members were properly classified which "stood in contrast to the trial court's determination that the *entire* class was misclassified."[63] In addition, the trial court selected a sample size without providing rationale for the decision and without input from the statistical experts retained by either party. The sample size appeared to be chosen based on convenience and manageability, but as the court noted, the same could be said for a sample of one and does not justify the use of a small sample.

Preliminary Assessment of Variability The court recognized that an appropriate sample size is influenced by the amount of variability within the population. The more variability between class members, the larger sample size needed to generate sufficiently precise estimates. However, no assessment of variability was performed in this case to help determine an appropriate sample size.

Nonrandom Sample In addition to sample size, the court noted problems with how the sample was selected. First, the two named plaintiffs were included in the sample. These two class members were not randomly selected and were already known to reflect a particular viewpoint. In addition, the two named plaintiffs were selected to replace four other previous named plaintiffs, each of whom later provided testimony that they believed they were properly classified. Second, the trial court excluded one randomly selected employee from the sample because his job duties were unique and not typical for the position. The court noted that this employee could have represented many other class members who performed work similar to him, and his exclusion imposed less variability in the sample that would have been found randomly.

Non-response bias Other randomly selected class members either opted out of the class after learning they would be required to give testimony or failed to appear to give testimony. Those who had weaker claims would be less motivated to provide testimony and opt out, leaving a sample that overrepresents those with stronger claims. Indeed, 4 out of 20 (20%) of those selected in the RWG chose to opt out compared to 2% from the rest of the class. US Bank also produced declarations from two of the members of the RWG who opted out stating that they opted out because the plaintiff attorneys urged them to do so. However, the trial court chose to remove and replace the four who had opted out.

---

[63] *Duran v. US Bank* (p. 14).

Implications   The court's ruling did not prohibit the use of statistical sampling in wage and hour cases but has had an impact on experts by raising the bar for what is acceptable. Since *Duran*, experts are generally required to fully explain their sampling plan at the class certification stage and present a sampling plan that is reliable and follows scientific standards. Though this decision was from the California court system, the reasoning of the court provides useful guidance to experts in all jurisdictions.

8.9.2   Tyson Foods, Inc. v Bouaphakeo et al.

Tyson was a class action FLSA case that involved a claim that workers at an Iowa pork-processing plant were not properly compensated for time spent putting on and taking off protective gear ("donning and doffing"). There were 3500 individuals involved in the lawsuit, between two separate classes that differed only with respect to time frame. The classes were certified, and the defendant was found to be liable for $2.9 million in compensatory damages. The case was eventually appealed to the US Supreme Court which issued a ruling on March 22, 2016. The central issue addressed by the Supreme Court was whether it was appropriate for the trial court to use the calculated average amount of time a sample of employees spent donning and doffing to certify a class and determine damages.

An expert retained by the plaintiffs conducted a video-based time and motion study in which he measured the time spent donning and doffing required personal protective equipment (PPE)[64] for a sample of employees. The court was forced to decide whether the statistical evidence can be used to establish class-wide liability. The dispute in this case was based not on the quality of the data collected but whether that data revealed enough variability to make class treatment inappropriate. In other words, the dispute was over the interpretation of the data, not the data themselves. Tyson argued that the degree of variability among class members made reliance on the sample improper and would result in recovery for class members who had no claims. Plaintiffs argued that differences between class members were minimal. The Supreme Court found in favor of the plaintiffs. An overview of the issues and the court's logic are provided below.

Data   Tyson did not maintain time records showing the time individual employees spent donning and doffing PPE. As a result, the parties were forced to rely on "representative evidence." This evidence came from 744 videotaped observations, in which the time employees spent donning and doffing PPE was measured across three departments. The study results showed that employees spend an average of 18 min/day donning and doffing PPE in the "cut" and "retrim" departments and an average of 21.25 min/day in the "kill" department. A different expert, also retained by the plaintiffs, then applied these averages to employee time records and calculated

---

[64] The PPE included protection against knife cuts which both parties agreed was compensable.

the amount of unpaid overtime owed to each class member.[65] This analysis showed that 212 class members were not entitled to any recovery, while the rest of the more than 3000 class members were. Tyson argued that the study overstated the average donning and doffing time but did not present an expert to oppose the validity of the data or offer an alternative study.

Variability The primary issue for the Supreme Court involved variability. Defendants argued that the classes should not have been certified for two reasons. First, there is too much variability in time spent donning and doffing. They argued that the method used assumed no variability by applying an average for all class members even though that is the key question that should have been answered prior to certifying the class. Second, the statistical approach used by the plaintiffs will provide recovery for some class members who have no claims, such as those who never worked more than 40 h in a workweek.

The court addressed both of those arguments. The court noted that unlike other cases in which class certification was denied due to high variability, the class members in this case all worked in the same facility, performed similar work, and were paid under the same policy. The question remaining was whether the time spent donning and doffing substantially differed from person to person. The court stated that this decision was appropriately made by the jury who found that employees spent roughly equal time donning and doffing. The district court could have denied class certification only if it concluded that no reasonable juror could have reached this conclusion. The court addressed the second argument by stating that Tyson could challenge the proposed method of allocating damages when they are dispersed. However, neither argument raised by Tyson persuaded the court to decertify the class.

Implications This case was notable because it provided an example of how representative evidence can be used effectively in wage and hour cases. However, the court also cautioned that the outcome of this case does not mean that similar approaches are useful in every circumstance:

> This case presents no occasion for adoption of broad and categorical rules governing the use of representative and statistical evidence in class actions. Rather, the ability to use a representative sample to establish class wide liability will depend on the purpose for which the sample is being introduced and on the underlying cause of action.[66]

This case is often cited by plaintiffs attempting to introduce statistical evidence to resolve wage and hour class actions.

---

[65] Some employees were compensated between 4 and 8 min for donning and doffing PPE. This time was removed as part of the calculation.

[66] *Tyson Foods, Inc. v Bouaphakeo et al.*, (p. 2).

8.10   Conclusion

Sampling and statistical analyses often play a central role in resolving wage and hour disputes. This chapter provides the underlying logic supporting many of the sampling and statistical approaches used by experts in these cases. In addition, I have highlighted several areas where the approaches can be misapplied or results may be misinterpreted and discussed how factors such as non-response bias and variability may impact the ability to reach meaningful conclusions about a population based on sampling and extrapolation. To illustrate these points, I've summarized two important cases that addressed sampling and statistics in detail. Together, this information is intended to provide a useful reference for those evaluating wage and hour compliance.

References

Allen, M. A., Hall, R. E., & Lazear, V. A. (2011). Reference guide on estimation of economic damages. In*Reference manual of scientific evidence* (3rd ed.). Washington, DC: National Academies Press.

American Statistical Association, Committee on Professional Ethics. (2016). *Ethical guidelines for statistical practice*. Retrieved from http://www.amstat.org/asa/files/pdfs/EthicalGuidelines. pdf

Babbie, E. R. (1990). *Survey research methods* (2nd ed.). Belmont, CA: Wadsworth.

Brase, C. H., & Brase, C. P. (2011). *Understandable statistics: Concepts and methods* (10th ed.). Boston, MA: Cengage Learning.

Bruckman v. Parliament Escrow Corp. (1987). 190 Cal.App.3d 1051, 1061.

DeGroot, M. H., Fienberg, S. E., & Kadane, J. B. (Eds.). (1986). *Statistics and the law*. New York: Wiley.

Diamond, S. S. (2011). Reference guide on survey research. In*Reference manual of scientific evidence* (3rd ed.). Washington, DC: National Academies Press.

Fienberg, S. E. (Ed.). (1989). *The evolving role of statistical assessments as evidence in the courts*. New York: Springer.

Finberg, J. M., & Thoreen, P. J. (2007). *The use of representative testimony and bifurcation of liability and damages in FLSA collective actions*. Prepared for the American Bar Association Section of Labor and Employment Law, Philadelphia, PA.

Gastwirth, J. L. (Ed.). (2000). *Statistical science in the courtroom*. New York: Springer.

Hanvey, C. M. (2014, May). Evaluating "statistically significant" within-title variability. In C. Hanvey (Chair), *Within-group variability: Methodological and statistical advancements in the legal context*. Symposium presented at the annual meeting of the Society for Industrial and Organizational Psychology (SIOP), Honolulu, HI.

Howell, D. C. (2010). *Statistical methods for psychology* (7th ed.). Belmont, CA: Cengage Wadsworth.

Kaye, D. H., & Freedman, D. A. (2011). Reference guide on statistics. In*Reference Manual of Scientific Evidence* (3rd ed.). Washington, DC: National Academies Press.

Krosnick, J. A., & Presser, S. (2010). Questions and questionnaire design. In P. V. Marsden & J. D. Wright (Eds.), *Handbook of survey research* (2nd ed.). Bingley, UK: Emerald.

Murphy, K. R. (2014, May). Describing variability: The coefficient of variation. In C. Hanvey (Chair), *Within-group variability: Methodological and statistical advancements in the legal context.* Symposium presented at the annual meeting of the Society for Industrial and Organizational Psychology (SIOP), Honolulu, HI.

Stetz, T. A., Beaubien, M., Keeney, M. J., & Lyons, B. D. (2008). Nonrandom response and rater variance in job analysis surveys: A cause for concern? *Public Personnel Management, 37*(2), 223–241.

Thompson, S. K. (2012). *Sampling* (3rd ed.). Hoboken, NJ: Wiley.

Wheelan, C. (2013). *Naked statistics: Stripping the dread from the data.* New York: W. W. Norton.

Witte, R. S., & Witte, J. S. (2010). *Statistics* (9th ed.). Hoboken, NJ: Wiley.

Court Cases

Duran v. U.S. Bank Nat'l Ass'n, No. S200923 (May 29, 2014).

Tyson Foods, Inc. v. Bouaphakeo, 577 U.S. ___ (2016).

Chapter 9
Pay Equity

Kayo Sady and Chester Hanvey

9.1 Introduction

Concerns about pay equity straddle the line between two legal arenas: wage and hour and sex/race discrimination. Although discussions of pay equity typically focus on concerns about discrimination in the workplace, this issue is ultimately about the wages that employees are paid. Indeed, the Equal Pay Act of 1963, upon which pay equity litigation at the federal level is often based (along with allegations of Title VII violations), was an amendment to the Fair Labor Standards Act to outlaw wage disparities based on the sex of employees. In this chapter, we introduce concepts of pay equity and present considerations associated with using multiple regression analysis to evaluate pay disparities between protected class subgroups.

9.2 What Is Pay Equity?

There are several perspectives from which to consider "equity" in pay, and failure of parties with different perspectives to agree on a common definition of "equity" upfront can result in unproductive discussions. Thus, to ensure a common understanding of what we mean by pay equity in the equal employment opportunity context, in the following sections, we briefly address the difference between "external equity" and "internal equity."

The original version of this chapter was revised. A correction to this chapter can be found at https://doi.org/10.1007/978-3-319-74612-8_10

9.2.1   External Equity

External equity refers to the degree to which an employee's salary is commensurate with the salary the employee could demand in the external labor market. Employees who think their salaries are below their "market value" may perceive inequity. Such perceptions might result in the employee leaving the organization or reducing level of performance. Two major factors that influence perceptions of external equity are (1) how the employer pays relative to the external labor market and (2) salary compression.

An organization's compensation philosophy with respect to where it sets salaries relative to the relevant labor market is often reflected in the values of its pay ranges (or pay bands).[1] Specifically, the philosophy is reflected in the relationship between the midpoint of each pay band and the market midpoint. Employers with pay band midpoints lower than the competitive labor market midpoints may experience more problems with negative external equity perceptions in their workforce compared to employers with pay band midpoints that are higher than the market midpoint.[2] Of course, there are other forms of extrinsic[3] and intrinsic[4] rewards that may make a particular position with an organization more or less attractive to an employee aside from their compensation.

Salary compression reflects differences in the influence, on salary, of external market forces versus internal market forces. Wages in the external labor market tend to increase at a higher rate than wages internal to an organization, such that an external hire may demand higher wages than a similarly situated internal hire[5] who has been promoted to a position from within the organization. Thus, salary compression can be attributed to the fact that the *external market premium* is often higher than the *loyalty premium*.

9.2.2   Internal Equity

Internal equity refers to pay equity between employees within an organization. Internal equity typically involves one of two types of comparisons: individual and group. With individual equity, an employee compares his or her salary with that of

---

[1] Gerhart (2000).

[2] Fitzpatrick and McMullen (2008).

[3] For example, retirement benefits or flexible schedules may compensate for relatively lower wages.

[4] For example, elements of Hackman and Oldham's (1976) job characteristics theory may influence an employee's satisfaction, thus offsetting sentiments of inequity if s/he is paid relatively low compared to the external labor market.

[5] "Similarly situated" is a Civil Rights Act (1964) Title VII standard. The Equal Pay Act (1963) defines comparators as those who are "substantially equal" to one another. Moreover, state laws have used even different language to define comparators, such as the "substantially similar" standard of the California Fair Pay Act (2015).

one or more peers. In doing so the employee informally considers a variety of input factors such as years of experience, effort, and performance. Effectively, internal equity refers to a comparison of input/output ratios between two or more employees. That is, the question of internal equity refers to whether the ratios of employee contributions and employee pay are equal between two individuals. In considering internal equity, it is important to distinguish between actual inputs and perceived inputs. Actual inputs are quantified employee inputs such as employee time in the organization (and the knowledge accrued as a result) or performance, whereas perceived inputs[6] reflect an individual's perspective on the contributions he or she makes to the organization. In labor law, perceptions of unequal input/output ratios may be the basis for a complaint lawsuit; however, comparisons of actual input/output ratios are the facts on which a case is decided.

The specific characterization of internal equity varies depending on the employees compared. For example, job evaluation procedures quantify the contributions of employees in specific roles by assigning point values based on defined job characteristics.[7] The points can be translated to compensation values to determine the pay of employees in the roles.

Group-level internal equity refers to whether there are compensation differences between similarly situated[8] employees of different protected class subgroup status (e.g., men versus women) that cannot be accounted for by legitimate, nondiscriminatory factors. Although such comparisons may take the form of a one-to-one comparison between two employees in different protected class subgroups, the remainder of this chapter focuses on a comparison of many similarly situated employees, in which both legitimate factors and protected class subgroup status can be accounted for statistically.

9.3 Defining Appropriate Employee Groups for Analysis

Grouping employees for analysis is one of the most important activities in an EEO pay analysis. If similarly situated status is not properly established, the statistical analysis will not account for major job characteristics that influence pay differences. As a general rule, employees of different FLSA status should not be grouped together for analysis. By definition, the job duties and pay models differ for exempt and non-exempt employees. Exempt employees typically hold more senior

---

[6] The concept of distributive justice, based on Adams' (1965) equity theory, reflects the extent to which an individual employee perceives that his or her work outcomes relative to his or her contributions match the work outcomes to contributions ratios of others in the organization.

[7] Milkovich and Newman (2005).

[8] Whether individuals are similarly situated depends on whether they share one or more important job-related characteristics that influence compensation. Characteristics may include similarity in tasks, skills required, effort, responsibility, working conditions, or complexity (cf. Sady et al., 2015).

positions within an organization and, depending on the exemption for which they qualify, have responsibilities that may include (1) managing other employees, (2) managing the enterprise, (3) exercising discretion and independent judgment on matters of significance, or (4) performing work that involves advanced knowledge.[9] Further, individuals in different pay grades will usually differ substantially in the type of work they perform and the skills, qualifications, and levels of responsibility required by the roles. Similar to an evaluation of FLSA exemption status, job title or job code alone may not accurately reflect the work an employee actually performs to the level of detail required to determine similarly situated status. If the titles or codes in an organization are broad and represent, within title or code, arrays of specific positions with fundamentally different work duties or level of skill, job title or code should be divided along lines of common duties prior to analysis.

Failing to group employees along job characteristics that make them similarly situated (such as the job duties, the skills and qualifications required of the job, the level of responsibility inherent in the job, and other major factors) can result in problematic analyses and misleading statistical results. It is our general recommendation to group employees at the most specific level of similarity that allows meaningful analyses for much of the workforce. Refer to Sady and Aamodt (2016) and Sady et al. (2015) for a more comprehensive explanation of grouping strategies and pitfalls.

9.4   Establishing the Employment Decision to Analyze

The most common pay equity evaluations focus on differences in base salary between members of different protected class subgroups. When analyzing base pay, it is important to annualize salary for part-time employees prior to conducting the analysis. Failure to do so will lead to results that indicate part-time employees are severely underpaid relative to their predicted pay based on the regression model. For non-exempt employees, annualizing salary for everybody (part-time or full-time) requires simply multiplying employees' hourly rates by 2080, which reflects the total number of workable hours across 52 weeks (i.e., 1 year) of 40-h workweeks. It is slightly more complicated to establish annualized salary for part-time exempt employees. For these employees, multiplying their annual salary (i.e., what they actually receive) by the following ratio will annualize the salaries, such that they can be accurately analyzed with full-time employees: (40 h)/(assigned hours in the part-time appointment).[10] Sometimes, full-time equivalent (or "FTE") proportions are available from the HRIS. The ratios represent the proportion of a 40-h workweek that an employee is assigned. Full-time employees will have values of 1; part-time employees will have values below 1. If FTE proportions are available, the base

---

[9] See Chap. 3 for more detail about FLSA exemptions.

[10] As an example: Assume an employee works 25 h per week and makes a total salary of $30,000 in a year. Their annualized salary would be calculated as $30,000 × (40/25) or $48,000.

Table 9.1 Pay factors commonly available in HRIS systems

Type	Factor
Time factors	Time in company (TIC)
	Time in job (TIJ)
	Time in grade (TIG)
	Experience prior to joining the organization
Non-time factors	Performance
	Starting salary
	Internal versus external hire

salaries for part-time employees can be annualized by (1) dividing 1 by the FTE values assigned to the part-time employees and (2) multiplying the results by the employees' base salaries.[11]

Other forms of compensation such as annual merit increases, annual bonuses, stock options, and overtime pay are increasingly included in pay equity studies. The different types of compensation are typically determined by different sets of factors (i.e., predictors in a regression model), so combining all forms into an aggregate of "total compensation" to analyze will produce confounding results. For example, service years are often related to base salary but not annual bonus, whereas performance ratings are highly correlated with bonus percentages but not with base salary. Thus, analyzing each form of compensation separately with a set of specific predictors suitable for the particular form will produce more meaningful, cogent results than an analysis of "total compensation."[12]

9.5   Pay Factors

Although there are myriad factors and decisions that influence an employee's base salary at any given time, many of these factors are not readily available in a database to be used in an EEO pay equity analysis. Several, however, are commonly available for retrievable from an organization's human resource information system (HRIS), which are listed in Table 9.1. If the major factors affecting compensation are unable to be accounted for in a regression analysis of compensation, it is prudent to be cautious in interpreting statistical indicators of discrimination, as statistically significant indicators of protected class subgroups may reflect differences due to the absence of a major, nondiscriminatory factor(s).

---

[11] As an example: Assume an employee has an FTE value of 0.80 (i.e., works 80% of the hours a full-time employee works) and makes $50,000 per year. Their annualized salary would be calculated as $(1/0.80) \times \$50,000$ or $62,500.

[12] Analysis of "W2 earnings" can be particularly problematic given the confounding of earnings and time in job for any employees hired during the calendar year.

9.5.1 Time Factors

Some of the factors most commonly used to explain differences in compensation between similarly situated employees are time and experience variables. This set of factors may be divided further into two main sets: experience factors at the organization (seniority) and experience factors prior to joining the organization.

9.5.1.1 Experience in the Organization

Three organizational tenure variables commonly calculated as part of an EEO pay analysis to be used as legitimate explanations of pay differences are (1) time in company (TIC), (2) time in job (TIJ), and (3) time in grade (TIG).

Time in Company (TIC) In theory, the longer that an employee has been with an organization, the more he/she should be making compared to others in the organization, ceteris paribus.[13] The idea behind the positive correlation behind TIC and compensation is that an effectively performing employee with more time in the organization should have higher levels of institutional knowledge and more years of merit increases to salary. In practice, TIC is sometimes curvilinear or negatively correlated with compensation due to the phenomenon of *salary compression* that we addressed in the external equity section.[14]

Time in Job (TIJ) The theory behind the relationship between salary and TIJ is similar to that of salary and TIC. Ceteris paribus, the more time a given employee accrues in a particular position, the more he or she is likely to be paid. Including TIJ in a regression model helps to account for differences in compensation due to the knowledge acquisition and annual merit increases associated with increased time in a specific job or role. Unlike TIC, TIJ is almost always positively correlated with base pay.

Time in Grade (TIG) It is generally the case that job titles or codes do not cross pay grade/band, such that employees within a specific title or code are all in one pay grade/band. If a title does cross grade/band and title is the unit of aggregation for analysis purposes, TIJ will not adequately account for differences in salary due to time in the title because TIJ is conflated with the amount of time in the pay grade/ band (TIG). In such cases, TIG is a necessary pay factor to include in order to account for legitimate differences in pay associated with different grades/bands. Adding a TIG factor in such cases, however, does not necessarily resolve issues with analyzing employees in different grades/bands together, as the influence of TIG on compensation may differ depending on the grade/band. Grouping employees

---

[13] A Latin phrase meaning *other things equal*. It is commonly used as a qualifier of general statements about relationships between phenomena in economics.

[14] Barbezat (2003).

such that only one grade is represented in any one pay analysis group is advised and avoids problems with grouping employees together for analysis who are not similarly situated.

In most organizations, job title does not cross pay grade/band, but modeling time in grade (TIG) as an explanatory pay factor is still helpful. Time in job may not represent the length of time in a particular grade if pay grades are broad and/or an employee has undergone a lateral transfer, such that the grade of his/her prior position matches that of the current position. Calculating and modeling time in grade allows an explanation of pay differences between employees that are due to the fact that employees with longer time in a pay grade tend to be paid higher than those with shorter time in a pay grade. That said, similar to TIC, the compensation returns to TIG tend to diminish over time in most cases. As an employee's salary approaches the maximum of the pay band range, the rate of increase to his or her salary will tend to slow. Employee compa-ratios[15] or range penetration[16] values are commonly used as indicators of an employee's position within the applicable range and markers of when compensation growth within the grade should be slowed. Creating a version of TIG that account for the slowed growth often improves model fit; squared TIG terms are a typical way to account for the curvilinear relationship between TIG and compensation growth.

9.5.1.2 Experience Prior to Joining the Organization

Modeling employees' relevant experience prior to joining the organization is complex and difficult because most organizations simply do not have complete, accurate, or accessible records of the background history for all employees prior to their joining the organization. Thus, the most common practice is to use employees' ages as a proxy (i.e., age-as-a-proxy) for the relevant experience they had upon hire into the organization. For example, if two employees have 5 years of TIC but one is 39 and the other is 26, it is a fair assumption that the older employee was hired with more relevant experiences than the younger employee. Although older employees generally have more work-related prior experience, age is an imperfect indicator of experience, and if actual *related, prior experience* is available, it should be used in the analysis instead of age.[17] In our experience, few organizations have these data available and/or useable in database form.

---

[15] This metric is used to determine how an employee's salary compares to the midpoint of the salary range for their position or pay grade. The ratio is calculated by dividing an employee's actual salary by the midpoint of the salary range for that position or pay grade.

[16] This metric is used to determine where the employee's salary falls within the entire range of salaries for their position or pay grade. It is calculated using the following formula (salary range minimum)/(range maximum − range minimum).

[17] For example, an established limitation of using age-as-a-proxy for actual years of experience is that it may overestimate actual years of prior experience more commonly for women than men. If women have been more likely to leave the workforce for more extended periods of time, using

9.5.2 Non-time Factors

Many other legitimate, nondiscriminatory factors may explain a sex- or race-based disparity in compensation beyond the time-based factors discussed. Although a discussion of each is beyond the scope of this chapter, we address three common factors considered: (1) performance, (2) starting salary, and (3) internal versus external hire.

9.5.2.1 Performance

Organizational compensation systems often incorporate an element of performance-based pay, such that higher performing employees have higher salaries than their similarly situated peers.[18] Unfortunately, accounting for compensation differences due to performance differences in compensation equity studies can be problematic for several reasons.

Limited Data One limitation associated with performance data is that they are often available for only a small number of recent years and may only be available for a subset of employees during those years. A limited number of years of performance data does not allow a complete modeling of how employees' performance histories influence current compensation; however, accounting for (1) most recent performance, (2) typical performance, (3) and maximum performance using the available data can be helpful in explaining compensation differences.[19] As a practical matter, missing data within and across years are typically imputed to allow incorporation of performance factors in the regression equation, and imputation procedures should be chosen carefully.

Range Restriction Even if performance data are available and complete, in many cases a group of similarly situated employees do not vary substantially in their performance ratings (i.e., differences in performance ratings between employees are small). In our experience, less than 4% of employees receive a performance rating of below average. In such cases, the performance predictor suffers from *range restriction* which will limit the extent to which it will correlate with compensation values and explain differences in compensation between protected class subgroups.[20]

---

age-as-a-proxy for prior experience when such employees are in a regression equation will overestimate the amount of compensation that should be credited to those employees.

[18] Cannon (2008).

[19] See Sackett et al. (1988) for a discussion of the relationship between typical and maximum performance.

[20] Cohen et al. (2013).

Arguments that Performance is "Tainted" If performance data are incorporated into the analysis and account for unexplained differences in compensation between protected class subgroups, they can be challenged as being *tainted*. Arguments that performance rating(s) are tainted rely on the veracity of two hypotheses:

1. Individuals making performance rating decisions are biased (unconsciously or not) in favor of one particular protected class subgroup or against one particular protected class subgroup.
2. The performance appraisal system does not have sufficient structure to prevent rater biases from tainting the ratings.[21]

The defense against allegations that performance ratings are tainted is to demonstrate that they are job-related and reflect actual on-the-job performance. Performance ratings produced by job-related standards and evaluations reflect true performance differences between employees rather than rating biases or behaviors unrelated to the job.

Validation research can demonstrate that performance appraisal standards and evaluations are job-related. Certainly, validation research is not a requirement of valid, job-related, unbiased performance appraisal systems and corresponding ratings; however, in the event that the system is challenged as an invalid explanation of compensation differences, validation evidence demonstrating the job-relatedness of performance appraisal content and process characteristics will counter arguments that the ratings are biased or tainted. Depending on context, a validation study may take different forms to answer the question of whether there is evidence that the ratings reflect important job-related criteria.

9.5.2.2 Starting Salary

Employees' starting salaries are often the primary determinants of current salary.[22] Because future salary increases[23] are typically a percentage of an individual's base salary, annual compensation growth is heavily influenced by initial salary upon entry into the organization.

If starting salary for a given group of employees explains a statistically significant disparity in compensation between protected class groups, it is prudent to consider thoroughly whether starting salary can be defended as a legitimate, nondiscriminatory pay factor. Arguments that starting salary is itself biased and/or discriminatory typically come in one of two forms:

1. The labor market is biased against a particular protected class subgroup, such that a different subgroup enjoys higher pay on average. Because prior salary is

---

[21] See Werner and Bolino (1997).

[22] Gerhart (1990).

[23] Increases result from cost-of-living adjustments, performance, promotion, or other factors.

often used to determine starting salary for a new employee, starting salary perpetuates labor market biases.

2. Hiring managers are more likely (a) to negotiate with applicants from one particular protected class subgroup and (b) to be persuaded by negotiation tactics employed by them, such that the negotiating subgroup is more likely to receive higher starting salaries than other protected class subgroups, ceteris paribus.

Related to the first argument above, some state legislation has barred employers from asking prospective employees about their most recent or current salary (e.g., Massachusetts and California state pay legislation). The reasoning behind such bans is that they should (1) limit the perpetuation of differences in salaries between protected class subgroups in the available labor pool and (2) require hiring managers to codify the worth of the position to the organization ahead of time.

With respect to the second argument above, if managers establish, ahead of time, what they are willing to pay somebody hired into an open position, arguments that starting salary is somehow biased can be neutralized. Some organizations do not engage in salary negotiation for certain positions. Instead, they have policies that formalize starting salary values to be offered to candidates based on a matrix analysis of experience, knowledge, and other job-related criteria that the candidate may possess. The recommended values may be accompanied by a small variance (e.g., 3%) that provides a range within which managers can establish the most appropriate starting salary offer for a specific candidate. A structured process such as that described provides a rebuttal to claims that employee starting salary is tainted and inappropriate to use a legitimate, explanatory factor for current salary.

The veracity of claims that starting salary is a tainted variable is situationally specific, but employers can defend the use of starting salary as a legitimate explanation of compensation differences by adopting certain practices around establishing starting salary. That said, the reality of the labor market is that starting salary and competition for jobs and human capital are tied to the health of the general economy and unemployment rate. In a booming economy, applicants with many options are in a position to negotiate higher salaries; in a withering economy, the same applicants may have fewer alternative options and less leverage in demanding salary levels. To the extent that protected class status proportions in the labor market systematically correspond to economic fluctuations, differences in starting salary will correlate with protected class status.

9.5.2.3 Internal Versus External Hire

As noted earlier, employees hired into a position from outside of the organization (external hire) may demand a higher salary than employees promoted into a position from within the organization (internal hire) due to wage compression. It may also be the case that an organization has difficulty finding employees within its organization who possess highly sought specialized skill set or competitive knowledge; fulfilling such human capital needs may only be feasible by hiring somebody away from a competitor. In any case, accounting for the difference between externally hired and internally promoted employees within a group of similarly situated employees will often improve the accuracy of the regression model and may account for previously unexplained differences in compensation between protected class subgroups.

9.5.2.4 A Note on Tainted Variables

The fact that a pay factor correlates with protected subgroup status may be misunderstood to mean that the factor is tainted. In fact, correlation between the factor and protected subgroup status is a necessary but *insufficient* condition for a sound argument that a pay factor is tainted. In order for a factor to explain a discrepancy in compensation between protected class groups, it must be both related to the outcome (compensation) and the protected class variable. A factor that is correlated with the protected class variable[24] is not inherently "biased" or "tainted" or reflecting discrimination. An actual "tainted" variable (explanatory factor) is one in which the values represent bias (intentional or not) associated with protected class status. For example, if differences in performance ratings between race groups are due to the bias of managers creating the ratings rather than actual differences in on-the-job performance, the performance ratings should be considered tainted. As such, the ratings in this situation should not be included as a legitimate, explanatory factor in a regression equation, regardless of whether the ratings account for the difference in compensation between race groups. As another example, if the managers setting starting salary for new employees are biased in favor of men (consciously or unconsciously), using starting salary as an explanatory factor of current base pay would be inappropriate, whether or not starting salary values explain the difference in compensation between men and women.

9.6 Conducting a Statistical Analysis of Pay Equity

Pay equity is typically evaluated using a statistical approach called multiple linear regression. This approach provides an objective standard to determine whether statistically significant pay differences exist between subgroups after accounting for ("controlling for") legitimate pay factors in a regression model. Space prohibits comprehensive treatment of the use of multiple linear regression procedures for analyzing EEO pay disparities, and detail on this topic has been covered in other

---

[24]Correlation between two variables/characteristics means that values on one variable/characteristic are systematically related to values on the other variables/characteristics. For example, if time in company is correlated with sex, it may be the case that men tend to have more time in the organization than women or vice versa. To the extent that TIC is not a reflection of sex bias and it explains a difference in compensation between two protected class subgroups, it is a legitimate pay factor for compensation differences that is both correlated with compensation and the protected class variable.

works,[25] but we cover some of the basic statistics for interpretation in this final section, which is separated into a discussion of model statistics and variable statistics. For further reference, Cohen et al. (2013) provide a comprehensive treatment of applied multiple regression procedures.

In the simplest case, two regression models are created for each group of similarly situated employees: one model that includes only the legitimate, nondiscriminatory pay factors and one model that adds a variable(s) representing protected group subgroup status. The former has been referred to as the compensation model and the latter the discrimination model.[26] Conceptually, when the discrimination model accounts for more pay differences than the compensation model, there is initial statistical evidence of discrimination; however, many statistical nuances should be considered, which are discussed below.

9.6.1   Model Statistics

Model statistics provide information about the degree to which the factors included in the model fit the actual data. The relevant model statistics in this evaluation are those associated with the compensation model. First, the model F-statistic provides an indication of the probability that associations between the predictor side of the regression equation (pay factor side) and the outcome side of the regression equation (compensation) reflect "noise" and are just due to chance. If the probability value associated with the F-statistic is less than 0.05, the model is statistically significant, and it is appropriate to conclude that at least some of the pay factors have reliable and systematic relationships with compensation. Further interpretation of any model or variable statistics is inappropriate if this first standard of evaluation is not met.

The second indicator of model fit is the R^2 ("R-squared") value, which ranges from 0.00 to 1.00 and indicates the proportion of total differences in salaries that are accounted for by pay factors. Ceteris paribus, the closer the R^2 value is to 1.00, the more strongly the pay factors relate to compensation. When evaluating the R^2, however, it is important to take into account the amount of variability in salary within the group. That is, a model that explains 25% ($R^2 = 0.25$) of the variability in salary among a group of employees whose salaries vary by $5000, on average, leaves fewer overall dollars unaccounted for than a model that explains 50% ($R^2 = 0.50$) of the variability in salary among a group of employees whose salaried vary by $20,000, on average. Thus, we recommend evaluating the model root mean squared error (RMSE) in concert with the R^2 to fully understand the extent to which salary differences are unaccounted for by the pay factors.[27]

---

[25] cf. Sady et al. (2015) and Sady and Aamodt (2016).

[26] Sady et al. (2015).

[27] Sady et al. (2015).

9.6.2 Variable Statistics

In EEO pay analyses, statistics in the discrimination model provide an indication of the extent to which race, sex, or some other protected class variable is associated with unaccounted for differences in compensation from the compensation model. Specifically, the regression estimate (b-weight) for the protected class variable(s) indicates the average difference in compensation between the protected class subgroups after accounting for influence of the legitimate pay factors on compensation. The t-value associated with the regression weight and its corresponding probability value indicate whether the regression coefficient is different from zero at a statistically significant level. Regression coefficients that are not statistically significant should not be interpreted as reflecting differences in salaries between the protected class subgroups. That is, a nonsignificant result means that differences in compensation between protected class subgroups may very well be due to chance.

The statistical significance of the protected class subgroup b-weight is driven by the gap between employees' actual compensation and their predicted compensation[28] from the compensation model. For example, if there is a statistically significant difference between men's and women's salary for a particular group of employees, such that men have higher compensation after accounting for the influence of the legitimate pay factors, this means that men, on average, have salaries above the value predicted by the regression model compared to the women who, on average, have salaries below the value predicted by the regression model.

It is important to consider the statistical significance of regression coefficients in the context of the compensation model's R^2 value. Recall, the R^2 indicates how well the pay factors actually predict compensation. In other words, the R^2 provides an indication of the extent to which the purported pay factors modeled in the regression actually correspond to differences in how people are paid. If R^2 is small, there is a reasonable likelihood that other pay factors could be identified as part of a follow-up analysis, and one should be cautious in interpreting a statistically significant difference between protected class subgroups as meaningful. The difference might simply reflect the absence of important pay factors yet to be accounted for in the regression model.

If, in fact, an unexplained difference in compensation between protected class subgroups requires remediation, salary adjustments should be carefully considered in terms of amount, recipients, and timing. Refer to Sady and Aamodt (2016) for an extensive discussion of adjustment strategies and considerations.

---

[28] In addition to variable statistics, the regression model results in a "predicted salary" for each employee based on the employee's pattern of legitimate pay factors (e.g., time in job, performance). Each employee's predicted salary based on these factors can be compared to their actual salary to identify discrepancies.

9.7   Conclusion

Equal employment opportunity pay equity studies are complex endeavors, requiring an understanding of both compensation systems and sophisticated statistical procedures. These studies usually involve an iterative process by which compensation models are improved through increased scope and clarity of pay factors. The complexity of the analyses, number of iterations involved in a typical analysis, and sensitivity of the results all justify that the research should be conducted at the direction of counsel and covered under attorney-client privilege. Failure to do so could result in significant liability despite an organization's best intentions and efforts to proactively identify potential pay inequities within its workforce.

References

Adams, J. S. (1965). Inequity in social exchange. In L. Berkowitz (Ed.), *Advances in experimental social psychology* (Vol. 2, pp. 267–299). New York: Academic Press.

Barbezat, B. E. (2003). From here to seniority: The effect of experience and job tenure on faculty salaries. In R. K. Toutkoushian (Ed.), *Unresolved issues in conducting salary-equity studies.* San Francisco: Jossey-Bass.

Cannon, M. D. (2008). Pay-for-performance: New developments and issues. In L. A. Berger & D. R. Berger (Eds.), *The compensation handbook* (pp. 543–558). New York: McGraw-Hill.

Cohen, J., Cohen, P., West, S. G., & Aiken, L. S. (2013). *Applied multiple regression/correlation analysis for the behavioral sciences.* New York: Routledge.

Fitzpatrick, I., & McMullen, T. D. (2008). Benchmarking. In L. A. Berger & D. R. Berger (Eds.), *The compensation handbook* (pp. 125–142). New York: McGraw-Hill.

Gerhart, B. (1990). Gender differences in current and starting salaries: The role of performance, college major, and job title. *Industrial and Labor Relations Review, 43*(4), 418–433.

Gerhart, B. (2000). Compensation strategy and organizational performance. In S. L. Rynes & B. Gerhart (Eds.), *Compensation in organizations* (pp. 151–195). San Francisco: Jossey-Bass.

Hackman, J. R., & Oldham, G. R. (1976). Motivation through the design of work: Test of a theory. *Organizational Behavior and Human Performance, 16*, 250–279.

Milkovich, G. T., & Newman, J. M. (2005). *Compensation* (8th ed.). Boston: McGraw-Hill.

Sackett, P. R., Zedeck, S., & Fogli, L. (1988). Relations between measures of typical and maximum job performance. *Journal of Applied Psychology, 73*, 482–486.

Sady, K., & Aamodt, M. (2016). Analyzing EO disparities in pay: Guidance in the application of regression analyses. In S. B. Morris & E. D. Dunleavy (Eds.), *Adverse impact analysis: Understanding data, statistics and risk* (pp. 216–238). New York: Routledge.

Sady, K., Aamodt, M., & Cohen, D. (2015). Compensation equity and title VII: Who, what, where, when, why, and how. In C. Hanvey & K. Sady (Eds.), *HR practitioners guide to legal issues in organizations* (pp. 249–282). New York: Springer.

Werner, J. M., & Bolino, M. C. (1997). Explaining US courts of appeals decisions involving performance appraisal: Accuracy, fairness, and validation. *Personnel Psychology, 50*, 1–24.

Statutes and Regulations

California Equal Pay Act. (2015), Cal. Labor Code § 1197.5.

Civil Rights Act. (1964), Pub.L. 88-352, 78 Stat. 241.

Equal Pay Act. (1963), 29 U.S.C. § 206(d).

Correction to: Wage and Hour Law: Guide to Methods and Analysis

Chester Hanvey

Correction to:
C. Hanvey, *Wage and Hour Law*,
https://doi.org/10.1007/978-3-319-74612-8

An error in the production process unfortunately led to publication of these chapters prematurely, before incorporation of the final corrections. The version supplied here has been corrected and approved by the author.

The updated online version of this book can be found at
https://doi.org/10.1007/978-3-319-74612-8
https://doi.org/10.1007/978-3-319-74612-8_1
https://doi.org/10.1007/978-3-319-74612-8_2
https://doi.org/10.1007/978-3-319-74612-8_3
https://doi.org/10.1007/978-3-319-74612-8_4
https://doi.org/10.1007/978-3-319-74612-8_6
https://doi.org/10.1007/978-3-319-74612-8_8
https://doi.org/10.1007/978-3-319-74612-8_9

© Springer International Publishing AG, part of Springer Nature 2018
C. Hanvey, *Wage and Hour Law*, https://doi.org/10.1007/978-3-319-74612-8_10

Index

© Springer International Publishing AG, part of Springer Nature 2018
C. Hanvey, *Wage and Hour Law*, https://doi.org/10.1007/978-3-319-74612-8

Druck:
Customized Business Services GmbH
im Auftrag der KNV-Gruppe
Ferdinand-Jühlke-Str. 7
99095 Erfurt